The DRAPER TOUCH

Other books by Carleton Varney

Decorating With Color
You and Your Apartment
The Family Decorates a Home
Decorating for Fun
Carleton Varney Decorates Windows
Carleton Varney Decorates From A to Z
Color Magic
Carleton Varney's Book of Decorating Ideas
There's No Place Like Home
Down Home
Carleton Varney's ABC's of Decorating
Staying in Shape: An Insiders Guide to the Great Spas
Be Your Own Decorator
Room By Room Decorating

The DRAPER TOUCH

The High Life & High Style of Dorothy Draper

By Carleton Varney

PRENTICE HALL PRESS

New York   London   Toronto   Sydney   Tokyo

Prentice Hall Press
Gulf+Western Building
One Gulf+Western Plaza
New York, New York   10023

All photographs courtesy of the author.

PRENTICE HALL PRESS and colophon are registered
trademarks of Simon & Schuster, Inc.

Library of Congress Cataloging-in-Publication Data

Varney, Carleton.
   The Draper touch.
   1. Draper, Dorothy, 1889   2. Interior
decorators—United States—Biography.   I. Title.
NK2004.3.D74V37   1988   747.213 [B]   88-25399
ISBN 0-13-219080-X

Designed by Irving Perkins Associates

Manufactured in the United States of America

10   9   8   7   6   5   4   3   2   1

First Edition

For my three sons—

Nicholas Varney, Seamus Varney,
and Sebastian Varney—

With lots of fatherly love

Acknowledgments

I wish to thank all those people who have contributed so much to this book: Elisabeth Draper, Susan Minturn Jay, George Jay, George Draper, John Wisner, Mrs. Nelson Jay, Ted Mueller, Leon Hegwood, Lester Grundy, James Amster, Robert Moyer, Jean Gordon Pease, Joan van de Maele, E. Truman Wright, Margaret Kappa, Mrs. Vincent Coyle, Nancy Tuckerman, Roger Tuckerman, Mabel Hakin, Hart Smith, Martine Gilcrest, Robert Winslow, Palmer Le Roy, Ethel Schneider Gould, Robert Conte, Gloria Rosselle, Edward Bragaline, Roy Sibert, Rene Carillo, Flora Miller Biddle of the Whitney Museum, The Metropolitan Museum of Art, The Tuxedo Park Library, Mary Lasker, Dorothy McCauley, Charles of New York, William Pitt, Joseph Ryle, Sister Parrish, Dr. Edmund Goodman, Mrs. Norman Vincent Peale, Mr. Neil Waldman (Director of Archives Development at CBS News), The Museum of Broadcasting, Mr. Ken De Bie of the *Architectural Record*, The Hudson New York Public Library, Mrs. Gertrude Adcox, Ms. Terry Gray, Public Relations Director of the Fairmont Hotel, Conrad Engelhardt, Heather Cohane, The Brearley School of New York, Esther Williams, and Ted Kleisher.

I also wish to acknowledge those on my personal office staff who have assisted in the day-by-day reading and preparation of this book: Susan van Berg, Molly Hayden, Irene Xinos, Patricia Justice, Blanche Bender, Luis Gallego, Tom Tortora, Daniel Parker, Charles Davis, Sara Beaudry, Elsie Lumsden, and Ethel Connon.

My special thanks go to my friend and writer-researcher, Catherine Revland; my literary agent, Rosalind Cole; my editors Bill Thompson, Pam Thomas, and Susan Friedland; and to Penelope and Harvey Buchanan for their generous help on every facet of this book.

Contents

Preface

When Dorothy Draper corresponded with her grandchildren, she sometimes sent them copies of the Declaration of Independence. Boldly circled in red would be the signature of her great-great-grandfather Oliver Wolcott. It was her calling card. Dorothy was a grande dame who could not make a small gesture, and red was her signature. "Look here!" it said. "This is who I am." It was an exuberant signature, rebellious, even stirring.

For all her life, Dorothy used her considerable influence to pursue the right to be an individual. She was born in 1889 in Tuxedo Park, New York, one of the most exclusive communities in American history. Edith Wharton called her grandfather Robert Bowne Minturn, "one of the few gentlemen in America." Dorothy's father called her "Star." She had nothing to prove to anyone but herself.

One of Dorothy's many dictums was "If it looks right, it is right." Because of her background, who could argue? Mrs. Draper's absolutism appealed to the socially insecure—the nouveaux riches and the readers of her *Good Housekeeping* columns, who most likely would never be rich. For both groups, the seal of her approval had the weight of divine right.

In her day, Dorothy was the prima donna of the decorating business;

her name was as synonymous with decorating as zipper was with the slide fastener. Her famous touch was a merger of her unique color sense—combinations never before attempted, plus her two favorites, dull white and shiny black—and a few good pieces. The formula was called the Draper touch: A powerful and magical thing, it is the subject of this book.

One of the leaders in professionalizing the interior design business, Dorothy Draper developed the concept of "design" beyond the arrangement of furniture and accessories and broke away from the historical "period room" styles that dominated the work of her predecessors and contemporaries. She invented "Modern Baroque," a style that had particular application to large public spaces and modern architecture. As an artist she was a modern, one of the first decorators of that breed, and a pioneer.

Fresh from college, I came to work for Dorothy Draper in 1960, and the last thing in the world I had in mind was going into the decorating business. But like many others before me, I was mesmerized by her, and she changed the direction of my life. A portrait of her circa 1930 still hangs in my office. In it she wears one of her stunning hats, which frames her equally stunning face. Draped over my office coat rack is her little fox fur stole. Because of the Crash of 1929, Dorothy could never actually afford the luxuries of the world she was born into, but the way she threw those little foxes over her imposing shoulders had the impact of twenty feet of ermine. She kept her ship of state afloat on the illusion of her wealth.

In 1988, one hundred years after her birth, examples of her work are surprisingly plentiful, not only in Manhattan (she virtually transformed sections of New York City in the 1930s and 1940s) but also in other parts of the United States. Her work remains intact in a lot of these places. After all, why change perfection?

She craved public space, the canvas on which she did her most inspired work. The most well-known example was the "Dorotheum," the ground-floor cafeteria at The Metropolitan Museum of Art in New York City. To Dorothy, public space represented a place for people to come and feel elevated in the presence of great beauty, where the senses could look and feel and absorb the meaning of a quality life. That any of her work remains twenty years after her death speaks volumes about her talent. Her touch has survived in a time that does not value the past. She was truly the last grande dame.

The DRAPER TOUCH

Mrs. Draper Receives a Ghostly Visitor

The *George Washington* ground to a halt in a cloud of steam as it hit the White Sulphur Springs depot, high in the West Virginia Allegheny Mountains. It was early in the morning of December 28, 1946, and still pitch-dark. The occupants of a hotel limousine waited in the depot parking lot for heads to appear at the top of the stairs to the sleeping car. The wait was longer than usual.

At last the first passenger from New York appeared—feet first, one in a cast. Several porters carried a woman, a rather large woman, down the steps.

"That will be Mrs. Draper," said the driver.

"And six more coming," said the porter.

Behind her, three men and three women, alternately yawning and shivering, descended the stairs. It was a small traveling entourage for Dorothy Draper, Inc., due to the conditions of the times.

Laughing at her own clumsiness, Mrs. Draper struggled into the middle seat of the limousine and was handed her crutches. Her staff settled themselves in the back. The hotel porter closed the car doors all around, and the members of the delegation leaned against the cushions of the luxury car and sighed. The *George Washington* may have been the most luxurious train in the world, but a twelve-hour train ride was a twelve-hour train ride. "Its wheels were square," someone complained from the back seat. It was good to be back on terra firma, even if the particular terra was slightly to the west of nowhere.

Mrs. Draper was her usual buoyant self. Complaining was not her style, and she could sleep anywhere, even in a cramped little roomette. She might extol the democratic virtues of train travel and its great potential under her magic touch, but her favorite mode of travel was still a slow luxury motor car drive past the local flora, which she never failed to appreciate.

Directly across from the tiny depot was the hotel. As soon as the car drove through the gates, it could be seen looming ghostly white in the predawn mist behind a screen of ancient oaks.

"Those trees . . ." said Mrs. Draper in a dubious voice, but she did not finish her thought.

Although the porticoes of the hotel were visible from the road, the impact of their dimensions could not be appreciated until one stood directly under them. Even in the uncertain light, one could see they were on an Olympian scale, as if a photograph of Tara had been blown up to the point where its outlines began to blur. Had Margaret Mitchell dreamed up the grandest plantation house imaginable, the Greenbrier would have dwarfed it, for the Old White, as it was still known throughout the South, was Tara in extremis.

Before the war, it had been a giant amphitheater for the enactment of the curious customs of antebellum times, a place where the very rich could take a trip through time and experience life as it used to be in the Old Dominion. The cynical Yankee called it "the last darkie enclave." During the war it had been bought by the government for use as an internment camp for Nazi diplomats and then as Ashford General Hospital. Now the time had come for it to be turned back into a pleasure palace under the magic hands of the most famous decorator in the world.

On either side of the massive pillars, the building seemed to drift out into infinity; the outlines of the farthest wings were barely visible in the gray light that was just beginning to dawn.

"Well, at least it's not a monster palace like the Quitandinha," said a male voice from the back seat.

"Not on the outside anyway," said another.

Mrs. Draper shuddered. Her staff was right. The Greenbrier was no cozy cottage. She did not enjoy the prospect of spending the night in such a big empty building.

Standing under the mammoth pillars of the north portico was a servant bearing a flashlight and a wheelchair.

"Mr. Jim," said Mrs. Draper cheerfully. "How very nice to see you again."

Of Richmond background, Jim McKensie was the perfect southern doorman. She was encouraged to know he would be opening the door to all the drama. He led them upstairs to an even more vast and empty "upper" lobby where a small group of local executives had risen early to greet her. Introductions echoed ominously through the halls. The air was charged with anxiety. The hotel executives were concerned: They didn't approve of what Mrs. Draper had done to a floor of the venerable Mayflower Hotel in Washington, D.C.; rooms intended for distinguished world figures were done dripping in satin like the set for a Jean Harlow movie. Was she likely to paint everything white, including the woodwork, as she had done at Chicago's premier nightspot, the Camellia Room in the Drake Hotel? Mrs. Draper had come to redo the Greenbrier with the full support of their top boss, Robert R. Young, king of the Chesapeake and Ohio Railroad, and his social-climbing wife, Anita. The Youngs had told the press they had given Mrs. Draper carte blanche to redo the hotel, and the Greenbrier executives had reason to suspect Mrs. Draper took that charge literally.

Mrs. Draper, however, was oblivious to their state of mind. What interested her was the grand but ghastly hotel. In spite of its obvious drawbacks and the chilling gloom, she thought it was the most potentially romantic of places, a dream of Tara and a certain flower that was not a rose. A rose wasn't southern enough. . . .

Roy Sibert, a member of the hotel executive staff, wheeled Mrs. Draper through the lobby past its forest of pillars. Sibert had been an

3

employee of the hotel since 1920, so there wasn't much about the place he didn't know. As he answered the questions of the talkative ladies and gentlemen who accompanied her, Mrs. Draper scanned the far horizon of the lobby, the length of two football fields away, shaded her eyes, and said nothing.

On reaching the mezzanine, Sibert braved a comment: "Well, ma'am, what do you think of our little hotel?"

"A Brobdingnagian monster of a bowling alley," she replied.

Boarding the train at seven o'clock the previous evening, the Draper group had missed dinner. After a short turn through the main lobbies, everyone's thoughts turned to breakfast. No matter where Dorothy was, she always anticipated mealtime with pleasure, even when dining on the luncheon special at Schrafft's. But time spent anticipating meals at the Greenbrier had always been a special kind of pleasure, a suspension in a gustatory never-never land where the concept of calories did not exist. For more than one hundred years the kitchens at White Sulphur Springs had served cuisine in the tradition of Versailles. Like the country larders of the kings of France, the Greenbrier's pantries were stocked with only the choicest local produce—prize beef and lamb from the 4-H clubs of Lewisburg, pheasant and partridge from mountain hunters, and Virginia hams cured fourteen months, meats more sumptuous than any she had eaten, even during her Italian travels.

Over the years, Mrs. Draper had enjoyed many meals at the Greenbrier. The dinners were especially memorable—languid, two-hour affairs, never fewer than seven courses of lavish French cuisine, southern-style, with biscuit girls at the elbow. Ravenous on the train the night before, she had lulled herself to sleep dreaming of the roast duck she had once enjoyed, a ritual of sacrament presided over by the stately Toman, who had also greeted them that morning. His concern over the amount of paprika had made her feel as if the weight of the world rested on her preferences.

Mrs. Draper sighed as that same Toman now walked slowly across a dining room so cavernous that the unlit chandeliers looked like stalactites. Frowning, Toman reported that not even coffee was available. The gas had been turned off due to a leak, and that plus a generator problem had put the kitchens out of commission. In the wake of the dismantling of the hospital by the military, many repairs had to be done before the place was even livable.

Thinking of hot biscuits, Mrs. Draper suppressed a sigh. Her staff, restless in their coffeeless state, now began to sound mutinous.

"But there's a coffee shop in town," said Sibert.

They piled into two hotel limousines and were driven the short distance to the main and only street of White Sulphur Springs. The coffee shop was right next to the quaint little depot. The food was quick and greasy, but at least the place was warm, unlike the hotel. Coffee was ordered.

"We had some experts down from New York," Sibert said. "Food experts—Horworth and Horworth. Do you know them?"

"Never heard of them," replied Mrs. Draper, cheerful despite the soggy toast.

"They wanted us to slice our steaks thinner to save money. We got them out quick!"

"Good for you, Mr. Sibert. You can't scrimp on quality."

"They were experts, alright," said Sibert, "experts in saving money."

"Quite right. Shame on them." Mrs. Draper laughed.

"People come down here and complain about the high rate. We just tell them, 'Well, why don't you go back home? You can pay the same prices there and not have six thousand acres of mountain to roam around in.' That shuts them up right away."

"Good for you," said Mrs. Draper, calling for more toast.

"Down here," he said, "we like to do things the old-fashioned way."

"My dear Mr. Sibert," she said, patting his arm, cosseting him, "I have come to know that's hardly *ever* the best way."

The people who worked with Dorothy Draper had come to accept the finality of her pronouncements, receiving them with bowed head as dictums from "On High." On the subject of which way to go, she was as fiercely devoted to her choice as a Scot is to the plaid of his clan. It was her way and no other, as the gentlemen from the South were about to

5

discover. In her day, Mrs. Draper had gone into battle with many formidable types—recent millionaire entrepreneurs who roared like Henry VIII, movie stars, politicians, and even members of the under-world—and she always had her way, without ever raising her voice.

The six people traveling with Mrs. Draper on that chilly post-Christmas trip to White Sulphur Springs were an extraordinarily talented group of artists whom Dorothy depended on to render her concepts into tangibles. They were the best designers money could buy, and she paid a cut above. As one designer crudely put it, "The oats are good in her stable."

When Mrs. Draper spent too lavishly at the office, she drew on her personal account, and in that postwar period, after five years of wartime rationing and a decade of Depression before that, the amount she had drawn had caused her brother Roger, the family conservator, considerable dismay. It was just not possible for Dorothy Draper to do things in less than the grand manner. For instance, there was no way she could travel to a major job without a draftsman, two decorators, a decorator's assistant, her secretary, and her confidant, Jean Gordon.

The designer on the Greenbrier trip was Glenn Boyles, who had designed Dorothy's famous cabbage rose chintz for the Hampshire House. A million yards of that fabric had been sold, brightening up Depression homes since 1939, and launching Dorothy Draper as the grande dame of the decorating business. Glenn understood her concept of roses—windblown, oversized, vivid, romantic and yet well bred, like English tea roses growing wild in an American meadow.

A wonderful artist, Glenn was a well-loved instructor at the Parsons School of Design. He was an emotional man, devoted and sweet-natured. Mrs. Draper adored him and treated him like family, which could easily include chiding when she felt like it.

Ted Stewart was the decorator on the Greenbrier job. Tall and exceptionally good-looking, he did nearly all the buying for the office. Dorothy had trained him since he was a seventeen-year-old schoolboy. She now trusted his choices completely: Ted had learned down to the last detail what perfection meant. Assisting him was a new employee, the current office gofer, Dick Harley. Dorothy thought he could learn a lot from Ted and especially from Glenn, because Dick had some design potential. He was also tall and good-looking with wavy dark hair.

Tall and vivacious Belle Clark was her executive assistant, a marvel of efficiency. Mrs. Draper couldn't travel anywhere without Belle and her steno pad. Another secretary, Georgette Kelly, had also come along. She was shy and inexperienced, and more or less under Dorothy's wing, placed there by an old Tuxedo Park friend. Although Georgette was slow to catch on, she was willing, and everyone was being patient with the young lady. Svelte Jean Gordon called herself Dorothy's expediter. She was also her confidant, and the only one who could successfully argue with Mrs. Draper.

The Draper delegation returned to the hotel for a thorough inspection of the public space and the guest rooms. The place was so big it took the entire afternoon to tour it, and it left them all feeling a little grim. There was a chill to the hotel colder than the outside air. Although the army had not repainted the walls in the usual drab military colors, a hospital atmosphere still prevailed. An elevator had been cut through one corner of the fabled Cameo ballroom, and the dining room had been converted into a mess hall with chandeliers. The historic President's Cottage, a miniature mansion where many heads of state had stayed when the resort was Washington's Camp David, had been turned into a headquarters for the Red Cross. Upstairs on the sixth floor, where belles had once changed their gowns between cotillions, thousands of soldiers had been operated on by vascular and neurological surgeons. Although the hospital equipment had been removed, a chill remained and the flaming logs in the fireplace did nothing to alleviate it.

Mrs. Draper and her staff reviewed their notes over another dreary meal in the greasy spoon and finished off with the strong, hot redneck coffee Mrs. Draper appreciated. Back in the Greenbrier, in spite of her jolt of caffeine, Mrs. Draper began to nod. Muted voices became whispers as the group of eight "Yankees" worked at a table in a corner of the dining room. Outside, snow gusted in eddies, and the windows rattled high up in the dome of the ceiling. No one wanted to leave the fire and venture into the dark, unoccupied wings. Only Mr. Sibert continued to talk, rather expansively, about the history of the hotel.

"Largest and oldest hotel of its kind in the South—maybe in the world," he said, and once again Mrs. Draper shuddered. The place was too vast even for her tastes, which was unusual. Nine times out of ten her objection to scale was "too small;" this was one reason she didn't like to do residential jobs. But here was a place whose dimensions made her shiver. The Greenbrier was haunted by too many unhappy memories. It needed a clean sweep of the cobwebs and plenty of bright, fresh, cheerful color.

"What is the state flower Mr. Sibert?" she asked.

Although he had already told the bright young ladies who hovered about their employer with pad and pencil, he repeated the information. Mrs. Draper was pleased to find out it was the rhododendron.

"A particular favorite of mine," she said.

Shortly after eight o'clock, Sibert excused himself.

"I'll be staying the night in the North Portico, not far from you," he said. "You can dial the front desk and they'll ring me if you need anything."

"Thank you, Mr. Sibert. It's most kind of you," said Mrs. Draper, and she stifled a yawn. It was approaching her bedtime. Still she lingered, not eager to be rolled through the caverns past hundreds of closed doors to her room on the mezzanine floor, while the others were sure to head straight to a bar. Conversation among her staff had turned to local lore. Ted and Glenn were great collectors of folklore, particularly ghost stories.

"And there's another one—most punctual—that hangs out in the hills above one of the cottages. I don't know which . . ." said Ted.

"And as the clock strikes twelve," interrupted Glenn, "she comes out in her wedding dress singing and playing her silver flute."

"How southern," said Jean.

"There are no such things as ghosts," said Mrs. Draper.

Glenn continued. "And that's not all. There's also Robert E. Lee, on his horse. He's been seen around here a lot."

"Old Marse himself," said Ted. "These hills are his old stomping grounds."

"Do these ghosts come into the rooms?" asked the timid Georgette.

"Just call Mr. Sibert, dear, if they do," said Mrs. Draper. "He is being a darling to stay with us tonight." She sighed and patted her lips. She approved of the texture of an old napkin she had found. It had a softness of patina that could only come from many launderings of good quality linen. She did not approve of the china. Perhaps she could change that; she considered a design of a big rhododendron trimmed with a pink edge—just like the camellia china pattern she had created for the Drake Hotel of Chicago.

Mrs. Draper reapplied her lipstick. Years ago, she had received an awful letter from her aunt Katie Leroy, who had apparently seen Dorothy whip out her compact and lipstick in the Palm Court at the Plaza Hotel in New York City. It was a terrible letter, but she didn't care then or now. Hope began to glimmer on the faces of her staff as Mrs. Draper completed her table toilette.

"Ted," she said, "would you please find that dear Mr. Jim and tell him to bring around my chair?" Ted left much too eagerly, and in no time the elderly head doorman was at her side.

"Do get a good night's sleep, everyone," she said. "There's much to be done tomorrow."

"Sleep well, Mrs. Draper," said Glenn.

"I will meet you all back here in the dining room at nine o'clock. À bientôt!"

Settled once again in her wheelchair, crutches balanced across her lap, Mrs. Draper was wheeled away by the elderly Mr. Jim. The voices around the fire rose in volume as he rolled her away, becoming raucous as an elevator emerged out of the shadows. Laughter broke out and became a roar as "DD" was lifted to the mezzanine.

"Thank God—I thought she'd never leave," cried Ted. Then, in the interest of upholding tradition—for wasn't the Greenbrier the birthplace of the mint julep?—they proceeded to a local saloon, in spite of the weather, knowing that their employer would be fast asleep before the second round.

But Dorothy Draper didn't care. As long as they appeared by nine the next morning capable of thinking, she simply wasn't interested in what they did or with whom. Her private life was sacred; she gave the same privilege to her employees.

At midnight she awoke, hearing bells. Something or someone was in her room. She was sure of that, for she could feel every hair stand on end.

"Who's there?" she commanded. Contrary to her earlier disclaimer, Mrs. Draper did believe in ghosts, but she knew how to deal with them. She had been visited by several of her illustrious ancestors over the years. They made sudden appearances, demanding to know what was going on in the world, and usually evanesced quickly enough when they discovered she couldn't tell them a thing. But southern ghosts were a different matter. Ted and Glenn told stories about them that really bothered her. If the alleged specter in her room was merely one of those pathetic creatures who had died for love in the southern manner—shot in a duel or plunged over Lover's Leap—that wasn't so alarming. All they wanted was an audience for their poignant little drama. But if she were being visited by the kind of southern ghost who materialized in the flesh—that wasn't fair!

Her foot hurt. As she fretted, reclining on the six pillows she always required, she forced herself to concentrate on pleasant thoughts. Whatever was she going to do with those cavernous spaces? The hotel was more of a challenge than the Quitandinha (built in the mountains above Rio de Janeiro), which was also too large, but the Quitandinha had no past to contend with. She would have to make a clean sweep of the Greenbrier and turn it into something cozy but grand. The first step would be to get rid of the prewar dark brown wicker on the porticoes.

Although her historic grasp of the South was limited, Mrs. Draper had a fondness for *Gone With the Wind.* She had seen the movie many times and had taken her staff to see it with her in preparation for the trip. But even without seeing the movie, she knew what the Greenbrier meant to the antebellum myth. She knew it in her bones, for she had grown up in Tuxedo Park, the northern version of the Old White.

Tuxedo Park was a resurrection of feudal England down to its faded cottage shingles and lichen-draped stones. Dorothy Draper knew precisely how such myths were created, and she could transform the Greenbrier with her eyes closed. She would enlarge the fantasy to mythic size, to movie-screen proportions, until it cried "Tara!" But how?

The air in her room no longer seemed disturbed. Mrs. Draper sighed—positive thinking to the rescue again.

In his chilly room in the North Portico, Roy Sibert was also having trouble falling asleep. He worried about what the lady decorator from New York was going to do to his hotel. Sibert had come there to work at age seventeen, a smart boy who didn't want to be a coal miner like his father. In twenty-five years he had worked his way up from night desk cashier to the executive suite of the Old White. (The locals still called the Greenbrier "Old White," just as present-day New Yorkers insist on calling the Avenue of the Americas "Sixth Avenue.")

In 1936, Sibert had played golf with Sam Snead from Hot Springs, a hollow so narrow the dogs had to wag their tails up and down. After one game, Sibert brought him over to the hotel and put him on the payroll. Sibert had overseen the hotel through its recent transformations from a society resort to a luxury internment camp to an army hospital to now only God knew what.

He had had no particular problem housing a thousand or so Nazi diplomats: At least they had known how to dress for dinner. But dealing with the army had been another matter. With them Sibert had had to be firm. When the military brass had wanted to turn the rooms into wards, Sibert had argued that it wasn't going to be a hospital forever: All they had to do was change the tumblers in the locks so that the doors would open out instead of in, and that way every soldier would have a nice private or double room.

Because of the attentions of Sibert and other local people the army had done minimal damage to the Greenbrier, although the military's stay certainly didn't improve Old White. At times bored, the officers had played darts against the sacred murals of the Virginia Room. Although they were not so barbarian as to do away with dart boards, they often missed the target. Small holes could be patched up, however, and the hospital elevator could be removed from the ballroom, and the mess hall could be restored to a dining room. What worried Sibert most was Mrs. Draper.

The lady didn't care a bit about tradition. From everything she had said so far, it was pretty clear she was going to modernize the Greenbrier, where every stick of furniture and every tree told a story and every room held memories of historical figures at play.

Even before she had been hired, Dorothy Draper had been the cause of sleepless nights for the executives of both the hotel and the Chesapeake and Ohio Railroad, which owned the Greenbrier. Mr. Romar, the treasurer of the C&O Railroad, had gone to New York to see Mrs. Draper in her office at 38 East 57th Street. When he walked in, she leaned back in her chair and said, "Don't say a word to me. I know what you're here for, and I want you to know I can go further in this thing than you can."

And she did. The lady prevailed over the nearly unanimous objections of the top brass of the C&O Railroad, for in her corner was the company's controlling stockholder, Robert R. Young. The future of the rail industry was in turmoil, and Young was at the center of it. Champion of the small investor, he was waging war against the combined forces of the sleeping car and railroad trusts *plus* the Wall Street bankers—a David and Goliath–type campaign that captured the hearts of millions and landed him on the cover of *Time*.

When the army put Ashford General on the market, some Hollywood types came by to look at it, but the place was too remote for their tastes. Young underbid them, over the objections of many in the C&O Railroad, who felt the place was now a white elephant and a relic of times past. But Young didn't care whether the hotel made a profit. He planned to use it for entertainment purposes, to woo society back to its doors. That the Greenbrier would be a place for serious social climbing was a foregone conclusion. Mrs. Young, the former Anita O'Keeffe, sister of the famous painter Georgia O'Keeffe, was a champion social climber. The couple from Texas planned to scale the heights with a boost from their good friends, the duke and duchess of Windsor, and the high-born Mrs. Draper. Sibert enjoyed the irony that Dorothy was a member of the very group Young accused of having the small investor by the throat.

Rumor had it that when Mrs. Draper was done with her modernizing, Young was going to throw an opening party to end all parties, which would bring society to the Greenbrier as in the years before the war, democratically mingling social climbers with aristocrats like the reuniting of North and South after the Civil War at the Old White. And at the center of it all, like the bride and groom on top of a wedding cake, would be the duke and the duchess of Windsor.

Only one thought kept Sibert from worrying until dawn's early light. If Mrs. Draper was planning on doing any "modernizing," the Greenbrier ghosts would be heard from all the way to Charlottesville.

Mrs. Draper woke long after her usual 7:00 A.M., still exhausted. Where had the night gone? Her appetite was roaring. She was in the dining room by half past eight, uncustomary dark circles under her eyes, but otherwise perfectly groomed and ready for the day, and expressed her gratitude to Sibert and George O'Brien for providing an in-house breakfast.

It was picnic-style, which she loved. With pleasure she selected one of each kind of roll (they were small) which O'Brien had brought from home, he said, followed by canned fruit and plenty of strong southern coffee from his thermos. Impatiently she waited for her staff. They were *not* all down by nine. In fact, Ted and Glenn did not appear until quarter after nine. She waited until they came to life over their second cup of coffee.

"The theme," she said, "is Romance and Rhododendrons." She paused dramatically as the note taking began. "For the corridors I see flowers, huge rhododendrons, perhaps. What do you think, Glenn? Up and down the halls on a sparkling white ground, bringing in as much light as possible. I see big, lush rhododendrons, big blue-green leaves, vines entangling them." Her ideas came faster, her gestures became broader. The staff scribbled.

She continued. "The color scheme—hunting pink and fuscia, cobalt blue and turquoise, lime and hunter green, and for punches . . ." She paused for emphasis: "Scarlet!"

"Divine! Divine!" said Georgette.

"Well, why not?" said Glenn.

"Scarlet in those antiseptic bathrooms," said Ted.

"Scarlet punctuating the golf course in the caddies' shirts," said Mrs. Draper. "Let our imaginations run rampant!"

Sibert and O'Brien joined the delegation in the main lobby, ready to go through the public rooms. They were flabbergasted at what they heard as they rolled her from room to room. No amount of foreboding could have prepared them for this. Red and green? Green and blue? Blue and yellow? Not only that, she wanted to tear the place apart and put it back together again—upside down; she wanted to move the lobby upstairs, tear down walls and floors, and install huge fireplaces. Nevertheless, the hotel executives maintained a grim silence.

Tensions rose when Mrs. Draper was wheeled into the Virginia Room, the resort's sanctum sanctorum, where the Cleveland artist William Grauer had been commissioned to portray the history of the hotel in murals that lined the room. Researching and painting had taken him a year, and they were the pride of West Virginia.

"Whatever happened to these murals?" she asked. "Look, they're full of holes."

"Tempera on paper," said Glenn, examining them.

"We've asked the artist to come and fix them," said Sibert.

"You may as well save yourself the expense. They have to go."

"I beg your pardon, ma'am?" said O'Brien.

"I know the painter was going for an antique sepia effect, and the murals are pleasant enough, but they don't fit into the color scheme. There's no room for that sickly color in the new Greenbrier."

"Excuse me, Mrs. Draper, but I think you'll find that would make a whole lot of people around here unhappy," said Sibert.

"A wide stripe," said Mrs. Draper, "a wide, wide, wide red-and-white peppermint stripe. How wide can it be made, Glenn?"

"Twenty-eight inches."

"That's not wide enough. We'll have to stencil them."

Once at Fraunces Tavern in New York City, another institution where pride was taken in keeping things the way they had been, Mrs. Draper had written "Paint lime green" on a wall in large letters. The clients had been taken aback, but nothing like the Greenbrier executives would be upon hearing what Mrs. Draper was going to do to the Virginia Room.

"Over my dead body," whispered O'Brien to Sibert as Mrs. Draper was wheeled toward the site of her next transformation.

"We'll have to call Mr. Bowman [the president of C&O]," said Sibert. "He's got to get through to the governor."

"This great hall is as cozy as an armory," said Mrs. Draper. "Let's enclose some spaces with walls and others with screens of chinoiserie lattice on the diagonal."

In one corner of the main hall she envisioned a special little nook. "This space will be a darling Victorian writing room. The walls will be that dark Victorian green we're using at the Fairmont and we will hang a gilt leaf chandelier with real wax candles. Hmm. I guess this little mirror can stay."

Of the hotel's most cherished antiques, the little girandole mirror was one of the few that had survived the war. The hotel's historical legacy had been reduced to a Sheffield chandelier, a Queen Anne table, five small chandeliers, and the mirror. Nothing else that Mrs. Draper saw inspired her at all. Southerners were too fond of massive pieces of dark wood, she thought, and she didn't like wood because it was brown and she hated brown.

That afternoon she commanded that one piece of each kind of furniture in the public rooms be placed in the lounge so she could get a general picture.

"Strip and repair," she ordered, moving among the pieces, her staff busily tagging each one. Her words made the hotel executives wince, but when she said the word "paint" they cried out loud.

"Now, now, gentlemen. It's done all the time. And if you can't decide what color to paint something, paint it black and it will disappear like magic."

The executives had an emergency caucus in the next room. Mrs.

Draper's ideas were beyond their comprehension. Only a Yankee would paint fine old mahogany furniture white and black and rhododendron pink. Someone had to be told she was taking this carte blanche thing to the limit and painting everything in sight like some crazy queen on the loose from *Alice in Wonderland*. She did everything but paint the roses red.

Mrs. Draper's attitude toward antiques was clear to all who knew her. Collecting them, she said, was a sign of personal insecurity—someone striving for something other than beauty. Although she would never have been so rude as to tell the locals that she suspected them of harboring feelings of insecurity, she was firm in her response to their objections.

"Gentlemen, furniture is either good or bad. You either like it or dislike it. It either serves its purpose or it doesn't. It's either lovely to look at or it isn't."

The hotel's executives placed calls to Romar and Bowman at C&O headquarters, claiming that Mrs. Draper was exceeding all their worst expectations. She was going to take the Greenbrier like Grant took Richmond.

Meanwhile, Mrs. Draper and her expediter, Jean, went to the greasy spoon for some coffee and a doughnut or two. "I won't leave here until I've come up with a china pattern," Mrs. Draper said.

"Then I think you'd better stay over, DD" said Jean. "Quite frankly, I don't see how you can meet Mr. Young's deadline."

"Oh, we'll meet it," Dorothy said airily.

"And it's so cold in there. I've never been in any place where I felt so cold that I thought I would never be warm again."

Mrs. Draper sent her coffee back because it wasn't hot enough.

"Heat the cup," she ordered the counterman. He did it furiously, poured the coffee back in, and Mrs. Draper burned her fingers. But she was a sport and laughed, and soon the counterman was laughing, too.

One last memo was sent to C&O headquarters that afternoon: "This lady is keeping us busy as heck, and she is now going to stay over tonight and return tomorrow."

Everyone retired early. Mrs. Draper and the cold were wearing every-body down.

Once again, Mrs. Draper slept badly. That was unusual. She prided herself on being able to fall asleep instantly anywhere. There was a knocking at the window that would not go away, and it was not an irregular sound like something caused by the wind. She was so exhausted her body hummed, but her eyes would not stay shut. Finally she broke down and called Sibert, who had agreed to stay one more night in the hotel.

By the time he arrived, she was in full regalia. Her eyes followed him around the suite as he checked behind doors and outside the window.

"There's nothing in sight that could be knocking against the win-dow," he said.

"Well, I feel rather foolish, Mr. Sibert, interrupting your evening like this."

"Don't mind a bit," he said. "And don't hesitate to call again if you're bothered."

She thanked him gratefully and he departed. The knocking sound stopped, but every now and then a strange light came through the draperies and seemed to flash even behind her closed eyelids. Only by matching up six hundred rooms with six hundred color schemes could she hope to fall asleep at all.

A bell chimed, or was it a radio? She thought she heard singing. The air was definitely disturbed.

"Sky blue and geranium pink, acid and kelly green," Mrs. Draper breathed as a spectral light moved across the room. From far away someone terribly unhappy was singing off-key.

"Rose, burgundy, and turquoise on a white ground . . ."

By the time she did the dining room, it was dark and quiet again. The air calmed down. By the time she began the upper lobby she was asleep.

Edward Lawless, Robert Walen, and John Stubblefield, other Greenbrier executives, accompanied Sibert and O'Brien when the Draper team went on its rounds the following day. Accompanying them were their secretaries, who took down every word Dorothy said. The Draper staff also took notes at top speed. War had been declared, but Mrs. Draper did not seem to notice. She had not only taken over the rooms down to the color of the soap wrappers (scarlet) but also invaded the kitchens, where she discussed adding something low-calorie to the menu, and then stormed the greenhouse.

"We must eliminate the use of gladiolus," she said. "They're impossibly stiff." Then she swept her arm across the lawn and called for a serpentine Jeffersonian wall of real plantation brick. Surely it could be found.

She even snooped around the sacred cottages, declaring her intention to make them "more cottagey." In the linen pantry, she found everything to be the wrong color. The draperies were of no use whatsoever. She needed to use her own man, who hand-loomed them. She even wanted to remove the historic chaperones' balcony from the ballroom because it was an anachronism.

Wheeled out to the front of the hotel and gesturing toward the center oval, Mrs. Draper threw down the gauntlet.

"Look at that one great big old tree in the middle," she said. "It disturbs the view completely. We should be able to catch a full view of the hotel at first glimpse."

"You mean . . ." said Lawless.

"You must cut it down."

Stubblefield was the first to find his voice. "It's a four-hundred-year-old tree!" he said, but Mrs. Draper stared at him uncomprehendingly.

She had decorating plans for the train station, and she had decorating plans for the golf and tennis pros' shops.

"Wait till Sammy hears he's getting decorated," muttered Sibert to Lawless. "He'll quit."

The only thing in the Greenbrier's existing color scheme she approved of was the blue of the outdoor ceilings under the porticoes.

"That's very innovative," she said.

"Down South we believe that mosquitoes don't bite under a blue sky," Lawless told her.

"Well, that's charming. We'll keep those outdoor ceilings blue, but not that blue—Jefferson blue."

It was the only concession she made all day.

By the end of the third evening, Mrs. Draper was well pleased. She had laid the groundwork for the gutting of the old hotel and the establishment of a new one, done in a single style—Great Beauty. It would be a house of whispers, where at night a sign went up that was not taken down until mid-morning: "Quiet, please. It's sleepy time down South." She would sweep the fustiness and unhappy memories out the door like so much dust in a pan, and give its worn old face a coat of sparkling color.

Mrs. Draper was exhausted but jubilant. Much had been accomplished in her short stay, despite the bad nights of sleep. But much remained to be done. Some of the staff would have to stay on. Ted had taken a liking to the Lee cottage. They could employ a cook. Although Mrs. Draper was beginning to find the constant complaining of the local people a bit tiresome, she was satisfied. In her trusted care, the new hotel would cry, "Tara!"

Dorothy woke up in the dead of night. She kept a lamp on, but was still able to make out a spectral light moving across the room as it had the night before. As she gathered her dressing gown together at the neck, the light grew brighter, like the approach of a train's headlights in a heavy mist.

"Help!" she cried, reaching for the telephone. The light grew dim, then brighter. With shaking fingers she dialed the night desk.

"Yes, ma'am?" said a sleepy voice, but before she could answer the light dimmed to a glow around the seemingly flesh-and-blood appearance of Robert E. Lee on his horse Traveller at the foot of her bed.

"Yes, ma'am?" repeated the voice in her ear.

"Mr. Sibert," she whispered, closing her eyes tightly. "Where is Mr. Sibert?"

"I'm ringing him for you now, ma'am."

She opened her eyes. The tableau was still there like a familiar bronze statue in a park but as real as real could be. The general's expression was extremely sad. Even the horse looked sad. She knew these southern ghosts couldn't be trusted. Why didn't Sibert answer? What could she possibly tell him if he did? That Robert E. Lee seemed to be mounted on his horse at the foot of her bed?

At last Sibert responded. "Yes?"

"There seems to be someone in my room," she said, trying to sound cheerful, closing her eyes again and making the supreme effort of her life not to give way to an unseemly emotional display. "Could you come right away?"

By the time Sibert arrived, of course, the tableau had dematerialized. She hobbled out of bed to talk to him through the door, as she had not had time to pull herself together.

"Oh, my dear Mr. Sibert, it was so good of you to come up right away, but everything seems to be alright now. I thought I saw something but it must have been a dream. So sorry to disturb you."

Sibert assured her through the door that he would be on call through the night should anything else happen. Mrs. Draper hopped back to bed, pulled the covers up to her neck, closed her eyes, and told herself that it was amazing what the mind was capable of when the body was denied a few nights of proper sleep.

There was another knock at the door. Although it was soft and accompanied by a low female voice, Mrs. Draper was startled all over again.

"Come in," she said.

"Some settling tea for you, ma'am," drawled the voice.

And that it was. As she lay suspended in the kind of stillness that can be felt only in the mountains, particularly in the dead of night, she began to breathe deeply.

At every moment in one's life one had a choice, she recited to herself—to be happy or unhappy. She could lie in a state of terror at the trick her mind had played on her or she could think pleasant thoughts. She could think about color. She could think about the shade of pink for the Cameo ballroom, one that would sing in the presence of turquoise. It shouldn't be a powdery bathroom pink like the one she had dreamed up for the Dorothy Grey "In the Pink" campaign, although that had been a hit. Ballrooms required another kind of pink, one with a sheen, the color of an abalone shell but more peachy . . . the color of pink in the blush of the cheeks of the thousands of belles who had promenaded through the centuries around that ballroom floor. . . .

As she dreamed of the perfect pink, her immediate surroundings began to lose their gloom. In her panic she had forgotten that she and the hotel—both important historical institutions—were safely in the care of the local residents who had watched over Old White for generations. It was a comforting thought to have so far from home. Yes, she was as safe in White Sulphur Springs as anywhere else in the world.

As she continued to lie in her pink cloud of positive thoughts, her surroundings became almost familiar. In many ways they were like the Tuxedo Park of her childhood. It was also in the mountains, miles from nowhere, and was also protected by a thick forest of bramble like a castle in a fairy tale. At Tuxedo Park, of course, there was the additional protection of the eight-foot barbed wire fence that she learned to hate. But in her childhood days she didn't know it was there, and it allowed her and her little companions much more freedom than children of the rich usually enjoyed.

Didn't a similar kind of freedom exist in her present circumstances? Of course it did. She had millions of dollars to spend and an empty canvas on which to create a masterpiece. She had not come to this moment to succumb to childish fears. After all, what could they actually *do*, these ghosts? She had no time to waste on apparitions. She had come to resurrect history, not to banish it as her critics would believe, and she would do so—her way. It was true she would not do the predictable thing and transform the Greenbrier with unnecessary homage paid to works of art from another era better forgotten, painted in all the wrong colors. She would perform the miracle *her* way, with *intangibles*. She would use her magic touch to make romance tangible, to make others feel it as she had felt it for real. She would make ordinary people feel like beaux and belles among the pink and turquoise and gilt. Crystals of light from one enormous Austrian chandelier would illuminate the ballroom. Perhaps she would design the chandelier herself, using as a guide a picture she had seen of one in the Russian imperial palace.

Floating now, as her dream took on the circular dimensions of a waltz (either the room was spinning or she was), Mrs. Draper felt the majesty of the opening quadrille of the Autumn Ball that had once been the prelude to each New York social season at Tuxedo Park. It was the same quadrille that they had danced at the Greenbrier, no doubt, her erstwhile night visitor at the hub with two young lovely belles on each arm. Or maybe it wasn't the same quadrille. Her ignorance of local history didn't bother her. A ballroom was a ballroom. She knew the big picture. Although she had left the exclusive Brearley school before the class studied the Civil War, she knew the history of the downstairs ballroom almost as well as that of the ballroom at Tuxedo Park, for the dancers were all members of the same big, old, happy family.

Dorothy Tuckerman Draper sighed. Her positive side was back in control once again. After a dreadful shock, the adult was back at the helm, and the child comforted. She became so relaxed she seemed to be floating just above her bed. Serenity melted her limbs. There was nothing to fear but fear itself. Even her ankle stopped throbbing. There was nothing the job would bring that she, Dorothy Draper, couldn't handle. Problems would melt away as she righted the place. When a sudden wind rattled the shutters, she did not flinch. The calming tea and the sage advice of Norman Vincent Peale had done their work. She slept soundly in the center of her six pillows.

Family History

On the resort circuit into which Dorothy Tuckerman was born, Tuxedo Park was the northern version of the Greenbrier, where society retreated in the spring and again in the fall to enjoy the healthful mountain air and the outdoor life. For both resorts, claims were made that food of such quality hadn't been served out in the sticks since Versailles. Both resorts were also favored by royals because people there knew how to behave. They knew, for instance, that royals were greeted *outside*, not inside, the homes of their hosts.

And both Tuxedo Park and the Greenbrier excluded whomever they pleased. According to Greenbrier historian William Olcott (author of *The Greenbrier Heritage*) there was a nineteenth-century major-domo at the Old White nicknamed "the Metternich of the mountains." He turned away George W. Featherstonhaugh, the founder of the New York Central Railway, with the words "Look ye, mister, I haven't room for a cat, to say nothing about your family" because Featherstonhaugh's money at that time was much too new.

The age of one's fortune was also the criterion at Tuxedo Park, although rejection was not quite so undignified. At Tuxedo Park members were voted in by the board of directors of the Tuxedo Club, a group of twenty men whose prestige spanned the alphabet from Astor to Winthrop, including Dorothy's father, Paul Tuckerman.

Under the shield of exclusivity, belles and debs alike could be mated to appropriate gentlemen without fear. The Old White had always been the official marriage mart of the South, where the far-flung aristocracy gathered to take care of the business of perpetuating dynasties. In the ballroom hung a long scroll of pink paper with the names of men whose backgrounds qualified them for what was quaintly called the "Billing and Cooing and Wooing Society." Matchmaking also went on at Tuxedo Park, minus the southern flamboyance. At either ball, one could be guaranteed that one's daughter would not be asked to dance by a Gould, an Armour, or (heavens!) a Morgenthau.

High society followed the seasons like migrant birds. They headed north with the sun to White Sulphur Springs for the Easter season. After apple blossom time in the Ramapo mountains, they departed for Newport shortly after the Fourth of July celebration, Tuxedo Park's biggest event aside from the Autumn Ball, which opened the New York social season. There, the current crop of debutantes were presented like brides to adult society.

As the northern hemisphere began to turn away from the sun, society journeyed south to White Sulphur Springs for skeet shooting and the holiday season, descending on the shores of southern Florida just as the January doldrums set in. In the sweet do-nothing pattern of the times, the resort circuit became a way of life, as predictable as the movement of the planets, as the very rich had perfected it since the beginning of time.

Dorothy Tuckerman was born in Tuxedo Park in 1889, but like a resorter she liked to tell people that her roots went back to the eighteenth century when her great-great-grandfather George Gibbs had seventy-five clipper ships in Newport harbor, which sailed to all parts of the world. At a time when White Sulphur Springs was still a collection of sheds and tents down by the springhouse, Newport was the most luxurious little island in America. Because the Gibbses came early to the island, Oaklands, their "farm," was one of its prime locations.

The settlement was named after Captain Christopher Newport, a seventeenth-century Thomas Cook who, in the employ of the London Company, transported the first lords and ladies from England to the New

World in 1610. The choicest real estate in the tiny colony was the largest island in Rhode Island Sound, which was shaped like a fish about to leap into the ocean; at its eye was Newport. From the beginning of colonization, Newport was the place for the upper class to summer.

There was a certain island mentality to Newport: Outsiders weren't discouraged, they simply weren't provided for. The inhabitants, said one observer, were people you were born knowing or died without meeting. Everyone else went to Providence.

Eighteenth-century Newport was nothing like the town that grew when a deluge of nineteenth-century new money built rows of *nouveau* stone palaces on the beach. Old Newport was strictly old money, like a backdrop for a modern ad for summer whites.

Newport before the Gilded Age was a family affair—old, old family and old, old money—and not at all baronial. On the contrary, *pique-niques* were served among the cucumbers and the melons prepared by French chefs at a time when French cuisine was still a rarity in most American households. The combined Newport dinner guest lists of Dorothy Tuckerman's ancestors and their close friends were the original social registers. They were members of English families (and in the early years, Dutch) who had come to New England during the seventeenth century. Over the generations they formed a society by intermarriage in the feudal manner of Old England. As entangled as the branches of a tree, it was a society so closed its members could deny its existence. Only the keeper of the family pedigree (and every family had one) was liable to reveal there was any attention at all paid to bloodline.

"Our family is of New England descent, exclusively," wrote Dorothy's Uncle Bayard, the Tuckerman family genealogist, in a book privately published for the family in 1912. "Up to our own generation there is not a single instance of the marriage of any other blood, and in nearly every case with a family that settled in the Northeast in the seventeenth century."

Before Abraham was, I am. One had to have been there for the creation to marry into the Tuckerman line, or at least for the Boston Tea Party: Aggassiz, Amory, Aspinwall, Cabot, Carey, Delano, Ellsworth, Gardiner, Gibbs, Greene, Griswold, Hartshorne, Kane, Kidder,

Kinnicutt, Leroy, Minturn, Parkman, Putnam, Roosevelt, Salisbury, Saltonstall, Sedgwick, Trumbull, Wendell, Wolcott. By the twentieth century there was hardly a noteworthy seventeenth-century New England family Dorothy Tuckerman's ancestors had *not* married into. Their blood was not just blue—it was indigo.

These "first families" married into other seventeenth-century families—the Van Rensselaers, the Van Cortlandts, the Greenes, the Livingstons, the Pells, and the Stuyvesants—the original lords and ladies of the manors that once stretched west from the early coastal settlements across Connecticut to the Hudson Valley.

Meanwhile, in the South, cash crops were being harvested by slave labor on a scale not known since the days of the Roman Empire. Life there was much more rugged and lawless. New England purebreds found no ladies and gentlemen worthy of the name in the southern colonies until the eighteenth century. Not that all New England aristocrats were to remain so pure (i.e., purely English and Dutch). By the eighteenth century, northern and southern accents blended harmoniously under an August moon on Newport's Bailey's Beach.

As a group, "they" had no name, only labels applied by outsiders. Henry James called them "The Real Thing." Ward McAllister, a self-appointed arbiter of the Gilded Age, called them "The Four Hundred," a term which is still in dispute. (Jan Morris calls the number "allegorical" [*Manhattan '45*, 1987].) The descendants of the original families will deny with some vigor that a special bloodline exists at all, noting indignantly that their ancestors fought a revolution to abolish the very idea of class in American society.

Not all deny it, however. In his classic *Who Killed Society?*, Tuxedoite Cleveland Amory quotes a member of the Otis clan as saying, "We didn't come over on the *Mayflower*. We sent the servants on that. We came over on the *Arabella*."

One thousand people settled in New England along with the ruling class on the *Arabella* in the first wave of migration in 1630. By 1642 sixteen thousand had arrived. People of all classes had reasons for leaving England, for the country was in the throes of a civil war that would end in regicide. The English upper class left regretfully, for they had lived a profitable and secure life for one hundred years under the Tudors, as had the next rung of English society, the local gentry, law enforcers, and merchants. Even the poor had had it good under the Tudors: In 1601, Parliament had passed a social landmark called the Elizabethan Poor Law, which charged the parishes with providing for the needy.

But when the House of Stuart came to power in 1603, the party was over for the upper class. Unlike the Tudors, the Stuarts wouldn't share the wealth. They also wanted divine right like the kings of France and Spain.

By 1630, during the reign of Charles I, conditions in England were so bad that many aristocrats left to settle in the colonies; so many fled that in 1638 the king refused to allow seven shiploads of them to sail to the colonies in order to staunch the flow of blue bloods from mother England.

But not only the rich emigrated. People of all classes decided to flee the Stuarts and the impending civil war. The first Draper emigrated to Roxbury, Massachusetts, shortly after the pilgrims arrived. He was James the Puritan, a weaver and cordwainer from Yorkshire. The Draper clan traces its origins to fifteenth-century Normandy. Like many of the other early colonists, James the Puritan came to find religious freedom in the New World. His great-great-great-great-great-great grandson would one day marry Dorothy Tuckerman.

The first Tuckerman to arrive in the New World was twenty-five-year-old John Tuckerman, whose family had owned a considerable amount of land in Devonshire since the fifteenth century. Tuckerman settled in Boston. His son was one of the few survivors of the Battle of Sudbury during the Great Indian War of 1675.

On Dorothy's mother's side, the first Wolcott, Henry, arrived in 1630. He was the son of an English squire with a manor in Somersetshire. He came in a ship chartered for his family, company, servants, and furniture and settled near the Connecticut River. James Gibbs settled in Newport, Rhode Island, where his son would rise to eminence as a grain merchant. Other ancestors of Dorothy Tuckerman who emigrated around that time were the Careys of Boston, who were sheriffs and mayors in sixteenth-century Bristol; Jonas Minturn from Leicester, England, whose ancestry on both sides consisted of "nature's noblemen" and whose sons would be some of the richest shipping merchants of their time; and the Parkmans, who settled in Dorchester, Massachusetts, and would one day play host to the Boston Tea Party.

Ralph Waldo Emerson described the majesty of the aristocrat as "bearing a train of great days and victories behind . . . that shed a united light on the advancing actor." The united light that shone on Dorothy Draper had the wattage of a bank of spotlights. They beamed their brightest on the eighteenth century and her ancestors' participation in the American Revolution. Unlike the histories of many other illustrious families, that spotlight shone down on both men and women.

The daughters of Oliver Wolcott, great-grandson of the founding Henry, melted the lead statue of George III, toppled at New York's Bowling Green in 1776, on the Wolcott lawn in Litchfield, Connecticut, to make bullets for the Continental army. Their father was a signer of the Declaration of Independence, a copy of which would one day be Dorothy Draper's calling card.

John Tuckerman's grandson Edward Tuckerman sat down at the Liberty Tree Tavern with fellow members of the "Loyal Five," a group that included Paul Revere, Samuel and John Adams, John Hancock, John Lowell, and Oliver Wendell. As described by the Tuckerman family genealogist, "An imitation of the hunting of a bitch fox was an entertaining feature of the occasion. All of the 'Sons' rose from the table sober."

The house of Edward Tuckerman on Dover Street was struck by a British cannonball during the siege of Boston. It was left embedded in a third-story beam as a badge of honor. Over on Temple Place, the front door of the Careys' house was made out of a piece of the *Constitution*.

On the Draper side, the wife of Captain William Draper, leader of one of Roxbury's three companies of minutemen, watched the British fire on the American volunteers at Ticonderoga and witnessed the disastrous retreat in which her husband died. Other Drapers were at Bunker Hill and the relief of Dorchester. At the Timothy Draper homestead in Roxboro, Vermont, Continental soldiers assembled to start for Lexington. Miss Sarah Draper kept the punch bowl from which they drank.

On Dorothy's mother's side of the family, Penelope Greene Minturn, cousin of General Nathanael Greene and wife of William Minturn, Newport's wealthiest merchant, traveled inland from Narragansett to Hudson, a city founded by her husband and other Newport ship owners to escape the bombardment of the British men-of-war. She made the perilous journey on horseback, wearing her entire wardrobe so that it wouldn't be taken from her.

Laura Gibbs was another intrepid woman in Dorothy's family tree. She was the daughter of Oliver Wolcott, Jr., who was appointed to the Treasury where he helped steady the ship of state after the Hamilton/ Burr affair. In gratitude, President Washington gave him two silver wine coolers that would become two of Dorothy's most cherished heirlooms. Laura Wolcott Gibbs (whose daughter married Dorothy's grandfather Lucius Tuckerman) was known for her artistic talent and her intense individuality. Dr. Henry Bellows wrote of her, "I always felt in the presence of Mrs. Gibbs as if I were talking with Oliver Wolcott himself and saw in her self-reliant, self-asserting and independent manner of speech an unmistakable copy of a strong and thoroughly individual character forged in the hottest fires of national struggle . . . a piece of the original granite on which this nation was built."

Laura Gibbs was an exquisite watercolorist. She executed a portrait of Alexander Hamilton as a young man that is often found in history book illustrations bearing the signature L. W. Gibbs. Her small, delicate painting of a peach was one of Dorothy's treasures.

Laura Wolcott Gibbs was not the only female ancestor who contributed to Dorothy's intense individuality. Mrs. Nathaniel Carey of Boston was outspoken in her condemnation of witchcraft during the hysteria that swept the Massachusetts colony in the seventeenth century. Soon after her husband left on a voyage to England, Mrs. Carey was arrested and imprisoned as a witch. Her daughter, with the help of a disguise, managed to get inside the prison and effect her mother's escape. Mrs. Carey fled to England on a ship more speedy than that of her husband,

and he was shocked to be greeted there by his wife. Family historian Bayard Tuckerman reports that his first words to his wife were "I really believe you are a witch and came over in an eggshell!" She is said to have replied, "Don't be a fool, Nat, like the rest of your countrymen."

The ancestors of Dorothy Tuckerman Draper thrived after the American Revolution, although not all of the founding families were as fortunate. The Reveres did not produce a dynasty; the Cabots were impoverished but, fortunately, married into money. From the beginning, American fortunes were plagued by violent economic mood swings. Fortunes were constantly made and lost. When Joseph Tuckerman appraised the estate of his friend John Hancock, he found nothing left for Hancock's heirs. Hancock, once the richest man in Boston, had been too generous in financing the Revolution, and his tastes ran to solid gold buttons. The famous family signature could not be cashed in to pay for a cottage in Newport and a house in town.

Dorothy's ancestors became rich in the early nineteenth century. "A cargo laid in at Canton will bring three for one in South America," wrote Joseph Tuckerman, Jr., to his father in the 1820s. Times had changed in Boston since the Puritan fathers had fined merchants for making too much profit. Returning home from a voyage during the Panic of 1837, however, he was greeted by his father, who threw open the window and shouted, "Joseph, we are ruined!" Fortunately, Joseph and his brother Lucius, Dorothy Tuckerman's grandfather, would recoup the family fortune many times over by mining iron ore shortly before the Civil War, but a lot of other old-money families lost everything in 1837.

While riding the train from Boston to New York one day, it dawned on Joseph Tuckerman that the future of the United States lay under his feet, in the railroads. Many other young men of the Eastern Establishment had the same idea. Joseph became a venture capitalist and bought into the iron ore business that was developing at Saugerties on the Hudson River.

Brother Lucius was pioneering in Chicago, a small town on the shore of Lake Michigan, with his bride, Elizabeth Gibbs Wolcott, when he received an urgent message from his brother to join him in his prospering iron business.

The brothers formed a company called J and L Tuckerman, and in twenty years emptied out the fabled Cheever ore pocket on Lake Champlain. It produced steel of greater tensile strength than any other made in the United States. Called Ulster ore, it made a huge fortune for the Tuckerman brothers. They had offices on the corner of Broadway and Wall Street in a brownstone overlooking Trinity Church, the spire of which at that time loomed high over the lower Manhattan landscape.

Lucius Tuckerman and Robert Bowne Minturn, Dorothy's maternal great-grandfather, were two of the small group of men who decided to establish a museum of European quality in New York. In 1863, they brought their own household treasures downtown to display, free to the public, in The Metropolitan Museum of Art's first location on 14th Street.

Robert Bowne Minturn also helped establish Central Park, and he was on the first commission designed to protect newly arrived immigrants from exploitation. According to the Minturn family history, the basement of his house on Chambers Street "resembled the outer courts of monasteries in olden times when the multitude came to be clothed and fed."

Lucius Tuckerman had six sons and three daughters, among them Dorothy's father, Paul. Lucius built a massive house at Sailor's Snug Harbor on Staten Island and kept a fast ship ready to sail at a moment's notice. In the cycles of boom and crash on the securities market, fortunes were made and lost in the blink of an eye, and a head start to Wall Street could mean the difference between riches and ruin. Later, he moved the family into 22 Washington Place, and when that neighborhood became overrun with new money, he moved uptown to 220 Madison Avenue on the outskirts of the city. The family spent their summers in Newport and Stockbridge, Massachusetts.

Unlike some other wealthy colonial families who enriched themselves on the country's frequent wars and then consolidated, the Tuckerman brothers made their killing, built mansions for their large families, and retired. The Vanderbilts chose a different path. Although they were a "First Family," the clan was slow in making its fortune. Fourth-generation Cornelius "Commodore" Vanderbilt began his career in poverty, running a ferry boat between Staten Island and Manhattan in the early part of the nineteenth century. He made his fortune running a fleet of leaky ships around Cape Horn during the Gold Rush, and then increased it a hundred times over by supplying well-aged meat to the Union navy. He then invested his bundle in a railroad system.

John Jacob Astor emigrated too late to be an official member of the Great Migration, coming in the late eighteenth century from Baden, Germany. According to one source, he was the son of a butcher; another source says he was the son of a flute importer. Astor got his start in business with a fur company owned by the Minturn family, which sent him up the Hudson River to buy furs at a good price from the Iroquois. Astor helped to deplete the Louisiana Purchase of its fur-bearing animals and amassed a huge fortune before his death in 1848.

By the Gilded Age, the House of Morgan had made the biggest fortune of all. Henry, the original Morgan, was a Caribbean pirate. The family fortune grew steadily from seventeenth-century Henry the pirate, to eighteenth-century Henry Morgan the stagecoach king, to nineteenth-century J. P. Morgan, the banking king. No other American family has been as consistently rich for so long. The half-million dollars the family earned during the American Revolution was a pittance compared to the money they made on the Civil War. It was said that when J. P. Morgan was on the high seas, he flew the skull and crossbones on his black painted yacht, the *Corsair*, in memory of his illustrious founding father.

The first man to be called a millionaire was Pierre Lorillard, the tobacco king, in 1843. A lot of other families were amassing new fortunes as well. James J. Cooke made one speculating in Union war bonds. Andrew Carnegie and James J. Hill began with nothing and ended up with millions by investing in steel and railroads, respectively. John D. Rockefeller piled up grocery profits in Cleveland and invested them in oil.

* * *

By the Gay Nineties, every twenty to thirty years, a cycle of panic (particularly the great Crash of 1873) on Wall Street would shake out small competitors. Sometimes, the demise of medium-size and even large competitors would follow. Families became corporations that ruled by divine right, for they could not be sued. They were as far above the law as any Stuart ever dreamed of being. Corporations joined together to become trusts, monopolizing entire industries. As the nineteenth century waned, more and more money passed into fewer and fewer hands, and the remaining victors became the ruling plutocrats for whom only one distinction counted—the size of one's fortune. They followed no code other than profit making. By the end of the nineteenth century, Rockefeller more or less owned the state of Colorado, and Carnegie was making twenty-three million dollars a *year*, tax free; the Czar of Russia managed his empire on half that amount. In fact, the cumulative wealth of all the civilizations of the world, from the pharaohs of Egypt to Czar Nicholas, did not equal the American fortunes that had been made playing the great Monopoly game of the nineteenth century.

Among the ruling class, battlefield distinction had been an important consideration since the days of Charlemagne, but the Civil War changed all that. Before the Civil War, aristocrats often led regiments into battle. But modern wars were not fought under the old code. Among the newly rich who paid someone three hundred dollars to fight for them in the Civil War were John D. Rockefeller, Andrew Carnegie, James Mellon, Philip Armour, and Jay Gould. Instead of earning aristocratic distinction on the battlefield, these new multimillionaires married it. Because of the volatile nature of the American stock market, there was always a plentiful supply of impoverished Old Guard from which to choose. A grocer baron from Cleveland could marry into the Aldrich family and become the lord of Pontico Hills—it was the American way. (In Maryland, the Du Ponts married each other until the head of the Dynasty forbade first cousins to wed.)

Before the Civil War, there were fewer than a half-dozen families in the country who spent more than sixty thousand dollars a year, a manageable number to invite to dinner. But the flood tide of new money that engulfed the enclaves of the Old Guard during the Gilded Age was completely unmanageable. Fifth Avenue was overrun with the newly rich, and they were spilling onto the side streets as far north as the Upper East Side.

The Old Guard had a number of names for the new people. Dorothy Draper used the bland "nouveau" when referring to her clients who reeked of large amounts of new money. However, she had no more disdain for them than a good schoolteacher has for her pupils. As far as she was concerned, they were just one more group of ignorant people who needed her good advice. Dorothy Draper did not shun them; she courted them, embraced them, and would move mountains for them. However, her ancestors went to great lengths to escape them. They lived in the Manhattan enclaves of the Old Guard, first in the elegant brick and brownstone homes of Washington Square and later moved uptown to the new enclave that began at 57th Street and ran from Central Park to Third Avenue. They belonged to the Union League Club, which also went to great lengths to exclude all but "family" from its membership.

The Old Guard called the newly rich by many names: the French *parvenu* and *arriviste,* the understated "go-getter," the parlor proper "newer element," or the more snobbish "outlander." Some of the more extreme blue bloods used terms like Emily Post's "vulgarian," also "mad dog," "robber baron," or even "the criminal element." Their fictional descendants would one day reign as the lords and ladies of East Egg.

In Newport the newly rich built castles of stone on the beach. Paul Bourget, commenting on the scene in 1894 (High Society at Newport), declared that Newport was finished. "At noon the women brought out their jewels . . . turquoises big as almonds, pearls large as filberts, diamonds large as their fingernails." The rustic *pique-niques* among the cucumbers and the tomatoes were replaced with lavish parties catered by New York's Delmonico's. There was such a crush at Mrs. Astor's ballroom door that she hired a distant relative named Ward McAllister to arbitrate. McAllister came from San Francisco, where everybody was a go-getter, and he never really understood who was in and who was out.

In his attempt to identify real society, which he referred to as "The Four Hundred," McAllister didn't even know that "real" society didn't clamor to get into Mrs. Astor's ballroom. Lady Astor was the self-proclaimed queen of New York society, the Leona Helmsley of her day. Nancy Langhorne, an Old White perennial and "family member" of the southern branch, referred to them as the "skunk-skinning Astors." (Nevertheless, she would marry one.) The running of society has always been the obsession of the recently arrived and the less secure. According to Lord Cecil, Ward McAllister's official "source," it took at least two generations to wash off oil and three to get rid of the smell of hogs. Ancestral portraits could be bought by the wall, but breeding took hundreds of years. The only way for the newly rich to acquire it was to marry it or have so much money that it didn't matter.

McAllister wrote a book (*Society as I Have Found It*) explaining how to enter the pearly portals of high society. He divided society into two groups—the nobs and the swells. A nob had to be to the manor born. A swell may or may not have the proper pedigree. A swell also had a lot of money. A nob did not necessarily have money. Advised McAllister, "A nob can be a swell if he spends the money, but for his social existence this is unnecessary. A swell creates himself."

The support of swells was necessary, he explained, "for society is sustained and carried on by the swells, the nobs looking quietly on and accepting the position, feeling they are there by divine right."

The Old Guard wasn't throwing any lavish parties for the nouveaux riches like the Astors, with favors from Tiffany's. Driven from Newport and the Manhattan enclave by a superabundance of wealthy people, nearly all of them strangers, the Old Guard drew its wagons in a circle and contemplated new vistas.

The old families were a private sort, so private that some of them remain virtually unknown. Shunning publicity became a way of life. One of the most powerful of Tuxedo Park's scions, George Baker, took pride in the fact that he had given one newspaper interview in his ninety years. His motto "Silence is Golden" made him extremely rich.

Real aristocrats lived in houses that could not be seen from the road, and anyone who played kiss-and-tell was never invited back. Their names did not appear in print except on museum plaques and road maps.

McAllister drew up a list of "The Four Hundred" and published it in the *New York Times*. He said that four hundred was the number of people who could be accommodated in Mrs. Astor's ballroom. The Tuckerman family name does not appear on the list, nor do the names of many of the founding fathers of Tuxedo Park, although McAllister could hardly have missed accounting for some of them.

It may be just a coincidence that the membership list of the Tuxedo Club was also limited to four hundred. Up on the Olympian heights there was no comment. Although the society press called the membership list of the Tuxedo Club "a guide to who is especially who in the four hundred," its founder, Colonel Pierre Lorillard IV, son of the first official millionaire, rejected the very idea as undemocratic. "I don't care a hoot if they're in the Social Register. Everybody's in the Social Register. What is a blue blood anyway?"

From the beginning, Tuxedo Park was designed as a refuge for the elite far from the din and clamor of those who were knocking on their doors. It was one of the most unique little towns in America. There has never been one like it, and most likely there never will be one again.

Tuxedo Park was the idea of Pierre Lorillard IV, great-grandson of the first official millionaire. He inherited a huge amount of land in the Ramapo mountains about forty miles from New York, which he expanded by playing poker with members of his family and winning. Lorillard belonged to the Union League Club, whose first president was Robert Bowne Minturn, as did the Tuckermans, Griswolds, Butlers, and Astors. From the Union League Club membership he formed a nucleus for a hunting and fishing community to be settled by invitation only. Its purpose would be "for the protection, increase and capture of all kinds of game and fish and for the promotion of social intercourse among its members." The few country clubs in existence at the time were small and unprepossessing. Tuxedo Park, with its five thousand acres of undeveloped wilderness, would be unique—an entire community completely in the control of the board.

The *New York Times* described the site as a beautiful wilderness where huge clumps of rhododendrons and dogwood grew. The woods were full of blueberries. It had once been a winter paradise for local Indians. Many sportsmen had enjoyed pulling bass from Tuxedo Lake (named, according to local legend, from Tauch Seeder, a local renegade who fought on both sides of the American Revolution). "Now the lake will be strictly private," lamented the *Times*. "Only members of the association or those persons who are so fortunate as to live within the limits of the park will be allowed the privileges of fishing in the park."

The building of Tuxedo Park during the winter of 1885 was a scene right out of ancient Egypt. Lorillard imported eighteen hundred workmen directly from Italy, built them a small city of shanties, and began blasting rock; the ambitious deadline of the spring of 1886 was set for the club opening. All through the summer and fall the workmen blasted and hauled tons of rock, ate in a mess hall called Lindy's, and slept in a bunkhouse on a street named Broadway. To make them feel less lonely, Lorillard had their bunkhouses painted bright pink and green to remind them of home. The New York names meant nothing to the laborers fresh from Naples and Sicily, but the press loved it, and published every available bit of news about what was going on in the Ramapo Mountains.

When in need of professional designing services, Lorillard turned to architect Bruce Price to design the park. He was from an impoverished Maryland family that had emigrated to America in the seventeenth century. Price had built cottages in Bar Harbor that he called "site-specific"—a concept far ahead of its time. His idea for Tuxedo Park was to blend the clubhouse and the "cottages" into the surrounding woodland so that the enclave would look as if it had been there for hundreds of years. The style was definitely Tudor. Price described the design of the gatehouse as "a frontispiece to an English novel." He managed to make the new look historic with plenty of natural camouflage. Walls of the gatehouse, post office, drugstore, and market were covered with moss and lichen. Shingles on the cottages were stained the deep russet and gray that come from centuries of weathering. The press called the style "shingle palace," and it intrigued many prospective colonizers, including the newlyweds Susan and Paul Tuckerman.

By the following autumn, the laborers had built eighteen miles of road, a water and sewer system, a village of stores that would serve the community, and a four-story clubhouse with a twenty-three-foot frontage, including a theater for the amusement of guests. There were one hundred bedrooms and one private bath, an oversight typical of the times. The immense stone walls of the gatehouse were like those of a fort. At the foot of the town that was owned by the club was the railroad station on a line owned by several of its members. And all around, like a moat, was an eight-foot fence and ten miles of bramble around that. Tuxedo Park was a self-contained, burglar-and-kidnapper-proof fortress right out of the Middle Ages.

Some club members were hesitant about living there. So much ground had been turned up at once, they feared the air was full of malaria. Others couldn't see how Lorillard's grand plans would ever prove financially successful. But Paul and Susan Minturn Tuckerman, married in March 1886, decided to colonize that first winter, as did their old friends the Grenville Kanes. The Lorillards settled the Park in the greatest numbers. Together with the Fosters and the Delafields, they made up half the Park's population. Price Collier, whose wife was a Delano, also signed up.

Tuxedo Park opened in October 1886 with the Autumn Ball. Hundreds of guests arrived on a special train from New York and were transported in open horsedrawn buses and tallyhos outfitted in the club colors of green and gold. As the buses made their way to the club, Orange County rustics appeared in gamekeeper garb, also in club colors and Tyrolean hats with black cock feathers. Lorillard hired them for the day to walk near the roads whenever they heard the buses coming. It was reported they hid in the bushes between appearances, afraid their friends would spot them.

At the gatehouse, good-looking policemen waved the buses through the gates. On the lakes that dotted the game reserve, eight-men rowing crews in snappy blue and white sailor suits manned barges filled with sightseers. The outside world roamed the hundred bedrooms and sought out the one bathroom. The atmosphere of the clubhouse was part hunting lodge, part palace, the sort of place where Henry VIII might have relaxed with his court at the end of a boar hunt. Guests in the manorial clubhouse sat on long leather sofas before wide, open medieval-style fireplaces burning five-foot logs. They were serviced by hallmen, footmen, and waiters, all dressed in full livery of green and gold.

The ballroom was circular, surrounded by built-in divans for the dowagers. The suspended parquet floor was reputed to be better than the one in the ballroom at White Sulphur Springs. Above, a domed ceiling gleamed like a jewel set among Corinthian columns. There was also a stage to provide for home entertainment, which was supplied by the amateur actors among the rich. It was fully equipped with footlights and draw curtains.

The opening quadrille was danced by the prominent fathers and mothers of the club. It was led by James Brown Potter, a member of the Tuxedo Park governing board, and his wife Cora Brown, flush with victory from her successful amateur theatrical performances in London. Later, Cora would shock the Tuxedo fathers by selling cosmetics, but in 1886 she was still easily cowed. That night Mrs. Brown was inwardly seething. Her guest, a Miss Fortesque, equipped with letters of introduction from prominent society people in London, did not appear at the festivities. "It is understood that this was in consequence of some objections made by members of the club," reported the *New York Times*. The objection was that Miss Fortesque was a member of the acting profession. Although Mrs. Lockwood had received Miss Terry that summer, and although Miss Fortesque "has never been a target for scandal beyond her breach of promise suit against Lord Garmoyle" the Old Guard at Tuxedo Park made it clear that what went on in the rest of the world had nothing to do with what went on inside the gates of Tuxedo Park. They would be entertained by members of the acting profession, but actors were not welcome as guests at the Tuxedo Club. Actors sang for their supper and they could be amusing, but they could not mingle with society.

Fashion history was created the night of the opening which made the name "Tuxedo" famous if not the town. Griswold Lorillard, one of the founder's sons, had just returned from England, where he had been the guest at the regatta ball where the Prince of Wales (later King Edward VII) had appeared with the tails of his dinner jacket removed similar to the short white jackets worn by the members of the royal yacht club. The Prince of Wales had tastes that were on the nautical side, which was why he was so popular with the Newport set. He creased his trousers on the side like the uniforms of the royal navy. But royalty had to modify. The jaunty Prince of Wales had his yachting jacket made in dignified black.

Young Griswold added a red vest. Society's gossip journal, *Town Topics,* claimed he looked "for all the world like a royal footman."

"Everyone wanted a jacket like Grizzie's," explained one of his friends. "Everybody just got tired of sitting on their tails," said another. The style eventually filtered all the way down to the lower classes as the *tuxedo,* although that word was never used in polite society, which continued to call it a dinner jacket.

The opening of Tuxedo Park changed not only the length of the dinner jacket but the very course of society. It shortened the New York season to a two-month revel in town, shorter even than that of London. The *New York Times* report on the change struck an ominous tone: "Small wonder is it, therefore, that city house after city house long occupied by well-known society people is rented and sold to the newer element which has not yet come to recognize the change in social conditions, and that the hopes of all young married couples are centered upon the selection of country and not as in bygone days, city homes. For the two months that New York society comes to town, houses, except to the very wealthy, are no longer possible luxuries, and hence the enormous and exorbitant rents that apartments and suites of rooms in hotels command from December until March.

"Now is the time for the student and philosopher to prepare his book, long discussed and anticipated, on New York society and to draw the 'deadly parallel' between it and that of older lands."

So much for classless society.

Growing up in the Magic Kingdom

Do not envy the rich, dear. Don't envy the society child.

—JAMES AMSTER

The first winter in Tuxedo Park, Paul Tuckerman kept a revolver in his bedroom and a megaphone to signal the night watchman.

"This would seem a bit surprising to anyone who knew Mr. Tuckerman," recalled George Rushmore in his account of Tuxedo days (*The World with a Fence Around It*), "for outwardly at least he was a mild-mannered gentleman of the old school, always rather formally attired and seemingly adapted to the most conventional surroundings."

Mrs. Tuckerman was decidedly unconventional. She was the first lady in Tuxedo Park to ride horses astride, in a divided skirt. When it came to convention, however, Tuxedo Park was much more unbending than the Greenbrier. At Old White the dowagers frequently had to pack their trunks and go to the nearby homestead when the celebrating got out of hand. Over the years, the Greenbrier dowagers saw belles drink champagne out of their slippers, as was the custom among the lower classes, and observed guests wearing see-through Egyptian pajamas on the porticoes. The dowagers of Tuxedo Park would tolerate none of that behavior. There was a fuss when Mrs. Tuckerman strolled around the lake wearing a tweed skirt that cleared the ground and showed her ankles at each stride. Despite the criticism, Dorothy's mother remained a style-setter—and a perfect lady.

The Tuckermans' honeymoon cottage was about a quarter-mile up the hill from the clubhouse. The surrounding forest nearly obliterated the outside world; they could barely see the cottage of their next-door neighbors, the Kanes.

During the first few years, there was a baby boom in Tuxedo Park. The word was out: Tuxedo Park was a grand place to go to get away from the influence of Mother and Dad in the family fiefdom. A young group settled there; they were willing to rough it until they had all the amenities. In other resorts people came and went with the season, but Tuxedo Park was so pleasant that many families with young children stayed year-round and made it home. A kitchen-table conviviality, reminiscent of Newport's atmosphere before the invasion of the newly rich, set the spirit in the cottages of the Tuxedo Park colonizers.

In 1889 there were thirty-seven residents living in Tuxedo Park. Paul Tuckerman was on the Committee on Amusements and the Committee on Tennis, and he and his wife were joyfully awaiting the birth of their first child. The winter of 1889 was a blizzard year. On November 22, before the worst of the storms arrived, Mrs. Paul Tuckerman delivered a baby girl. They named her Dorothy, but from the day of her birth Paul Tuckerman called her Star. Their neighbors, the Kanes, were also raising a family: By 1891 they had five daughters. The Tuckermans saw their nearest neighbors frequently because Kane refused to have a telephone installed in his home. His youngest daughter was a grown woman before he relented. Kane was renowned for his thrift. The family used the same paper Christmas tree each year. The Kane governess had a mule instead of a donkey to draw her cart. One of Kane's peers said if he ever got a check out of Kane he'd frame it. Every year, however, the Kanes sponsored a fancy dress lawn party where their five accomplished daughters could entertain their friends: It was the height of the children's social season. A group photograph of one of the Kane spectaculars reveals Averell Harriman as a mandarin, Eleanor Alexander (later Mrs. Theodore Roosevelt) as a French peasant, and Dorothy Tuckerman in a Japanese costume.

There were plenty of other children for little Star to play with in Tuxedo Park. The Alexander girls lived nearby, and they had a real stucco-and-beam, Tudor-style playhouse down the road from their house. The Harrimans built a large house not far from the north gate. When the neighborhood children came over to play with their ponies, Mrs. Harriman served ginger ale and little French cakes.

In Tuxedo Park, children were given much more freedom than was usual for the offspring of the rich. Founding father William Waldorf Astor told the press that he had bought an estate in England because America was too dangerous to live in: The risk of burglars and kidnappers was too great. But Astor's children played safely in Tuxedo Park; a private police force on guard day and night at each of its four gates patrolled its eight-foot fence. Some residents didn't lock their doors. Unlike Newport, where detectives hovered nearby as the children of the rich built castles in the sand, in Tuxedo Park they roamed free.

In the winter Little Star skated on the black ice in the cove across from the clubhouse. There she and her friends practiced the grapevine and continental styles of skating, imitating the Park's champion skater, "Count Cravatsky," a descendant of Montesquieu who earned his nickname because of his flowing necktie. The Scotts brought back bobsleds from St. Moritz. There was an electrically lit toboggan slide a half-mile long. The hills were dotted with skiers and servants dragging sleds. The roads were well packed by sleigh runners, and sleighbells jingled between the great houses. On Sunday afternoons the children were allowed in the clubhouse under the supervision of their nannies and governesses for hot cider and sugared doughnuts.

In the summer, horse shows and dog shows were held on the racetrack but the highlight of the season was the Fourth of July. On that day Tuxedo Park was open only to the villagers and their friends. A procession of them came in through the gates after breakfast, chattering in many languages. Club members got up a purse for prizes. Bicycle races were a big favorite, often wild and bloody affairs. A red-haired Italian boy named Red Amaroso won several years in a row. Little girls in white dresses waved flags.

* * *

Tuxedo Park was famous for its outdoor life. Once a favorite playground of Indians, the club never became a haven for hunting and fishing. The children had domesticated the wilds. The deer wore pink ribbons. The artificial shooting parties where beaters flushed imported pheasant and quail toward the hunters failed. The birds escaped to the open fields where they preferred to live. Lorillard had stocked the lakes with one hundred thousand bass and German carp, but the carp grew up and ate the bass and that was that.

But the atmosphere remained sporting. During evenings around the clubhouse fire, the Marquis de Mores, who had a chateau outside Fort Lincoln in Dakota territory, would tell the gathered elite stories of the Wild West, whose mystique appealed to the Tuxedoites, always ready for a new thrill. The French were especially drawn to it.

Exclusiveness was what the upper crust wanted in sport. Tennis and golf eventually became democratized, but court tennis did not; therefore, it was a preferred sport for the upper class. In fact, it was played only in Tuxedo Park and a few other very exclusive places. Even sportsmen who could discuss the relative merits of one- or two-masted yachts could not always hold their own when court tennis buffs began talking of sloping buttresses and penthouses on the hazard side. The game was so complicated people studied it for years. Onlookers also had to study, just to understand the rules. The sport was so arcane that sometimes some-one won a tournament just by showing up to play.

Unfortunately, the "go-getters" infiltrated the game. When "mad dog" Jay Gould won the tournament two years in a row, the Tuxedo Park founding fathers abandoned court tennis at the club.

The sports that really mattered were the equestrian events. Saratoga was the center of the horsey set, but Tuxedo Park's horse shows were high points of the social season.

Little Star was not enthusiastic about sports, but she participated nevertheless. In such an environment, she had no choice. The Harriman daughters, Mary, Cornelia, and Carol, were all fine equestriennes, as were the five Kane girls. Mrs. Draper would later say with amazement, "I raised three equestrian children. I don't understand it." Nevertheless, when she was only eight years old, she held her own against a gang of Julliards, Lorillards, Harrimans, Bakers, and Poors. In the horse show of 1900, in Class Nine, children's ponies under fourteen hands driven by children younger than seventeen, Henry Poor won first place and Dorothy, driving her pony Jack Ugly finished third. Incidentally, Jack Ugly lived to the ripe old age of thirty-three.

Watching in the box was Dorothy's father, by that time a Tuxedo father as well. He had been a member of the Committee on Amusements and the Committee on Tennis since 1888. In a more serious vein, he led the fight for a library for the town. Hundreds of thousands of dollars had been invested in homes, he chided, but none in a library. "There can be no finer charity than to supply one's less capable neighbors with the opportunity to train their minds," he told the *Tuxedo News* in its one and only edition in November 1900. The publication lasted in Tuxedo Park about as long as the bass.

Paul Tuckerman was president of the board of directors of the Tuxedo Stores Company, which was truly a *company* store. According to the *Tuxedo News,* the board "provided the best the markets could afford at a regulated cost." With a large working capital, perfect delivery system, and a policy of no more than two months' credit, there was "a decline in prices and wonderful improvement in the quality of the food."

The town was run like Liechtenstein. The chairman of the board was also the chief executive. The ruling body sold land in the Park to selected members and rented it in the village, where shopkeepers were tenants at the sufferance of the residents of the Park, upon whom they relied exclusively for business.

Tuxedo Park had its own police force. No visitor could get by the gatehouse without the guards telephoning ahead. The stream of servants came and went with special passes. Only one man actually earned his living in the Park—Dr. Rushmore.

Because so many residents commuted to Wall Street, Tuxedo Park qualified as the first bedroom community in the United States, although the number of bedrooms per home puts it in a special category. With the proliferation of the telephone, it was no longer necessary for an investor to keep a fast ship ready to sail to Wall Street when panic struck, and commuting from Tuxedo Park was an easy matter with the railroad station outside its gates.

Many special train privileges were granted with all the railroad czars living in the Park. Although the quality of train service was a national scandal, the Tuxedo Park express was not only on time but also usually a few minutes ahead of schedule. With a short run of sixty-four miles, it was the flagship of the Erie Lackawanna line. By displaying the club badge, an oak leaf pin of solid gold, any member of the Tuxedo Club could stop any train on the line, even one that didn't stop at Tuxedo Park, and the schedule would be made up elsewhere. The Western Express even stopped for members down by the signal tower a mile below the Tuxedo station.

Paul Tuckerman was part of the group that made the daily commute. Like many other heads of households, he was a member of the "trustee generation," sons of fathers who had made a killing. These men were often mild-mannered like Mr. Tuckerman—in contrast, perhaps, to their lion-hearted father—and some developed a genius for making, not earning, money. They played the stock market like chancellors of the exchequer. At his office at 32 Cedar Street, Paul Tuckerman was trustee for his brothers, sisters, and cousins. As his cousin Bayard put it in the family history, "[Paul Tuckerman's] abilities have been advantageously employed for the benefits of our family and others whose interests have been confined to his care." But he was a conserver, not an aggrandizer. His income was eighty thousand dollars a year, a pittance compared to what the go-getters in the Park made; they had footmen behind every chair. By comparison, the ten servants he employed were a modest-size staff for the Park. Because of Lorillard's rule regarding the employment of servants (stablemen were stablemen and gardeners were gardeners), there was no such thing as a small staff in Tuxedo Park.

The period of greatest opulence in Tuxedo Park was around the turn of the century. William McKinley was in office, and that was good for business. The spread of organized labor and the graduated income tax were still a bad dream. Within the gates of the Park, the dawning of the new century could not have looked more rosy. Tuxedo Park had never been so popular, or so difficult to get into. A person who wanted to be a member asked someone in the club to propose his name for membership and another member to second the proposal. Then he waited. People who bought a house in the Park before getting elected to the club (which was technically possible) were usually blackballed for their inability to delay gratification. At the annual meeting in June, new members were admitted by ballot. One negative vote in seven would mean exclusion.

In the beginning, the vast majority of the Tuxedo Club membership lived outside the Park. At the turn of the century there was a building boom, and homes had never been more magnificent. The original Bruce Price cottages on Tower Hill that blended so modestly into the background became an anachronism. Victorian Gothic dinosaurs with porches on every flank topped by turrets and domed towers, gargantuan Renaissance chateaus, and gray stone-and-timber mountain abbeys rose on every side. The interiors were as irregular as the exteriors. Rooms of odd shapes spanned several levels. Flights of stairs led nowhere. Rooms were laid out like a funhouse maze but were not much fun: Often they were dark and stiff of texture. Every surface was encrusted with inlay and gilt. Precious works of art never saw the light of day in overstuffed parlors and dimly lit halls.

The goal was splendor in the dark. Dark walls were a foregone conclusion: Vast swathes of mahogany were varnished every year until their patinas were as dark as the oak that was stained to look like them. Replicas of castles included windows that had once been made deliberately small, high, and narrow for the purpose of fortification. But size didn't make a difference. Even when windows were large, they were swathed in as many layers of drapery as women were in petticoats.

Sanford White designed a large brick Tudor house for Henry Poor at the top of Tower Hill, just below Imlaugh, the original Lorillard cottage. Unfortunately, Poor went bankrupt shortly after it was completed and sold it to Henry M. Tilford, the president of Standard Oil of Ohio, for a half-million dollars. The Monroe house was built in the style of a French chateau. The Spencer Trask house was an Elizabethan abbey.

Meanwhile, in New York City, the craze for a bigger and better house was running rampant. Up and down Fifth and Madison Avenues mansions that looked like architectural salads were being erected, the owners apparently afraid to leave out anything impressive.

Tuxedoites were eager to install the latest amenities. In the early years they had been the first community whose residents were simultaneously wired for telephones (except the Kanes, of course). They were also among the first communities to break the Victorian tradition of de-emphasizing the existence of bodily functions. The Tuxedo Club had been built with one hundred bedrooms and only one bathroom, but the mansions had many bathrooms, each as large as bedrooms. A guest in the A. D. Julliard house recalled asking a footman for directions to the toilet, and upon discovering a chaise lounge and a fireplace on the other side of the door, decided he had made a mistake and had entered a bed chamber. Not so, a footman assured him. It was the bathroom.

When Dorothy was four years old, she and her family moved out of their Bruce Price honeymoon cottage on the west side of Lookout Road, into a new home designed by the architect James Brown Lord. It was in the ancestral Tudor style, ignoring the current fashion. According to the Tuxedo Park registry of houses, "The style, mainly decorative, is subordinate to the expression of elegance and wealth." The ornate scrollwork, etched copper drain troughs, and exquisite sundial were more in the American decorative tradition—the useful made an object of beauty—than in the continental manner of art for art's sake.

In 1899, the size of the Tuckerman family had increased to four with the birth of a son, Roger, the year before. The family finally succumbed to the rage of building a bigger mansion and moved across Lookout Road into a Romanesque villa (National Register of Historic Places, inventory #1-99). Majestic in location, it was surrounded entirely by woodland. Its stone carriage house had more dignity than Manhattan's most lavish mansion. The villa was majestic of proportion as well—three stories in height. It had sandstone mullions, leaded windows, and a slate roof—a fairyland house.

Its structure did not reflect the weather of the English countryside as the first Tuckerman house had; rather, its vast open courtyard spoke of more temperate climates, although it had the obligatory English lawn of clipped velvet. A dream house, it was impeccably decorated: Mrs. Tuckerman was a standard-bearer of good taste all of her adult life. The interior of the Tuckerman house was not a backdrop for the display of recent purchases, as was the custom in the homes of the newly rich.

Dorothy's parents didn't buy much furniture, preferring to use what they already had. There was a desk that had belonged to Oliver Wolcott, signer of the Declaration of Independence, and the silver wine coolers given to his son by George Washington. There was French furniture brought over in the ships of George Gibbs the Elder, after the Revolution of 1789. There were also the Minturn family treasures, which were packed in green tea for the voyage to America on the *Sea Witch*, the ship that made the Canton to New York run in seventy-seven days, stocked with goodies bought cheap to sell dear. The Tuckerman family historian notes, "In those days, all that came from China was the finest and best—screens, silks, furniture, and carvings brought by people who picked them out for themselves."

Dorothy Tuckerman grew up surrounded by ancestral portraits done by Gilbert Stuart, Chester Harding, John Singleton Copley, John Trumbull, and Thomas Sully. The Stuart portraits were particularly distinctive because Colonel Gibbs was a great friend of the painter: His portrait is considered by some to be the finest of all Stuart's works. The home that little Star grew up in was chock-full of the best—Gainsborough drawings, Whistler etchings, Turner watercolors, Venetian glass, Clevenger's bust of Oliver Wolcott, eighteenth-century Newport hurricane globes, and Dutch inlaid cabinets filled with "Famille Rose" Lowestoft china.

With such a collection of "hand-me-downs," there was no need to impress in the Tuckerman home. The Tuckermans could not rightfully be called snobs, nor could they be held accountable for their acceptance of the prevailing doctrine of snobbery—it was the climate of Tuxedo Park. Snobbery reached great heights: Excluded were all races and creeds except White Anglo-Saxon Protestant (and many of them were shut out as well). Perhaps they were deliberately blind to life in the real world, but they were not snobs.

"The rich are different," wrote F. Scott Fitzgerald, but his depiction of the East Egg scene and life among the swells wasn't different at all: Infidelity, treachery, display, and blood on the highway—such are the usual elements of night-time soap opera. The scene at Tuxedo Park was as different from the scene at East Egg as Camelot is from *Dynasty.* The code of behavior the Park's residents tried to live up to wasn't just different—it was unique. "Obedience to the unenforceable" was the motto of the Auchincloss clan. Mark Twain called good breeding "concealing how much we think of ourselves and how little we think of others."

The ruling classes from East Egg to West Podunk emulated the nobs on high, and that behavior was eventually codified for the general public by a Tuxedo Park resident, Emily Post, the daughter of architect Bruce Price. But ordinary people had as much chance of acquiring good breeding by memorizing the table settings in her *Bluebook of Social Usage* as putting together an assemble-it-yourself Rolls Royce. The purr wouldn't be there.

Daughters of the newly rich were sent to finishing school to learn the form if not the content of what Dorothy Tuckerman and her friends learned at their mothers' (or, more likely, nannies') knees. But the end result was not the same. Ward McAllister claimed that Mrs. Post was one of ten women who could gracefully walk across a ballroom floor alone. One did not learn overnight or even in a semester to walk into society's spotlight and not seem to notice a bit. According to Mr. McAllister, that self-possession took centuries to develop.

Mrs. Post used the term "thoroughbred" to describe the manners of those to the manor born. Without breeding, people went wild in the presence of large amounts of money, especially if a lot of money was acquired very suddenly. Children of the nouveaux riches often lived scandalous lives because they were not properly bred from an early age. By contrast, the life of the aristocratic child was spartan. One toy was removed from the toy closet each day. When a child was packed off to boarding school at a tender age, he or she learned the meaning of delayed gratification in a way that a child who brings a videodisc of the "Care Bears" to a birthday party to ward off the possibility of boredom never will.

How *did* a woman learn to walk alone across a ballroom floor with grace? "Do not swing your arms as if on a golf course or rest your hand on your hips but glide like Pavlova dancing," advised Mrs. Post. Dorothy Tuckerman learned the social graces under the tutelage of Miss Robinson, a severe woman remembered for her black accordion-pleated skirt. In the Tuxedo Club ballroom, prepubescent boys wearing long herringbone pants and Eaton jackets, and girls wearing miniature "mommie" dresses, learned how to curtsy, waltz, and promenade in the popular quadrilles, which were not dances so much as chances to show off one's outfit.

Children of Tuxedo Park honed their skills at parties chaperoned by their governesses and nannies. They were sometimes boisterous. They liked Punch and Judy shows and shouted loudly when the whacking started, and they cut loose like a tribe of Mohicans when playing "Musical Chairs," the children's version of the games their fathers played on Wall Street, where gilt chairs fell with a smash.

Of course, such behavior was frowned upon by the Tuxedo fathers and dowagers, who had been much too staid to even mildly participate in the Gay Nineties. George Rushmore recalled a crazy but brief exception to the rules of comportment during the time of Dorothy's childhood. It took place on the clubhouse stairs. The game was to toboggan down the stairs on silver Tuxedo Club trays. Girls used boys as pillows to land on, and boys enjoyed catching them. The youngsters enjoyed the game immensely until James L. Breese was overheard commenting on the view from the landing. That was the end of tray tobogganing.

Becoming a thoroughbred wasn't all play. Children graduated from nannies to governesses, most of whom were French. Governesses sometimes merged with the family until they became known as "the Monroe's Mademoiselle" or "the Tilford's Fraulein." Dorothy was educated by the Tuckerman's Mademoiselle. The Kane girls also did not go away to school: They had an English governess, Miss Dusenberry.

Tutors were employed as the children grew older. Miss Hale, who taught in Tuxedo Park for awhile, found it impossible to teach a class that changed as frequently as the seasons. The Monroes came in the summers and occasionally in the winters. The Hamilton Fish family were autumn residents. The Seatons spent summers in Tuxedo Park if they didn't go abroad. Others followed the resorts and were there for the "season," two months in the spring and again in the fall. Although the Tuckermans considered the Park home, they were also constantly abroad. Only the Kanes and the Rushmores were year-round residents.

Dorothy spent two years at the fashionable Brearley School in Manhattan, between the eighth and the ninth form. Her grades were not spectacular, average and below average. Dorothy hated Brearley, and rarely mentioned that she had even attended. Why did she leave? In a 1940 article in *Harper's Bazaar,* Janet Flannery reported "[Dorothy] was removed from school because she was supposed not to be strong, which on looking back, [Dorothy] does not believe."

Dorothy did not do much reminiscing about Brearley. In fact, she rarely mentioned her one brush with formal education, following the code, "Never complain, never explain." Dorothy was a visual person, not a scholar. "I don't read. I think," she would one day explain to those who asked her how she prepared herself for her career. For whatever reason, her time spent at "dreary Brearley" was not a period in her life that the positive-thinking Mrs. Draper dwelt upon.

Dorothy's inability to adjust to the Brearley mentality was early evidence of her iconoclasm. Her insistence on the right to her individuality was always one of her major strengths. Brearley girls were not bred to have the kind of strong opinions Dorothy was not only allowed but encouraged to have by her parents and Mademoiselle. Her refusal to defer to the model of the Brearley girl resulted in her withdrawal from school and return to her understanding parents. Thirteen-year-old Dorothy happily returned to Tuxedo Park to romp once again in the rose garden and the mountains beyond it, her explorations interspersed with lessons from Mademoiselle and other tutors. They all had trouble capturing Dorothy's attention, which had a way of wandering into the realm of fantasy. Still, she learned excellent French and acquired a zest for knowing about those aspects of the world she found interesting.

Her education was broadened with yearly trips to Europe. Travel abroad increased the Tuckerman women's appreciation of fine things. The beautiful clothing, jewelry, and decorative objects of Vienna, exquisite hand-made works of art, captured their fancy. They marveled at the Fladermaus Café, perfection of form down to the coffee spoons. In Florence they gasped at the quality of the color and the light. They toured museums, cathedrals, and royal gardens; Dorothy's mother would comment enthusiastically on the flora. Susan Tuckerman also had a zest for life and a curiosity about everything she saw.

Mrs. Draper did not talk much about her childhood and adolescence, even to her own children. Although she passed on her knowledge of her ancestral history in minute detail, down to the ages of the crew of Gibbs's *Flying Cloud* ("Not a one over twenty-one, including the captain"), she did not talk about her own history, except for an occasional memory of jingle bells through the snow. The adolescence of a very tall girl is a well-known horror tale, and perhaps Dorothy's reticence to talk about her early years can be traced to self-consciousness about her height.

For the first ten years of her life, Dorothy was a pretty little girl, perfectly normal in every respect. The gangly Star of twelve or thirteen was not that different from her coltish friends who played in the Tuxedo hills. Perhaps Dorothy was just a bit ganglier than the Alexander and Kane girls. But then distance began to separate her from the rest of her peers, girls and boys alike. Dorothy went beyond gangly to tall, and then beyond tall to very tall—5'9" of adolescent taking off irregularly in all directions.

At the age when a person's self-image is the most precarious, Dorothy saw herself as out of scale, too big for everybody. Without her consent, she had become larger than life. Boys who had been her comrades in play now squinted up at her, angry and uncomfortable at the way she towered over them. They didn't want her around because she made them feel so small. From Dorothy's perspective, the boys made her feel big and ungainly. An aversion to small men remained with her for life.

Throughout Dorothy's trial, her mother was her only hope. Susan Tuckerman was a beauty to her bones. She had exquisite shoulders and a swanlike neck, and cheekbones that met the forehead and chin at the right aesthetic angle. That Dorothy would emerge from her grueling "finishing" to look like her mother was what the young girl prayed for. Her mother's sense of humor also helped. Susan's sister Katie Leroy was critical of her free-spirited niece, but Susan and Dorothy just laughed it off.

Other imperfections made themselves more evident in Dorothy's world as she grew. For instance, she learned that there was a fence around Tuxedo Park. What she had been led to believe was a playground for grown-ups and children was actually a fortress, and she reacted to the news as if the fence were there to keep her from getting out, not to prevent predators from getting in.

Dorothy's ancestry was different from that of many people in Tuxedo Park. Her mother's ancestors were from Rhode Island, the state that was originally a colony established by Roger Williams for iconoclasts like Ann Hutchinson. The Minturns and Gibbs of Newport had the free-spirited island mentality as well. Dorothy really took to heart the Rights of Man her Revolutionary ancestors had fought and died for. Although she grew up in the summer citadel of the plutocrats, she believed absolutely in the democratic ideal of the classless society. The naïveté of her patriotism, which she would one day display with red, white, and blue élan at *Good Housekeeping,* came not from drills learned at school but from tales around the family fire. Dorothy was a true believer, and because of that she was a great communicator. She democratized.

But the adolescent Dorothy had no way of knowing that her current discomfort would one day become her liberating force, that her name would be a voice in the wilderness urging people to break the bonds of social dicta. The miserable girl was for the moment trapped, like Alice in Wonderland, in her much too little house, growing much too big for Tuxedo Park.

But nothing lasts forever, not even adolescence. In France around the time of her sixteenth birthday in 1904, Dorothy came down to dinner and heard a man at a nearby table say, *"La jeune fille—quelle jolie."* Not *la* grande *jeune fille*, just *jolie*, which she had begun to confirm for herself. Now someone else confirmed it for her. The height she had once propelled through space with such difficulty she now bore to devastating effect. It made her commanding, like a fun Eleanor Hall. The woman that Dorothy became had inherited her mother's swanlike neck, exquisite shoulders, and strong patrician bones. Added to that was the Wolcott majesty, which made her entry into a room an occasion. All eyes could not help but be drawn to her. Dorothy had a way of gliding through space that was grander than that of her diminutive mother, and more majestic than that of the dainty Mrs. Post. Dorothy Tuckerman came into a room in full sail, like the flagship of her great-great-grandfather Gibbs's fleet of seventy-five clippers.

Becoming a Thoroughbred in the Edwardian Age

Edwardian: reflecting the self-satisfaction or opulence characteristic of the reign of Edward VII.

Dorothy Draper came of age in the Edwardian era and remained Edwardian in attitude throughout her life. An Edwardian lived by a highly prescribed code of behavior: Attracting publicity was one taboo among many others. In Tuxedo Park, the maintenance of privacy was carried to the point of catatonia. The wives of certain scions were not allowed to address their husbands by their first names. Not even children were called by their first names outside the immediate family. This custom was one of the things about Tuxedo Park that made the exuberant Dorothy want to scream.

Another taboo was the discussion of personal matters. Dorothy Draper had a way of looking through people who confided in her about personal matters and acting as if she hadn't heard a thing. Even her closest friends were spared her tales of woe about husbands and children. As Emily Post described it, "To be courteously polite and yet keep one's walls up is a thing every thoroughbred person knows how to do. A vulgarian has no walls."

Behind those walls, a thoroughbred revealed no more about his or her feelings than does a good poker player. Vulgarians, on the other hand, displayed every emotion they felt—anger, excitement, fear, embarrassment, passion—privately and in public. A thoroughbred suffered no embarrassment by little social mistakes. Knock over a glass? A servant will clean it up.

The mark of good breeding was not how one conducted oneself on a sunny day in the rose garden: That behavior could be easily learned by rote. How one behaved when the chips were down was what counted. Ignoring hardship was a trademark of the British Empire, and the source of "Only mad dogs and Englishmen go out in the noonday sun." Complaining about matters that were beyond one's control was useless and vulgar. Besides, no discomfort lasted for long. At the end of it was a hot bath and a massage, a light soup and a heavy salmon.

No matter what the occasion, true thoroughbreds did not make a fuss. Even at funerals they displayed none of the emotion that the rest of the world indulged in.

From high drama to everyday matters, thoroughbreds did nothing with a splash. Every detail spoke of understated elegance. The paper they wrote on was of the weight of a starched shirt front, but it was never scented or oddly shaped. Their correspondence was equally reserved: They signed off with "sincerely yours" in the British manner and never the innovative "cordially yours" or "hastily yours" or the unspeakable "warmly yours." Effusive Americans often reversed good form, as in their passion for initials. The last name was good enough for a duke and just the first name was good enough for a queen.

Modesty was the thing. The royal walk, hands behind the back, was the most nonthreatening of gestures. Only the truly powerful were allowed to display such a sign of weakness. And one never, never criticized. The code of Thumper's mother, "If you can't say something nice, don't say anything at all," prevailed. Compliments were considered impolite. There was never any doubt about the quality of the food or the decor, so nothing needed to be said. Besides, flattery was always suspect. A well-bred person also avoided superlatives: An estate was a farm; a mansion, a cottage; a limousine, a car; and a chauffeur, a driver. Only the nouveaux riches used the word *suite* instead of *room*.

Punctuality was another point upon which the well-bred and the ill-bred differed widely. Being fashionably late was vulgar. A thoroughbred was taught that punctuality was the politeness of kings. The well-bred Edwardian gentleman or lady could not be late, or discuss religion or politics, or talk about money. (J. P. Morgan once said when asked about the cost of a yacht, "If you have to ask you can't afford it.") Acceptable topics were few: the weather, horticulture, sports, bird watching, and the nonscandalous news. Talk about the royal family was always appropriate, except for news of the Prince of Wales. It was forbidden to mention him in the presence of ladies.

Fortunately for Dorothy, her mother and father paid no attention to the more restricting elements of the code. Beyond an insistence on social responsibility and kindness to all, Dorothy was not burdened with rules of behavior, although she kept many of the taboos throughout her life.

"A lady does not improvise," admonished Miss Graham at her finishing school on West 12th Street in New York City. There, the daughters of the newly rich were turned over to her to prepare for entry into society. She was extremely strict: Any student who failed to become a top debutante had her name struck from Miss Graham's records. Miss Graham's rule that ladies did not improvise might have been true for most of society, but not for Dorothy Draper and her mother.

When a graduate of Miss Graham's finishing school had her portrait done, the proper place to go was to Rosina Emmett Sherwood, a few blocks away on the west end of 10th Street near Sixth Avenue. There, an entire building full of artists gave society a taste of Bohemian life along with their likenesses in oil. But the Tuckerman ladies didn't go there for Dorothy's portrait. They went instead to the Fenway, in the upper stratosphere of Boston's Back Bay, where the grande dame of high society innovators, Isabella Stuart Gardner of the Scottish royal family, was the patron of the artist John Singer Sargent. Mrs. Jack, as she was called, took her innovation seriously. She walked the streets with a lion named Rex on a leash. She drank beer. She studied the Eastern mystical religions and received her guests while perched in a tree. She formed her own club, called the "It" club.

In her palace brought stone by stone from Florence, John Singer

Sargent painted the adventurous women of her class. He did several of his patron, too. One revealed her as curvaceous in a low-neck black dress with a rope of pearls around her waist. It nearly caused a riot when it was exhibited in 1889, and Mr. Gardner had it removed from the show.

A woman whose motto was *C'est mon plaisir* was dangerous to society. In Connecticut, Roger Wolcott forbade his wife to accept an invitation from Mrs. Gardner. But Mrs. Paul Tuckerman and her daughter had no such restrictions put on them.

Susan Tuckerman had her portrait executed when she was in her late teens. She is portrayed with a long neck; straight back; short, sleek dark hair; prominent facial bones; and luminous, somber, arresting eyes. Dorothy Tuckerman's portrait at age twenty was executed in charcoal by John Singer Sargent at his studio in Isabella Gardner's palace. It shows a proud woman with her mother's long neck, finely boned shoulders, and large eyes, but the eyes are not somber. There is a challenge in the set of the jaw and the straightforward glint in the eyes. Both faces are similar in their artlessness, strikingly without pose. Having nothing to prove to anyone, they were simply themselves, and the world found that more than sufficient.

Liberated from the need to prove themselves, Susan and Dorothy Tuckerman were free to imagine who they were and then create themselves. What they wrought was fearless. Eleanor Hall Roosevelt did settlement work rather than charity balls like the other women of her class. Susan Tuckerman also went out into the world to try to do some good. Tasting pork chops for the first time in the kitchens of the state institution for the insane (until that moment she had not known people actually ate pork), she pronounced them "absolutely delicious."

Individualism seemed to flow in the genes of the Tuckerman women, but there were restrictions imposed upon them at Tuxedo Park. The ultra-individualists resided at the Greenbrier, where the custom of champagne with watermelon for breakfast loosened up the atmosphere considerably. Down at the Greenbrier, the racy Mrs. William K. Vanderbilt rode a bicycle wearing bloomers and told her following, "Brace up, my dears, and pray to God. *She* will help you." Meanwhile, on Bailey's Beach in Newport, where Tuxedoites took the sun, Mrs. Tuckerman and her daughter would emerge fully clothed from the water to be wrapped immediately in long bathing capes, lest their forms be seen.

Although Tuxedo Park drew a more restrictive line at individuality, Mrs. Tuckerman continued to shake up the dowagers even after she became one of them. However, she didn't go as far as the shocking Rowena McKim, who smoked, swore, flirted, and used makeup. Susan was more of an innovator.

Around the turn of the century she appeared in her pièce de résistance, an evening dress that kept the Tuxedo tongues wagging over many an afternoon tea. It was a tightly fitting black sequined evening dress with long sleeves and a train. At the end of the train was the tail of a snake in brilliant green sequins that wound around her body, its head resting on one shoulder.

Tuxedo women could display their individuality in the Park, but they could not make a career of it in the outside world. Men and women alike could perform as amateurs but never as professionals, especially in the acting profession, which Pierre Lorillard did not approve of. Fortunately, Dorothy was not the first one to break through that barrier. Around 1890, Emily Price Post had first appeared in an amateur theatrical production at the Tuxedo Club and was a sensation. According to her son Edwin's biography of his mother (*Truly Emily Post*), Lorillard complained to Bruce Price, "She's too good. You must not let her go on." Emily's mother agreed that her daughter must be prevented from the kind of public exposure that actors received. Emily's stage career ended that night, but she found another way to express her creativity— writing.

The stage careers of Elsie deWolfe and Cora Brown Potter were also launched at Tuxedo Park. Elsie, who was to become one of the first professional interior decorators, was not a member of the Tuxedo set. She was born on the unfashionable West Side of Manhattan, not far from the present site of Macy's. But Cora Potter was a Tuxedoite through and through, and she went professional in spite of Lorillard's rules. She caused an uproar when she sent out letters of endorsement of her Harriet Hubbard Ayer line of cosmetics on Tuxedo Club stationery.

But the loosening of restrictions in the Park was not enough for Dorothy. There was still its wretched fence, its stuffy attitudes, its dank and airless rooms swathed in dusty velvet, and its deadly dull conversation that centered around gossip in spite of the code bluebloods were supposed to follow. Dorothy was not interested in sports, was an indifferent card player, and did not care to mingle in the usual social intrigue. The atmosphere suffocated her, and she yearned to find a way out. While the rest of society clamored to get into Tuxedo Park, Dorothy Tuckerman couldn't wait to get out.

Escape

Dorothy's one experience on her own outside Tuxedo Park was not a pleasant or successful one. Her stay at Brearley had not been her finest hour. She realized that within the Manhattan enclave she was just a country girl with a DAR card. Bereft of formal education, she was afraid she lacked the sophistication to maneuver through society alone. She daydreamed of escaping Tuxedo Park on the arm of a husband and enjoyed conjuring him up: tall, of course, and handsome, but also worldly, a scholar or a professional man, an intellect.

George (Dan) Draper met Dorothy Tuckerman several years after she had been presented to society at Sherry's in 1907. The details of that first meeting were never revealed, although it was known that Dan was smitten by Dorothy's beauty, a case of love at first sight. As in many of these cases, especially when opposites attract, reason seemed to have little to do with it. Dan Draper was everything Dorothy wanted in a husband; he was tall, handsome, witty, and a doctor. He came from an impeccable family. His father, William Draper, was a noted physician, and both father and son had graduated from the Columbia University College of Physicians and Surgeons.

Their basic difference was a matter of temperament. Dan Draper was quick, curious, and light of foot. Dorothy was dignified, statuesque, self-contained. He was spontaneous—throw out an idea and he would run with it. Dorothy was more likely to look on mournful-eyed when the animated banter started. But they made each other blissfully happy. Dorothy liked to call Dan "the M.D."

The wedding was scheduled for September 14, 1912, in Tuxedo Park. The bride's photo for the society page was not the usual kind, with the subject in a wedding gown, her eyes gazing heavenward or modestly cast down through a mist of tulle. Instead, Dorothy was photographed in a gown in the Spanish style, black and form-fitting like her mother's famous python dress and about as bridal, dripping with embroidery and jewels. Briskly unfolding her fan, chin held high, hand on hip, she dared society to be ready for Dorothy Draper.

More than fifteen hundred invitations were sent out, including three hundred fifty passes to ride a special train from Hoboken via the 23d Street ferry. Three thousand invitations had been sent for the Turner–Bishop wedding, which was the most important in the Berkshires that season, making the Draper–Tuckerman nuptials a medium-size upper crust wedding for the time. Still, three hundred to the house was a lot. The ceremony took place under a canopy in the piazza of the Tuckerman villa before an altar covered with roses. It rained. If only the weather had cooperated, the ceremony would have been held on the lawn.

The bride and groom honeymooned in Canada while Dorothy's parents sailed to England for some R and R. Dorothy wrote them letters nearly every day, describing the furbishing up of their honeymoon house at 164 East 63d Street. The Upper East Side of Manhattan was the place for young couples of her class to raise their families. It did not offer some of the safety features of Tuxedo Park, but it provided the children with more cultural disparity.

"The M.D. has gone down to order oil cloth for the kitchen from Wanamakers, and a few other chores," she wrote. "It is really wonderful the interest and care with which he attends to household details." Still in the honeymoon phase, the newlyweds acted in a manner unlike their behavior for the rest of their lives: Dorothy gleefully economized and Dan involved himself in petty household matters. They were still in a state of bliss. She was enjoying her role as thrifty wife. There was novelty in it, and it gave her a chance to express her creativity; for example, her husband's bedroom was decorated with blue denim: "twenty cents a yard!"

The house was small but charming and furnished with heirlooms from the Stockbridge home of Emily (Auntie Mee) Tuckerman, her father's sister. "The dining room is a roaring success and Auntie Mee's side tables go under the windows, and my old chest as side board with the two old silver candlesticks and altar cloth hanging from the beams. . . ."

There was a wood-colored carpet and "old blue coarse stuff at the windows and brown and green stuff on the sofa and chairs." Her description of her first decorating job reads a little like one of the letters she would later receive as a newspaper columnist from desperate housewives writing to "Ask Dorothy Draper."

"It seems more like a little country house," she wrote. "Everybody is most enthusiastic." Dorothy had traveled far and wide to Europe every season, but at heart she was still a country girl, and her favorite atmosphere was more Newport than Tuxedo Park.

The newlyweds had a busy social life. Dorothy's best friend and maid of honor, Helen Kane Coster, spent two days a week in town campaigning for the Bull Moose party of Teddy Roosevelt. She went into drugstores with Bertie Pell and got people to buy stamps for the fund. Dan's friend Franklin Roosevelt lived a few blocks away, at 49 East 65th Street, and was already busy raising a family. Their friendship went back to Groton. Franklin's mother and father were both related to Dorothy.

They went to the opera regularly with the Costers, the Harrimans, the Cuttings, the Thornton Wilsons, and other prominent New York families. It was the center of society life in those days. Boxes on the first tier, the famous "dress circle," were held by those who had founded the Metropolitan Opera Company. The tier had to be extended to accommodate all the patrons, and the acoustics suffered for it. The music was secondary, anyway; the object was to be seen. The charmed circles of the first and second tiers were about as close to a royal court as a democratic society could tolerate.

Dorothy was glad she didn't have in-law problems on the scale of her friend Eleanor Roosevelt, whose mother-in-law lived next door and could burst through the double doors of the dining room at any time (access had been made between the two brownstones for Mama's convenience). Nevertheless, Dorothy's in-laws did cause her problems of a nature she had not dreamed possible when living in Tuxedo Park. They actually made Dorothy Minturn Tuckerman feel inferior. It was an intolerable, unfamiliar feeling. At the Draper Sunday lunch table, the size or vintage of one's fortune meant nothing at all. They had the same opinion of Tuxedo Park as Julia Ward Howe—white of an egg. Dorothy lay low. The Drapers used the English language with the precision of a skewer. They were witty and clever and terribly well read. Dorothy was a thin-skinned Edwardian lady and an easy mark, and she quickly learned to protect her vulnerabilities. She suffered much and said little.

And there were so many Drapers. The oldest daughter, the literary Dorothea, was married at that time to Linzie Blagden, a banker. After he died, she married Henry James, a nephew of novelist Henry James and the son of William James, the famous Harvard philosopher and psychologist. Dorothea herself was a formidable intellect. Her tongue could also slice the skin off an elephant. Charles, the oldest son, was a conventional banker. Another daughter, Alice, was married to Edward Carter, a missionary and a pacifist who would later head the Institute of Pacific Relations. Alice traveled all over the world with her husband. Another son, Paul, was a well-known lieder singer who led the Bohemian life in London with his clever wife, Muriel, entertaining the brightest stars of the avante garde. The baby of the family was Ruth, and she was everybody's favorite, incredibly sensitive and a natural mimic.

It was a strange turnabout. In Dorothy's family, the women had been more interesting than the men, but even the Tuckerman women were not as interesting and unusual as the bluestocking Draper women.

The two families were already related. There were Kinnicutts and Minturns intermarried on both sides. However, the Drapers didn't give a fig about family history. Unlike some of the Tuckermans, who liked to sort out the Yorks from the Lancasters back to the mists of Avalon, the Drapers couldn't care less about bloodline. How you lived your life was what mattered. To lead a quality life one had to uphold certain standards which had nothing to do with who your parents were. This ideal had always been America's greatest appeal, and many people who marched to the beat of a different drummer had emigrated to the United States because of it.

There were many abolitionists, Whigs, Progressives, advocates of women's rights, transcendentalists, free-soilers, and Lincoln Republicans in the Draper line. Rich Drapers had helped finance the Union army. Members of the Draper clan had invented the scythe snath, the fly shuttle handloom, the first threshing machine of record, and the road scraper. They had discovered fossil footprints of extinct birds in the wilderness.

Dan Draper's grandfather was Charles A. Dana, owner and editor of the *New York Sun;* he had been born in poverty, orphaned very young, and sent to Buffalo to live with an uncle who had a country store near a Cherokee Indian reservation. There, he learned to read and write in several languages by candlelight, nearly ruining his eyes. He got a scholarship to Harvard but left school to join Brook Farm, the country's first commune, where he met and married Eunice McDaniel. (Their daughter Ruth married Dan Draper's father, William Draper, a physician and trustee of Columbia University.)

The Old Guard was forever asking Charles Dana to join their clubs, but he kept them at arm's length. The Century Club invited high-class artists and even a few actors, and did not discuss sports so much as the others, but Dana sent his regrets to them, too.

Ruth Dana was a superior woman, an accomplished pianist. Paderewski had written inside her piano, "This piano is a marvel." She not only played duets with him in the Draper drawing room but also published poems and stories in *Scribner's* and *Harper's Monthly.*

Her musical ability was passed on to her son, Paul, the lieder singer. Stravinsky, Casals, and Diaghilev and his dancers came to the parties at Edith Grove, the London home of Paul and his beloved Muriel. Especially popular were their midnight musicales, which Arthur Rubinstein called "the supreme musical euphoria of my life."

There was an unpleasant side to the London story. Paul was a drinker and a gambler. When luck was with him, he was able to underwrite Edith Grove and keep its wine cellar well stocked. When his luck ran out, he borrowed and lived at the mercy of creditors. Their staff was known as "the miracle maids," for they could apparently live on music while waiting to be paid.

And then, of course, there was Dan's youngest sister, Ruth, the darling of the family. From an early age she had been a natural mimic. This evolved into a highly distinctive art form. Ruth created rooms full of people and held conversations with them. She had a sense of projecting herself and acting the part of other people that delighted and astonished her friends. Henry James was forever urging her to go on the stage professionally. "My dear young friend," he had told her, "you have woven yourself a magic carpet. Stand on it!"

Dan's father had put himself through Columbia University College of Physicians and Surgeons by playing the organ. Dan played the saw; the Dana musicality had been lavishly passed on to the offspring. Other traits were passed on as well. In contrast to the strong democrat-to-socialist bent was a conservative republicanism when it came to money. Brother Charles could not have led a more conventional life. Dan abhorred the concept of credit, and always paid in cash.

Dorothy had not failed to notice her husband's frugality. She referred to her diamond engagement ring as "this little dreary thing" and left it in the powder room of a hotel shortly after her engagement—it was better to wear nothing at all!

Still, the Drapers lived well. The Manhattan enclave was a fairly concentrated part of the city—the sixties, seventies, and part of the eighties between Fifth and Third Avenues—and stayed within those boundaries until Mrs. Draper led the way to Sutton Place. In many ways it was like an urban Tuxedo Park. People were in walking distance of each other, and everybody was affluent and of Northern European extraction.

Doctors did not make a lot of money then, and it was not common for a doctor's family to have a staff of live-in servants. But Dorothy had to have a personal maid. Having never in her life picked up after herself, she simply dropped her clothing on the floor. There had always been somebody there to do that for her. Dorothy was also spectacularly undomestic. It never occurred to her to learn how to cook, so kitchen help was essential.

The newlyweds wasted no time starting a family. Their first child, Diana, was born in 1913, and a second child, George, was born two years later. Over on 65th Street, the Franklin Roosevelts were also busy raising a much larger family. Grandma Tuckerman drove down from Tuxedo Park to visit first her grandchildren and then her cousin Sarah Delano. Little George Draper called FDR's mother's cousin Sally and played with his sons Franklin and John. The Roosevelt boys were hellions, and someone was sure to get in trouble before the visit was over.

Dorothy did a lot of visiting in those days as her husband became increasingly involved in his profession. He had certain obsessions. When she asked him what he was doing, he told her he was studying human constitution and variances in human physiological types. He studied his observations late into the night in his laboratory at Columbia Presbyterian Hospital, which was then on Park Avenue in the seventies. He also specialized in poliomyelitis. In the early years of their marriage, Dr. and Mrs. Draper had attended the opera and had dined at Sherry's. Dan had been fun to be with, a man about town. Now he was a man devoted to his work. A brilliant physician, he got great satisfaction out of his career. He shared that satisfaction with his colleagues, but Dorothy was not really a part of it. The husband who measured the kitchen linoleum with her was gone forever. Dorothy wasn't really surprised or even disappointed. Men and women lived separate social lives in her world and saw far less of each other than the modern-day husband and wife.

Eleanor Roosevelt also had a husband who didn't come home to dinner. She went to sewing classes with her mother-in-law, often spending weekends with Sarah Delano at Hyde Park. Eleanor was often alone with her mother-in-law and the children for weeks on end while Franklin built his political career. It is doubtful that either Eleanor or Dorothy spent much time wondering whether she had a happy marriage. The goal was to try to make something meaningful out of one's own life. Eleanor had always been a serious person. She was very involved with charity and women's issues, putting her considerable energy into projects with other "she-males," as her husband called her feminist friends.

Dorothy, at that time in her life, was more interested in social life than social change. Dorothy's idea of social change was rearranging the furniture. Although a sensitive and thoughtful person to individuals, Dorothy was uninvolved on the political level. Politics had been one of the forbidden topics of her childhood, and she remained densely ignorant of subjects relating to it all her life; in fact, she was ignorant of current events and history, except as they related to design.

Eleanor's childhood made Dorothy's seem like a fairy tale. Although Dorothy grew up adored by her father, mother, and brother (even Roger called her Star), Eleanor had been cared for by a series of aunts, cousins, nurses, nannies, and governesses, none of whom stayed long enough to be a stabilizing influence.

Never having had a good nanny, Eleanor didn't even think to make sure that her brood (and dutiful Eleanor had so many) was nurtured by someone warm and loving. Until it was too late, she was oblivious to the fact that several of her children had suffered under the care of one of those sadistic nannies who enter the profession for some kind of twisted revenge.

Things were much different at the household of Dr. and Mrs. Draper. Their children were cared for by Frances Somson, a nanny secured for the Drapers by Dorothy's Anglophile mother. Frances's father was gardener at Lambert's Palace, the home of the Archbishop of Canterbury. Frances was always either writing to or receiving a letter from the Archbishop. Although it was not common practice for a doctor and his wife to employ a nanny in those days, Dorothy's parents made sure their grandchildren had the benefit of a warm-hearted, motherly type who would never leave them.

Many years later, Frances Somson died of a heart attack while reading to a child. She was buried in the Tuckerman family plot in Newport, loyal to the end. (There was quite a disagreement with her last employers over her interment, though; they wanted her buried in *their* family plot.)

. . .

The nation's capital became the place to be when the United States entered World War I. Dr. Draper was stationed there in the army medical corps, and his family moved down, too, staying in Washington while he served out his duty in France. There were lots of parties; many of the young people of Dorothy's set who weren't in the service lived there. Dorothy had family in Washington as well: Her cousins the Leroys had a house in the city and knew everyone. The Roosevelts had made the move as well because Franklin had also been called to duty.

In Washington Dorothy met Mae Laudenberg Davie, who would become a close friend for life. Mae was very active in the Republican party and eight or more years younger. She became a younger sister to Dorothy. Mae had a reputation for being a rather cold person, but Dorothy brought her out of her shell. Together they became popular hostesses in Washington during World War I.

Returning to life in Manhattan after the armistice, Dorothy was restless. She decided to take up sculpting. Life on the party circuit was not enough. She had always had a creative bent that she didn't know how to channel. She did a bust of her husband and another of an Auchincloss. They were good, but sculpting was too lonely an occupation. Dorothy had to be with people. She needed gaiety. If her husband were reluctant to join her in a social life, then she would bring that life home. He could hardly avoid a party thrown in his own home. Besides, entertaining in the home was more economical.

When she was growing up, her mother and father had been constantly occupied with blueprints and floor plans; the Tuckermans held a record for building homes in Tuxedo Park. In fact, they were thinking about building again, this time on a hilltop. The villa was too cavernous for two people, and Susan wanted to do something in French Normandy. It was only natural that Dorothy would have a proclivity for designing and decorating.

Refurnishing her house in order to throw more successful parties was a less solitary way to express her visual side than sculpting or painting, and she loved hearing the compliments from her guests. They were sincere; in fact, people wanted to buy her house and move right in. Selling the house would give Dorothy an opportunity to start all over again with fresh ideas, so the Draper family decided to move down the street, leaving behind everything except their personal items and a few heirlooms. When the new house was finished, someone once again made her an offer she couldn't refuse. Her husband wasn't terribly happy about the constant moving, but he spent much more time at his research lab than he did at home anyway, and he realized his wife had special talents and a great need to express them.

One of her fans was her friend Gertrude Whitney. Dorothy was thrilled when Gertrude asked her to help decorate a new museum in a brownstone at 147 West 4th Street in Greenwich Village. Decorating houses was limiting, and she had ideas about museums that had never been executed before. Why, for instance, did they have to be so dreary?

Gertrude's museum would accommodate exhibition galleries on the ground floor and low-cost rental space for artists to live and work in upstairs. Gertrude was well known for her eccentricities: The Whitney Studio Club even possessed a Ouija board. But she had a practical side, too, and saw the need to support artists as well as the arts.

The furniture was made at the Greenwich House, where Gertrude was the director. It was colorful and most unusual. Dorothy approved whole-heartedly and supplied more of the same. She designed sapphire blue satin curtains lined with a new yellow-green shade called *chartreuse*, with a bright scarlet cord.

The nanny that Dorothy's mother had found was such a jewel that DD, as her friends called her (for her given name somehow did not suit her), was free to exercise her self-expression to the limit. Her wifely obligations were all too few. Her husband had no interest at all in a social life. His idea of the ideal evening was to stay home and read a book. Dorothy wasn't disappointed, though: She had had no expectation of happily ever after. Her husband was tall, handsome, and distinguished. What more could she want?

His failure to make a proper income upset her, however. When Dorothy steered society patients his way he was as likely to insult them as to cultivate their business. One of Dorothy's friends had become a steady patient, bringing her daughter to his office frequently. The mother was unable to accept the child's condition as psychosomatic. "What is wrong with the girl?" she demanded of Dr. Draper. "You should know by now." He told her bluntly that her daughter's problem was her mother. She never came to him again.

He was of a similar opinion in the case of his distant relations, the Kinnicutts. One of their children nicknamed Sister (later, Mrs. Henry Parrish) had been brought to him in spite of her father's great animosity toward Dr. Draper. Miss Noland, the head mistress at Foxcroft, had suggested that Sister be taken to New York to be examined by a doctor because she was behaving badly at school. Unaware of the family connection, Miss Noland had suggested Dr. Draper because she knew he specialized in such cases. Mae Kinnicutt brought her daughter to the office, where Dr. Draper gravely asked her for her full name, age, address, and other particulars. Then he said, "Sister, you may go, and Mae, you may stay."

On another occasion, Mr. Kinnicutt had a terrible siege of hiccups that lasted four days. One specialist after another was consulted but no one could help him. Finally, he relented to see his nemesis, Dr. Draper.

"It's simple what I'm going to do," Dr. Draper said. He called for a ball of string, which put Mr. Kinnicutt into even more of a rage, weak as he was. But while the doctor tied it around his waist, the hiccups miraculously stopped.

Family would make allowances for him, but the society patient would not, so he lost that lucrative potential income. Dorothy was glad she had loving and generous parents.

In the summer of 1921 a terrible thing happened that took Dr. Draper away from home more than ever. By that time he was an established specialist in the treatment of the baffling disease known as poliomyelitis. Dr. Draper frequently presented his findings before medical societies.

One August afternoon, Dr. Draper took a phone call from Dr. Robert Lovett, a specialist in orthopedics who had heard of Dr. Draper's research on poliomyelitis. Dr. Lovett had an emergency referral. When Dr. Draper heard who the patient was, he told his colleague to send him to Columbia Presbyterian Hospital at once.

The patient was Dan's Groton schoolmate, Franklin Roosevelt. He had been out of politics since the disastrous Republican landslide of 1920, biding his time working for a Wall Street firm until he could run for governor of New York on the Democratic ticket. He had been sailing on his employer's yacht up in Campobello, New Brunswick, when he had fallen overboard into the ice-cold water. The next day, he had swum across a lake, run two miles, put out a forest fire, and then come home to a cabin heated by only a driftwood fire in the fireplace. Instead of changing into dry clothing, Franklin sat by the fire soaking wet and went through the mail.

The next morning he had awakened racked with stabbing pains all over his body and a temperature of 102°. By the time a local doctor was called in, Franklin was paralyzed from the chest down. Eleanor started calling people until she located a surgeon vacationing in Bar Harbor, Maine. By the time he arrived, her husband was totally paralyzed. The doctor failed to diagnose his condition as poliomyelitis; the disease was still rare. It was not until a third doctor was called in that Franklin's case was correctly diagnosed.

The trip from Campobello to New York was made in secrecy, but with great difficulty. Franklin managed to elude the press, but drenched with sweat, and an unlit cigar between his teeth, he was ready to flash his famous smile if reporters suddenly appeared as he was being transferred to or from the train. So far, no one outside Campobello knew of the tragedy. By the time Franklin was examined by Dr. Draper, he could not move so much as a big toe. Dr. Draper was appalled when he heard the surgeon from Bar Harbor had recommended massage, which Eleanor and Franklin's right-hand man, Louis Howe, performed around the clock, causing Franklin excruciating pain and increasing the damage that had already been done to his tissues. Nevertheless, Dr. Draper minimized the severity of Franklin's condition, and told the press he would not be permanently crippled. Franklin, meanwhile, insisted he had a case of lumbago and begged to be taken to White Sulphur for a cure in the springs. Dr. Draper postponed telling his famous patient the truth about his condition, fearing it might crush his spirit.

But after six weeks in Columbia Presbyterian Hospital, while

Franklin was able to turn himself in bed by use of his muscular arms, he still lacked the ability to twitch a muscle below the waist, and Dr. Draper told him his recovery was uncertain.

There was no need to keep FDR in the hospital, for the doctors there could do nothing more for him. Franklin came home and began a strenuous exercise program which worried everyone, especially his physician. Three weeks later, he suffered a relapse. The pain was worse than before, shooting right into his eyes. The tendons in his legs began to tighten. Dr. Draper put both legs in plaster casts so they wouldn't jackknife under him, but the pain from keeping them straight was nearly unbearable.

The tragedy had a dreadful impact on the family. Eleanor and Sarah were at each other's throats. The children were terribly bewildered that this could have happened to their father, for he was like a deity to them.

By the following February, Franklin was wearing leg braces and once again embarked upon a strenuous routine of exercises, which he performed each day until he dropped. Dr. Draper supervised these exercises with more authority and his patient was compliant. He approved of using the parallel bars but not of the other therapies Franklin sought because his old friend offered so little hope. There were heat treatments and oxygen tanks, rowing machines and the Coué method of autosuggestion. Everyone got into the act. His mother even sent away for an electric tricycle. When Dr. Draper dismissed some of them as quackery, Franklin chided him.

In the difficult months that followed, Dorothy's husband was called over to 65th Street countless times and consulted with the Roosevelts by telephone with even greater frequency. At times Eleanor saw more of Dr. Draper than Dorothy did. As great as Franklin's struggle was, the one between Eleanor and Sarah Delano equaled it. Dr. Draper would be called on to mediate. Sarah Delano wanted her son to spend the rest of his life rocking on her porch at Hyde Park. Eleanor violently disagreed: She felt he should be allowed as much activity as he was capable of performing, and they all knew how voracious he was when it came to being active. The doctor took Eleanor's side and also felt Franklin should not be considered an invalid. Because of his support, Eleanor won the struggle with her formidable mother-in-law, and Franklin returned to public life. Dr. Draper saw it as a considerable victory.

The strain Franklin's illness put upon Eleanor was great, but she prevailed and took even more tasks upon herself. She assumed the responsibility of active fathering, took skating and horseback riding lessons, and tried to do "fatherly" things with the children. In the summer of 1923, she planned an ambitious camping trip to Lake George, Lake Champlain, Montreal, and Quebec for two of her sons, Franklin and John, seven-year-old George Draper, Jr., and her nephew Hall, plus two of her "she-male" friends. Crammed into the family Buick along with tents, stove, and camping gear, the three women and four boys took off for Montreal. It was a disaster from day one.

Not the best driver, Eleanor drove into a ditch in upstate New York, and in the process of being pulled out had a collision with a lumber wagon, which spilled its contents onto the road. Halfway to Quebec, Franklin cut his foot with an axe, trying to chop down a tree on a French farm. Then he cut his finger falling over a seesaw. While working on their boats, Henry Hall threw a pillow at George, which hit Franklin, who promptly cut himself again. Eleanor sternly intervened. Meanwhile, Franklin and John were very successful in doing everything possible to irritate their mother's friends.

When there were no public camping sites available, Eleanor would try to talk farmers into allowing them to camp on their property. Although persuasive, she was not always successful, for rural New Yorkers were unaccustomed to the sight of women unaccompanied by men.

Somehow they reached Quebec in one piece. There, Johnny and George decided to go off by themselves and sightsee. By practicing their schoolboy French on the citizens of Montreal, they managed to get around quite well, and came back from their stroll several hours later; Eleanor was nearly hysterical. They did not return home all in one car. Eleanor's friends decided to spare themselves that pleasure and went back to New York on their own.

Dr. Draper had become involved with a new, controversial area of medicine—psychosomatic illness. Why did so many of his patients have maladies that did not seem to have a physical cause? Was the source of their suffering in their minds?

While Dr. Draper pursued the elusive psychological factor, his wife busied herself redoing yet another house, this time a former carriage factory near the corner of 64th Street and Third Avenue, on the fringes of the Upper East Side. There, she was going to turn her little world upside down—literally.

There were certain problems to brownstone living she was determined to solve. Dorothy had spent most of her life in the country, where one could expand majestically outward; in the urban "flat," however, one had to expand majestically in another direction—upward. Living in a vertical house had always been difficult for the rich who lived in town, but unless they were a Dodge or a Vanderbilt and could live in an urban manse, they had to learn to cope with the brownstone's inconveniences: the endless stairs to climb, the lack of light (the railroad car had more light than the center room of the townhouse), and the dark and dank backyard where nothing but mushrooms and alacanthus might grow— fit for cats but not for people.

She resolved the problem of the too-shady backyard by extending the ground-floor to the back of the lot and putting a garden in a series of terraces on the roof of the extension. There was another advantage to eliminating the backyard—a huge ground floor living room big enough for two hundred in which she would give sensational parties.

By eliminating the first floor, she solved the problem of not enough light; thereby giving the ground-floor living room the kind of majesty she had once known in Tuxedo Park. Happy to the point of delirium, she crawled all over the house, even though she was in an advanced stage of pregnancy.

Just about everything in the Upside-Down House was unique, and people began to comment on it even before it was finished. To the back of the living room was the kitchen. Upstairs was a dining-sitting room looking out onto the garden on top of the back-floor extension and the servants' quarters. On top of the house there was a big studio—very grand and well lit and full of sculpting equipment, marble, and clay, just in case. But over the years it became a storage room. Finally, by slithering around the city ordinances she had even secured permission for the greatest urban amenity of all—a garage.

In 1923, the family moved into the house, the last they would occupy together. Dorothy's third child, Penelope, was born that year, on the kitchen table of her grandmother's apartment on Park Avenue; Dorothy shunned hospitals and saw them as places that emphasized sickness, not health. Also that year Dorothy threw her first Christmas caroling party. It would become a life-long tradition.

The Upside-Down House was Dorothy's first taste of recognition. It was mentioned not only in the society pages but also in the real estate section, where it really counted. Her unusual talents were finally being recognized as something more than a society matron's diversion. Dr. Draper urged her to go into business. What she did for her own houses she could also do for others without the constant need for them to move. Friends also encouraged her: Brooke Marshall and her sister-in-law Evie (Mrs. Marshall Field, later Mrs. Diego Suarez), who was Penelope's godmother, Mrs. Fairfield Osborn, and, of course, Mae Davie. She was more than good at what she did, they said. She was sensational—magical!

The idea of a career appealed to DD for another reason. Ruth Draper had recently become a professional actress at the urging of people like Henry James. For years, her sister-in-law had been out in the world, getting lionized. Why couldn't she, Dorothy Draper, do the same?

Going into business held another appeal: It was expensive to live the life she was accustomed to. She was married to a doctor who did not cultivate society patients but was content to live on a researcher's salary. She had acquired a new attitude about wealth: There would be no mansions in her future but that was fine with her. She was happy living on East 64th Street. Besides, lavish display was no longer in vogue. Few of the residents of the Upper East Side had that kind of money anymore. The war had abruptly ended the Edwardian era, leaving them with their taste for quality and drastically reduced incomes. Fortunately, they had enough furniture in the family already that they could make do for some time.

Different sorts of people were getting rich after World War I, a new brand of go-getters, international in their business dealings, and sooner or later they came knocking at society's door. Meanwhile, the residents of the Silk Stocking District lived their lives like the impoverished aristocrats of Europe. It was the same everywhere, and if you were clever, you sold your taste to those in need in order to make ends meet—it was all perfectly honorable. Dorothy had heard that Pierre Lorillard had been disturbed about Emily Post's acting because it had been too good, too "professional." Had anyone said that to Dorothy Draper, she would have laughed out loud.

Dorothy's father, Paul Tuckerman, in 1894—the quintessential Edwardian sportsman.

Dorothy's mother, Susan Minturn Tuckerman, in 1894—a quintessential well-bred English beauty.

Three generations of Minturn women: Dorothy's maternal grandmother, Louisa Aspinwall, baby Dorothy, and Susan Tuckerman, 1889. It was the once extremely glamorous Louisa who married into the great fortune of John W. Minturn.

Dorothy Tuckerman, ca. 1900.

Dr. and Mrs. George "Dan" Draper in Washington, D.C., 1917. Dr. Draper wears his Army Medical Corps uniform, and Mrs. Draper one of her early memorable hats.

Dorothy around the time of her debut in 1907, in a gown of silk satin.

Dorothy Draper by John Singer Sargent, 1919.

Newlywed Dan Draper in a Norfolk jacket, ca. 1913.

A silouette of Dorothy Tuckerman (ca. 1910), featuring the double-folded scarf that became one of her fashion statements.

Dorothy and Dan Draper feed the pigeons in Venice in the late 1920s.

Dorothy Draper with her third and youngest child, Penelope, in 1923. Her left hand may belie the story that she "lost" her engagement ring in a hotel powder room.

Dr. and Mrs. Dan Draper greet their guests in their Tudor Garden on East 63rd Street in 1923. Foliage and shawl conceal Dorothy's late stage of pregnancy.

Back view of the 64th Street house, an early example of DD's magic touch as she replicates her past in a Manhattan back yard. Lavish use of diagonal trellis work screens out the city and creates a Tuxedo Park look; the country plantings evoke Newport.

Dorothy at home in Washington, D.C., in 1917 with Diana and George, Jr.

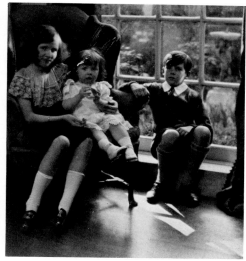

Penelope, ca. 1925, on the lap of Diana who remembers being forced to wear the heirloom Irish lace collar ("and I mean forced"). George sits on the window ledge in the drawing room of the house on 64th Street.

Susan and Paul Tuckerman with Penelope at Tuxedo Park, ca. 1935.

Dorothy's daughter, Diana, carrying on the family tradition of patrician beauty, and her father, Dr. Draper, en route to her marriage to Nelson Jay in 1935. She wears her mother's wedding gown of silk satin and Austrian rose-point lace.

Penelope Draper, left, with her cousins Cynthia and Nancy Tuckerman at Diana's wedding. When admonished that she had forgotten her "mitts," Penelope replied, "I don't have to wear them. I'm the maid of honor."

Two ladies in the height of fashion, Newport, 1933. Dorothy, left, and her sister-in-law Betty, wife of Roger Tuckerman.

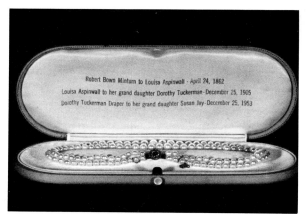

Robert Bown Minturn to Louisa Aspinwall · April 24, 1862
Louisa Aspinwall to her grand daughter Dorothy Tuckerman · December 25, 1905
Dorothy Tuckerman Draper to her grand daughter Susan Jay · December 25, 1953

Three generations of women in Dorothy Draper's family so far have worn the double-strand pearls whose diminished value due to the cultured market Robert Bown Minturn could not have foreseen.

Dorothy Draper during the Hampshire House restoration, 1937.

She Goes into Business

Years later, when Dorothy was at the peak of her fame, she was interviewed for *Current Biography* (1941). She was asked if she had difficulty managing both a career and home life. Absolutely not, DD replied: "A great deal of superfluous nonsense is talked about women combining careers with a normal home life. The way to combine the two is to combine the two and not dramatize them."

Although she must be given credit for having had children at all (few of her competitors had been both mothers and career women), Dorothy failed to explain that her emphatic attitude was helped along by a household staff of at least seven: two live-in maids, a live-in cook, a nanny who lived in the nursery, a day cleaning lady, and a furnace man, plus a secretary or two for her business.

"But," she said to the interviewer, almost as an afterthought, "American women are divided into two classes, the happily married and the decorators."

Dorothy Draper was not your typical American mom. She loved her children but was not particularly close to them. Family "togetherness" was a concept of the future. Such closeness did not exist among families within her sphere, and there were no books or magazines to tell her that she should adore her children and be affectionate with them, no group of peers who also felt that way. She did not think it was cruel to send seven-, eight-, or nine-year-old children to boarding school, sometimes all the way to England, where they would live the spartan life to prepare them for adulthood.

Nevertheless, she made it obvious that she was not really interested in children; after all, they were so little. By the time her brother had come along she was already ten, too old to play with dolls. And she certainly had no interest in appearing maternal. Penelope liked to watch her get dressed in the evening. Dorothy liked to wear low-cut gowns because she was proud of her décolleté and often put a rose there.

"You know, Mummy, you're so beautiful," said Penelope, watching transfixed as her mother made wonderful faces in the mirror. Her mother had a special look when she got herself ready for an evening.

"I am?" Dorothy said.

"Like a pear tree in bloom." The veil lifted and contact was made; the memory of the smile the child received was indelible.

Often, Penelope gazed at a photograph of Dorothy smiling confidently out at the world with a halo of feathers around her head, her lovely hands folded under her chin, and then tease her mother about how she always looked so glamorous.

"Oh, Ma," she said, "can't there be a picture of you where you look like a mother?"

The children turned to Nanny for soft, motherly affection. The most cuddly nanny in the world, she was short and stocky, with a sweet face and a comfortable bosom, truly a surrogate mother to all of the Draper children, although she came on the scene too late to nurture Diana in her early years. The children saw their mother in the morning for a few minutes and again in the evening. The rest of their time was spent with Nanny.

Nanny had a little crystal radio set. Very early in the morning, a sleepy child would often go into her room, which was next to the nursery, and rest beside her for awhile. Then Nanny would turn on the little crystal radio, and they would listen to the sound of Big Ben, which would bring tears to Nanny's eyes.

Nanny would read for hours and never skip a page. Under her method the children learned to read by the age of four and were joyfully devouring books before they went to school.

George was first sent to Indian Mountain boarding school near Keville, Connecticut, when he was nine. Then he went to Avon, a highly progressive school his father approved of, for three years. For awhile the school fell apart, and he went to Brooks in North Andover, which he detested. Fortunately, Avon got itself straightened out, and he returned there for three years. Diana was sent to Foxcroft at age fourteen.

Between boarding schools and Nanny's tutelage, George rarely saw either his mother or his father and rarely ate with them. George recalled only one time when his mother took charge of him and his sister; Nanny was off in Tuxedo Park. She gave them bread and chocolate for lunch in the European fashion. It was, he said, the only time he remembered receiving food from her hand.

Short breaks from boarding school for Thanksgiving and Easter and summers were spent in Tuxedo Park with the grandparents; Christmas was the only family occasion. The children would come home from school, and the family would decorate the tree; George put the star on top because he was the tallest. The candles were then lit, a big pail of water and a sponge kept nearby as a precaution.

At the Christmas parties the children sat at their separate table and dined on creamed chicken and rice, presided over by Nanny, who made sure each child got a favor. Their table was in the dining room; the adults were in the drawing room. Sooner or later Uncle Charles Draper would come upstairs and slip them his Christmas present—a five-dollar gold piece, which was immediately taken out of their hands and banked. The Draper children were kept on tight allowances. Money was never discussed, so they didn't know there was any until they were old enough to figure it out for themselves.

In 1925, with the older children in school and two-year-old Penny in the care of Nanny, Dorothy Draper opened a business called the Architectural Clearing House, operating out of her home. Her parents gave her five thousand dollars to start and every encouragement. Their Star would shine. After sending out announcements of her new venture, DD received her first response from a man selling fire extinguishers. She ordered two and gave him forty dollars; he was never heard from again. As her father remarked, it was a relatively inexpensive first lesson in learning how to run a business.

Her mother was particularly thrilled. She was aware that her daughter was no ordinary talented society woman. Dorothy was unique, and it delighted Mrs. Tuckerman to see her daughter reach for more than she could possibly have grasped. Susan Tuckerman had little choice but to be content with staying within society's boundaries, never to display her creativity except at a private masked ball or in a tableau for charity. She never would have had the courage to go into business, to handle her own money like a man. She was very proud of her daughter.

The business of the Architectural Clearing House was to match up Dorothy's favorite architects with her society friends who wanted to build or renovate. Dorothy's lack of formal training didn't bother her. Already she had developed the knack for putting things together and had even done some of her own architectural drawings when designing the Upside-Down House. She was familiar with the styles of well-known architects, so all she had to do was put them together with the proper friends.

Traditional twenties' decorating was boring and predictable, à la Charles of London. There was red in the living room, which was hung with the obligatory damask draperies; yellow in the dining room; and blue in the bedroom. Dorothy delighted in breaking through the conventions for her own houses, but redoing a house and then selling it eliminated the dilemma she now had to consider: the client's tastes and idiosyncracies. It didn't make her happy. Even when she had decorated the homes of friends—Mrs. Frank Vandelip, Mrs. Owen Young, or her good friend Mae Davies—there had been frequent awkward moments. Her ideas were simply much too bold for the average society woman to understand.

Her work on residential jobs was limited by her clients' tastes and that took away a lot of the fun. Dorothy needed more freedom. In fact, she preferred dealing with hard-boiled tycoons than with vacillating society hostesses, who were forever changing their minds with each new opinion from their friends. Men tended to be ignorant of such matters; in fact, most men didn't want to hear about the details at all.

Still, the Architectural Clearing House was a success as far as it went, because there was a lot of money around in the mid-1920s. Resort life was booming, and new enclaves were springing up all over. The C&O Railroad had bought the Greenbrier and had spent $2.5 million redoing it; the register was full in and out of season.

In the overheated market of the late 1920s, with speculation rampant and people spending money like there was no tomorrow, the Architectural Clearing House had enough business to keep Dorothy busy.

When the Decorators' Club got together—Diane Tate, Marion Ball, Elsie Cobb Wilson, Mrs. Brown of McMillan, Elisabeth Low, Ruby Ross Wood and her talented assistant Billy Baldwin, and others—Dorothy Draper was not among them. They had been meeting since 1915; before that time decorating wasn't considered a profession.

Some of the group were quite well known. Elsie Cobb Wilson didn't get much publicity for the ocean liners she decorated, but everyone knew they were floating palaces. Done in the conventional framework allowed by "polite society," they didn't reflect the style Dorothy Draper yearned to express. Polite society didn't have much to say about sapphire blue draperies with chartreuse linings and scarlet trim, but Dorothy had never cared very much about the opinions of anyone else, not even a so-called expert.

The members of the Decorators' Club were not innovators like their predecessors. DD could identify somewhat with Elsie deWolfe and Syrie Maugham, although she couldn't have had less in common with her friend Elsie. In 1913, when Dorothy was decorating her rustic honeymoon house on East 63d Street, Elsie was doing her most famous job, the second floor of the house of Henry Clay Frick. That job made her a millionaire and a celebrity, as well as making decorating a profession.

Elsie grew up the hard way, born in an unfashionable part of town near the site of what is now Macy's. Although Dorothy had been born beautiful, Elsie was exceptionally plain. Still, she knew how to cultivate charm, and became quite well known as an actress, making her stage debut at Tuxedo Park. It was there, she said, that she observed the limits to which people would go to be accepted by society.

Already an outcast as a professional actress, Elsie didn't give a fig about what society thought from an early age. Uniqueness was her trademark: She stood on her head at parties and tinted her hair lavender blue. She flew with Wilbur Wright. She lived with her "long-time companion" Elizabeth Marbury. Elsie was international: She combined the more interesting elements of society with artists from around the globe, creating what was known as café society. Elsie and Elizabeth's house on Sutton Place became a showcase of twentieth-century style, breaking from the claustrophobic Victorian tradition with sunlight, white walls, and lots of beige.

Being small, Elsie deWolfe was fond of small scale. Her rooms were diminutive, intimate to the point of secrecy. She also hated red. In those two ways Elsie and Dorothy couldn't have been more different. Elsie was particularly fond of French furniture, which she bought cheap from impoverished aristocrats and shipped to America for her clients. Then she went beyond beige to white—stark in the extreme—and furbished up the women-only Colony Club all in white, with light and airy white latticework and ferns.

Syrie Maugham, wife of the writer Somerset Maugham, was best known for the sparsely furnished, all-white room, a severe contrast to the style of the Victorian era. After the clutter of that time, with knickknacks spilling over onto every surface, wallpapers with multiple patterns, stenciled friezes, highly embossed ceilings, and exuberant decorative paintings, the sweep of Syrie's white was a startling break that many found soothing indeed.

At the beginning of her career, Dorothy Draper used what she would later call "gravy" colors. The day would come when she would banish beige from her palette. But one can never completely ignore the influences of one's childhood. The impressions made are too vivid to be eradicated. Dorothy had grown up during an era that could not have been more excessively baroque. The American spirit of "more is better," reflected by the architecture of the Gilded Age, is an object of wonder in our slicked-back era. At a time when even doorknobs and hinges are neatly hidden from sight, the excess display of that age is almost endearing.

The homes of Dorothy's childhood were replicas of the most ornate periods in history, well stirred. In one structure, the Renaissance might be combined with the Second French Empire, the time of Queen Anne, the splendor of ancient Greece, and the opulence of the Byzantine Empire, with verandas, towers, and bays thrusting out every which way. Victorians did not welcome the new: They demanded historical precedent, and it didn't matter to them if the styles of the periods didn't match. Like spiraling through a time tunnel from ancient Egypt to the recent past and back again, the result could be dizzying. Accumulation was the goal.

Dorothy Draper's style was a reaction to that incredible clutter and closed-in atmosphere. In her rooms there was no accumulation of bibelots on the table. She did not completely escape from the influence of her Victorian childhood, however. She did not reject the period so much as select certain classical aspects of it and expand them to the maximum, sweeping out the rest, and bathing what remained in sunlight and color.

Dorothy kept the plasterwork and got rid of the wood, painting it white like her predecessors, without a thought to generations of future restorers, who would curse as they wielded their heat guns and dental picks. She hated wood, posts and pillars, spindles, wainscoting, panels, spandrels, shutters, moldings, and beading and fretwork. "Paint it all white," she said, "and it will disappear."

She got rid of the sconces and brackets and replaced them with a few enormous lamps with black shades all the same height. She kept the wallpaper, especially the romantic floral prints. Her favorite motif was the cabbage rose, a romantic, richly petaled, windblown rose, which had been a favorite since her childhood romps through Tuxedo Park's rose garden.

When she landed her first commercial job, redoing the lobby of the Carlyle Hotel, through Douglas Elliman, a family friend, she chose a classical motif in black, white, and gray with muted colors. Nothing about the lobby foretold her later surrealism, but the marked difference between what she did with it and what had been done in hotel lobbies before—stuffy and impersonal work—was evident.

She did the lobby in High Roman Empire, with busts of heroes; friezes of gladiators, horsemen, and runners; Roman emperors' chairs; and marble columns. She softened the look with satin draperies and circular banquettes elaborately tufted and tasseled. She bought one perfect rug for the lobby floor, and two French tapestries from Rose Cumming. Chintz and wallpaper were in the oversize patterns she already preferred; the marble tile floors were in black and white. Some of her trademark features were present in this early job, but on the whole it was safe but grand, derived from things she had seen on her travels or in books. The job got a lot of attention, however. She had the knack for that from the start.

In 1927, she got involved in a real venture—the Piping Rock project. Dorothy and her favorite architect, Pleasants Pennington, had acquired thirty-seven acres near Locust Valley, New York, on Long Island, and planned to divide them into plots of from two to four acres. By using clever architecture and walled-in gardens, they would manage to make the plots look like large country estates. The smallest house would have three bedrooms and two maid's rooms; the largest house would be twice as big. It was an ambitious project, and it took her away from home a great deal, which she enjoyed.

Despite the notice Dorothy's work received, she was still obscure compared with her sister-in-law Ruth, who made the front pages of the arts sections. In 1927, Lord Balfour, England's most famous statesman, had surprised a London audience by coming on stage before Ruth's first appearance and delivering an impassioned five-minute paean to her. Ruth's great talent for the spoken word had always left Dorothy speechless, feeling like a pretty object by comparison, bred for show but without substance.

Ruth's career, like Dorothy's, got off to a slow start. Ruth turned professional in 1920 at the age of thirty-six, and the decade of the twenties was a steady, dignified climb to the pinnacle. In ten years she had the world at her feet: She performed at the White House for four presidents—Teddy Roosevelt, Taft, Wilson, and Harding. In 1925, she played at the American Embassy in Brussels before the king and queen of Belgium. The following year she played Windsor Castle, the Palladium of royal houses; the British worshiped her to the point where she had become a cult figure. The fondness of the British for the eccentric and Ruth Draper's fondness for the English character were a perfect match. She even performed before Mussolini, who didn't know what to make of her. When in Warsaw, Arthur Rubinstein made her feel at home. Among her fans were Judge Learned Hand, Ellen Terry, Eleanore Duse, Sarah Bernhardt, Alexander Wollcott, William Butler Yeats, and Helen Keller. George Bernard Shaw came away from a performance and commented, "That's not acting. That's life."

Amazingly, Ruth did not get a big head about all the adulation. She did not have such an exalted opinion of herself. In fact, she was a little amazed by the attention. Her forte was the understatement; she was so subtle when compared with the posturing of the divas of the day. The most insignificant negative remark could make her react as if she had been deeply wounded. The sensitivity she gave to her characters came out of her own ability to be hurt. She refused to be interviewed about anything personal and gave her press agent, Russel Crouse, a difficult time when it came to doing his job.

Before Ruth moved to 79th Street in Manhattan, she would sometimes stay with Dan and Dorothy. She was always made to feel welcome, and she could play another role she relished—the fond aunt—to their three children, whom she adored. Like all the Drapers except Paul, Ruth was thrifty, and her tastes ran to the spartan. Only 5'4" tall and birdlike, she could not have been more different from the flamboyant Dorothy.

In 1927, Ruth Draper grossed one hundred ten thousand dollars. In the United States, Ruth never received the accolades she got on the other side of the Atlantic, but she was at the top of her form. When she opened Christmas night in 1928 at the Comedy Theater in New York, however, her performance was sold out for its nineteen-week run.

Ruth's satire, like that of Mark Twain, gave Americans insight into their character, which was a caricature of the Old World–type. It was difficult to get a clear picture of the American character, but Ruth's monologues of American types were so accurate they came to life.

Still, Dorothy had what Ruth wanted most. More than fame, Ruth wanted marriage. It was more than just a yearning for romance. Living as a single woman was difficult, no matter how famous or cared for the woman was. The world revolved around the couple, and Ruth was tired of being her own helpmate. There were few people with whom she was truly intimate. One of her close friends said there was something elemental in her nature—like a gypsy or a Druid or something very ancient and distancing—that kept her from being intimate.

Ruth wanted someone poetic. She made a living by finding just the right word that had a certain rhythm and cadence that fit her voice like a custom-tailored garment. So it was not surprising that at forty-four she fell in love for the first time with a poet, a young man named Lauro DeBosis. When she met him he was at Casa Italiana, an Italian-American society at Columbia University, trying to organize a resistance group, the Alleanza Nazionale, to work for the overthrow of Mussolini and the Fascist party that had taken over Italy. DeBosis advocated a liberal monarchy. Ruth was madly in love, like a girl of fourteen, and saw him as often as she could between her touring engagements and his political activities. Her family was discreet about the affair.

Dan Draper was also becoming a bit of a celebrity. For nine years he had been working day and night in an old, crowded building at Columbia Presbyterian Hospital on a controversial medical theory: the relationship between the conformity of the body and disease, which he believed confirmed the "doctor's hunch," the ability of an experienced practitioner to diagnose at a glance.

Having measured hundreds of patients over the years with rulers, tape measures, and calipers, he had proved to his own satisfaction that there was a relationship between the measurement of face and temperament and between the measurements of the body and disease. According to Dr. Draper, people with short faces and wide-set eyes were likely to be musically and theatrically inclined. Big-boned men were often humorous. Hypertensive people were likely to have long heads. The idea could not have been more out of step with the times; it was regarded by most of the members of his profession as quackery, in the realm of the phrenologist or the palmist, not that of the medical doctor.

Nevertheless, Dr. Draper stood by his claim and insisted the pendulum was swinging from an emphasis on studying the disease back to studying the whole patient. He likened the study of the whole human being to a Japanese screen with four panels—anatomy, physiology, psychology, and immunity. The complete picture appeared only when the panels were grouped together.

Dr. Draper was one of those natural healers whose very presence makes people feel better. When William Douglas, who would one day become a justice of the U.S. Supreme Court, came to Dr. Draper with a migraine, he recalled in his autobiography, *Go East, Young Man,* "Tears filled my eyes, for I knew intuitively that I had come to the right man." Dr. Draper had an exquisite Chinese painting in his office that showed a man looking up at a full moon beside a lake. Its caption was "If I could only collect the moonbeams I could cure all the ills of mankind."

The doctor and the future Supreme Court justice became good friends. "Find your kindred spirits in the law and they will help you find your lodestar," he told Douglas. Would that Dr. Draper could have done the same, but his approach to medicine was far ahead of its time. To him, healing went beyond the microbe and the scalpel.

In treating the whole patient, he included the intangibles, for so many people came to him with illnesses that could not be found, let alone diagnosed. He believed that the fears of early childhood often controlled the adult, sending one in all directions without recognizing that a force existed within oneself besides one's will which, when disturbed, confused the past and the present.

These beliefs were not appreciated by many of his contemporaries, most of whom denounced the man who would one day be called the father of psychosomatic medicine in the United States.

In 1929, his search for kindred spirits took him to Zurich, where he studied with the famous disciple of Freud, Dr. Carl Jung. Dorothy accepted the temporary separation as a professional necessity; she was too preoccupied with her flourishing business to give much thought to his absence, although she missed him a great deal—the separation lasted for eighteen months.

Dorothy was brimming with optimism in the summer of 1929, and felt positive about being on the verge of success. She faced no competition in decorating for the luxury housing market. She had a clear field. No one else of consequence was doing lobbies. She loved to tackle public areas, making them grand and intimate.

Dorothy paid little attention to all the talk about the overheated stock market. That was the concern of her brother Roger, who had followed Paul Tuckerman into the business of handling the family's investments. It was a shock when he told her in October that the Tuckerman fortune was no more. They hadn't been wiped out completely like some people, but they were no longer rich, only moderately wealthy.

Because of the Crash, the ideal home colony in Locust Valley would never be, and the Coyle family lost the Carlyle Hotel. It went bankrupt as she applied the finishing touches to the decor.

When Dorothy didn't think things could get much worse, her husband came home one day and told her he wanted a divorce. He moved out the same night, disproving the adage that lightning doesn't strike twice in the same spot.

Depression

Dorothy reeled in the aftershock of her husband's announcement for weeks. On the subject of marriage her beloved Auntie Mee of Stockbridge used to say, "I've always had the best of the second best." The best was to marry and have a family, which Auntie Mee never did. Dorothy Draper now knew what the worst was, something Auntie Mee had spared herself. The worst was to be deserted by one's husband for another woman—a younger woman, of course. Being rejected at forty for the fresher item had its special sting.

The thought that her husband might prefer another had never occurred to her. Well, perhaps in passing, but she didn't bother herself much about what he did. If he had been seeing another woman year after year, avowing that he would not be able to divorce his wife until the children were grown, she had pity on the "other woman." But to divorce! Dorothy had always thought of herself as a beautiful woman, a great prize. How could he have preferred another? How often had she heard of another woman's similar plight and felt smug that she had succeeded in keeping her privileges as a "Mrs." intact?

Quickly she learned what those privileges were. Single women were social pariahs, threats to other women; the easy camaraderie had vanished. Hosts were compelled to locate the suitable single man to pair off with her at dinner. All in all, it was much easier to invite couples. The world revolved in pairs, two by two; the divorced hobbled around on one leg, out of the social whirl quicker than you could say Las Vegas.

Two pieces of unsolicited advice her husband had given her over the years stayed in her mind: Never fight with machinery and keep your eyes on the road. Dorothy tended to live in her imagination, in a fantasy world where machinery was run by others who watched the road as well while she soared to the heights. Now that the pain of reality was too great to bear, she fled into her imagination for comfort and became as driven as any man at her work.

Even when Dorothy was married she had made no bones about the fact that she believed her career was as important as her husband's. Most women would dissemble on that point, bending over backward to be the extra good wife. Dorothy didn't have time for that. Her career was the most important thing in the world. It was not merely a business, it was a mission. While Dr. Draper helped his patients by finding illnesses in their minds that couldn't be located in their bodies, Dorothy pursued her mission: to bring hope to the unhappy. She would rescue people from their pale and drab existences like a magician armed with a paintbrush instead of a magic wand.

She was slow to develop her unique color sense, however. Finding the colors she craved was difficult. Her eyes constantly scanned flower stalls and shop windows, seeking the blue-based magenta or green-based ultramarine that swam in her mind.

Still, no matter how energetically she tried to preoccupy her mind, the reality of being a divorcée was galling. It hit her cruelly before dawn each morning when she became aware of it all over again, suddenly awake, groaning with the strength of the first blow. Dan had stung her, and she was totally unprepared for this rejection: Her father had all but worshiped her.

Worst of all, her private life had been made public, and that intrusion hurt most. Divorce was a public airing of one's most private affairs. More distressing than the pain of the sudden and complete loss of Dan's company, which she had always enjoyed immensely, even if she didn't have the faintest idea what he was talking about, was how it *looked*, which was always her major concern. The idle gossip about the identity of the "other woman" (her name wasn't revealed) pained her until she wanted to cry out loud. Dorothy didn't want to know. She said she hadn't the faintest idea who the woman was and didn't care. What was over was over. The machinery had been broken and could not be fixed. Dorothy tried to keep her eyes steadfastly on the road—a new road for which she had no map.

Instead of falling apart, she went out and drummed up some badly needed business. She formed the River Club, which she called a country club in the city. It was organized like the Tuxedo Club, with founding members investing in it. The Old Guard connection was a big hit with the new money in town. Dorothy was amazed by how much new money there actually was, in spite of the Crash. Suddenly, her commercial business was booming.

The River Club was an immediate success. Once the club was formed and a suitable location found at 52d Street and the East River, Dorothy decorated it, including the two huge tennis courts and the swimming pool, to unanimous acclaim. A story with photos was published in the papers. Then she did the new Sherry's, which had moved uptown to 300 Park Avenue. Her work there was described as "restoration and elaboration." Dorothy Draper Incorporated was off to a great start.

She shed the old name of her company because Architectural Clearing House seemed so earthbound. Too much of her role had been matching up the personalities of her rich friends with the architects she knew, and the scope of that was too confining. There was no room for her big ideas in it. She loved being Dorothy Draper Incorporated. She loved the swoop of those double *D*s. They made her company look as if it were sailing off into the future on gossamer wings.

DD's wounds did not heal that easily. Contrary to the impression she gave of being self-assured, confident, and bold, she often felt inferior out in the world beyond Tuxedo Park. Her arrogance was nothing but a defense against her feelings of inadequacy, which she aggravated over the years by comparing her intellect with those of the brilliant Drapers. Dorothy knew she was not an intellectual. She couldn't play golf or bridge. She towered over most people, and she hated it when she towered over men. In the business world or in the small circle into which she was born, she was protected by her credentials, but in the rest of the world she was vulnerable, an uneducated country girl. When she felt shy and awkward in that world she armored herself with her credentials—out came the society matron's voice, "that unfortunate voice," and the society matron's stance. But that was not how Dorothy wanted to be at all, and the divorce had attacked whatever self-confidence she had: Her faith in herself, even in her creative abilities, her precious vision, was badly shaken. Then, in 1930, she sought help, along with half of Manhattan, from a psychiatrist.

Recognizing that psychoanalysis had helped Dr. Draper break through his reserve to achieve what he really wanted—a life without her in it—Dorothy went beyond the hurt of that realization to acknowledge what Dan's time on the couch had done for him. His position in his field was more important than ever, for there were very few Jungian psychoanalysts in Manhattan in the 1930s. Most psychiatrists were disciples of Freud. Knowing little about such matters, Dorothy sought out a "society" psychiatrist and chose Smiley Blanton.

Dr. Blanton was a Freudian. He didn't say much, and Dorothy didn't say anything at all. What could she say? For several weeks she lay back and decorated his office in her mind, but soon that got boring—and expensive.

She found Dr. Blanton to be fascinating, even though he didn't say anything. He was tall and distinguished. She could not possibly go to anyone who was not, of course, but more than that, he was mysterious, as if he knew some deep and wonderful secrets about her that she didn't know herself.

Unfortunately, words were not Dorothy's forte, and on the couch, where she was supposed to search her soul, she had no words at all. She had heard other people talk about their psychotherapy, and it sounded like they spent most of their time talking about their parents and all the terrible things they had done to them as little children. But she had no bad memories. Her problem wasn't with her darling parents, who were cheerfully footing the bill for her therapy three times a week. She had no idea whether she had resolved her Oedipus and Electra complexes. When it came to understanding psychotherapy and how it worked, she was as dense as she was when staring at the innards of her Chrysler.

Dorothy had not come to Dr. Blanton to discuss her personal life. She wanted to be a star, to fulfill the prophecy her father had made the day she was born. She wanted her name in the papers. She wanted to be as famous as Ruth Draper. If she had a complex, that was it. But she couldn't possibly tell *that* to Smiley Blanton.

And so she went to him three times a week for a year and didn't say a word.

Dr. Blanton was a member of the board of directors of the Marble Collegiate Church, the oldest congregation in continuous existence in America. He recommended that Dorothy go down and hear Dr. Norman Vincent Peale speak, which she did. Soon she was going two or three times a week, and also on Sunday. She told people that Dr. Peale put her on the right track and that life was going to be beautiful.

Dorothy found life at this time to be difficult, much more difficult than she had ever thought possible. She found that raising children was a simple matter, but coping with adolescent rebellion was not. Always having had things her way, she didn't know what to do. Her children's impertinence galled her. Going through adolescence did not give them license to act in any way they pleased.

When the divorce came, Diana was seventeen and George was fifteen. There had never been much in the way of family life during the marriage; both father and mother had been preoccupied with careers. There were no family activities except at Christmas. The older children had been away too much of the time to feel as if they had belonged to a family in the first place, and when the divorce came they had no nanny to cling to like their younger sister.

Diana had been rebellious for years. Although she was everything a girl was supposed to be—attractive, charming, musically talented, popular—she and her mother fought a great deal. Diana complained bitterly to her aunts that her mother was too critical. For all her positive attributes, the girl had a terrible self-image and a tendency to punish herself.

For comfort Diana looked especially to her aunt Ruth, who opened her arms to the bewildered child as she did to all refugees and the unloved, furious with her brother Dan over the divorce. Ruth's love affair with Lauro DeBosis had just ended tragically, and it made her especially sensitive to the suffering of others. In October 1930, flying low over Rome to drop anti-Fascist literature over the city, his plane disappeared over the horizon and crashed. DeBosis was killed. For weeks, news of his martyrdom was splashed all over the European press. His action had deeply angered the detested Mussolini. Members of the DeBosis family were arrested, tried for treason, and acquitted. Their case was a cause célèbre and a great morale-booster for anti-Fascists all over Europe.

But DeBosis's death was completely ignored on the other side of the Atlantic, which made Ruth Draper's suffering all the more painful. A two-inch notice appeared at the bottom of an inside page of the *New York Times*. Her family discreetly did not bring it up and offered no sympathy.

Sensitive to Diana's needs, she listened to her niece and did not try to solve the girl's problems, as Dorothy was likely to do. To a young woman starved for old-fashioned motherly affection, Ruth was a balm. Diana could weep and Ruth would never chide. Then Ruth would tell her a funny story and they would laugh. Diana went to museums and concerts with her famous aunt and enjoyed the attention.

Aunt Alice was another motherly type who came to Diana's rescue after the divorce. She had a special soft spot for Diana. Dorothy felt forsaken when her daughter turned to these other women for support and understanding. Mother-daughter relationships have their treacherous aspects; they are especially tricky between women of great beauty. The source of their difficulties was not lack of affection on Dorothy's part, for she poured it out on Penny. Diana had grown up to be a mirror image of Dorothy at twenty-one, a stunning beauty even more popular and social than her mother had been. Perhaps there was not room for a younger version of herself in Dorothy's life.

Diana had been sent to Foxcroft at the age of fourteen. Once Mrs. Draper had paid a visit to the head mistress to find out how her daughter was doing. She was told, "Wonderfully. We're going to have her hunting by Christmas." In spite of her mother's misgivings, Diana graduated from Foxcroft, spent a year in Italy, and became a deb in the time-honored way, her debut paid for by her Tuckerman grandparents. On the surface she looked like a well-behaved and wholesome miss, but her after-hours behavior, jazzing it up in the clubs of Harlem, left much to be desired as far as her mother was concerned. But there was no talking to Diana. Together in a room the mother and daughter were like time bombs; one or both were likely to explode before long.

Fifteen-year-old George was also a problem. George had been a wanderer since the days of his exploration of Montreal with Franklin and John Roosevelt. He went where his curiosity took him and hardly paid attention to his mother's or father's opinions. He found it was easy to discover what was going on in the world—leave the neighborhood.

When the stock market crashed, George was old enough to wonder why it had happened. He had often discussed history and politics with his grandfather Tuckerman, the family member he was closest to. His grandfather was quite knowledgeable about American history and liked to talk about it, so they had had many long conversations over the years. Paul Tuckerman believed in capitalism, having benefited so much from it. His father Lucius had made a bundle, and Paul had protected it well enough to be able to assist his children and grandchildren.

Grandfather Tuckerman told George about the Tuckerman preacher in Boston who had urged people to save their money and not drink so much, and about George's namesake on his mother's side, George Washington Tuckerman. George Washington's father was a rich Boston import-export merchant, but the son didn't want to work in the family company. He would rather go to the wharves and fish all day. One day George Washington Tuckerman dropped from sight. Fifteen or twenty years later one of his sisters received a letter from "Don Jorje" Tuckerman, a cattle rancher from Corientas, Argentina. Young George began

emulating his wandering namesake by traveling every summer, beginning with a trip to Wyoming at age fourteen.

In 1933, Dr. Draper helped get his son a nonpaying job on the *New
York Evening Post.* George worked there all summer, going out with
reporters as a gofer. He sat next to a reporter who got him interested in
the problems of the unemployed.

That summer he lived with his Uncle Charles the banker, who had a
little brownstone on 72d Street between Lexington and Third Avenues
with his two Irish maids, Lora and Dora. Charles was away much of the
summer of 1933, and George stayed there. On his way up from the *Post*
every evening he began stopping off at Union Square, where political
splinter groups gathered and constantly clashed with the police. What
he saw and heard there opened his eyes a little further.

Later when he attended Columbia University, he learned about what
was going on in Europe. Since DeBosis formed the Alleanza Nazionale,
the campus had become a place where Americans could connect with
anti-Fascist resistance movements.

With George and Diana gone most of the time, Dorothy sought comfort
in Penelope, who suffered less from the divorce than her brother and
sister. Penelope hardly remembered her father at home, so having him
gone was not a drastic change. The only thing about him she could
remember was watching him shave with a razor and a strap. When he
was home, he slept in the dressing room where there was a bed, but that
was not unusual; her grandparents also slept in different bedrooms.

Four years after the divorce, in 1933, Nanny left and ten-year-old
Penelope moved downstairs into the room that had been her father's.
Occasionally she and her mother did things with George, but seldom
with Diana. Penelope had lunch with her father on Friday after school.
She both adored and respected him. He had a marvelous mind and was
funny. She was also very special to Ruth. In the summer, Penelope would
be sent to her grandparents at Tuxedo Park to escape the city heat, or to
the Draper summer cottage in Maine to be with Ruth. Everybody in the
family was supportive of the youngest child.

When DD was working in her office on the ground floor of the

Upside-Down House, Nanny would read stories to Penelope. She also told wonderful bedtime stories about bad and good little girls. Dorothy also loved to read aloud to her little girl, often in bed after her breakfast. She liked to read a little bit each day until a book was finished, but Penelope couldn't stand the suspense. She had been a voracious reader since age four and was unable to keep herself from finishing books on the QT. One morning, while reading to Penelope, Dorothy noticed her attention was wandering. Didn't she like the book? Why wasn't she listening? Finally Penelope admitted she had finished the book already. Dorothy was terribly distressed. Her one moment of contact with her child had been spoiled. She could not understand her daughter's passion for books.

Nanny had taught Penelope the Calvert system at four, and the child read so fast by the time she was ready for school that her father couldn't believe it and used to quiz her on what she had just read. At six she read *Black Beauty.* The Drapers sent their youngest daughter to the Horne school and then to Brearley, her mother's erstwhile alma mater and only brush with formal education. There, Penelope was put ahead a year, skipping the third grade. She did poorly in school after that, which did not disturb her mother very much. After all, Dorothy hadn't done well at school either, and look how far she had come without schooling. Penelope's father, on the other hand, was upset over her miserable grades.

When Penelope went to Tuxedo Park during the summers to be with her beloved "Margee" and "Muggy," the grandchildrens' pet names for their grandmother and grandfather, respectively, she was free to roam the hills as Tuxedo children had always done, although there weren't many other children in the Park by then. Tuxedo Park's population had aged along with the town. Young families now lived in Manhattan. Tuxedo Park was hardly the place for forward-looking society. All its flaws became more obvious as the years went by. The comments of outsiders were mild compared with those of former residents who had grown disenchanted with the place long ago. The quaintness of its customs, its servants in livery, and its gamekeepers in Tyrolean hats, were first anachronisms and then embarrassments. The country set now preferred Saratoga, where the Gideon Putnam would soon get the Draper touch and triple its business in one year. And White Sulphur Springs was still au courant. But the world had passed by Tuxedo Park when it failed to keep up with modern times. It was an old folks' home now.

The Crash of 1929 continued to send its shock waves around the world. The rich had immediately begun to withdraw billions of dollars in gold from American banks and deposit it in European banks because of the well-founded fear of bank holidays. When liquid assets went up in smoke, it was better to turn them into solid gold.

Within the upper class were people who were not enlightened about the poor. Unlike the Drapers, the Tuckermans, the Roosevelts, and others who moved in their circle, some very rich people hated the sight of the poor. Often these were the newly rich who had bought their way onto the high court of the Diamond Horseshoe ring at the Metropolitan Opera. Afraid of displaying their jewelry in public, they threatened to stop subscribing to the Metropolitan Opera until the breadlines were removed from the vicinity. Patrons were furious that the Diamond Horseshoe had become a symbol of the two-class system along Union Square, and there were demonstrations in response to the removal of the breadlines that were noisily put down by the police.

The theory among the unenlightened rich was that a revolution was imminent and would begin in the big cities. People began to stock up on canned goods: It wasn't long before there wasn't a tin of caviar to be had on either side of Manhattan. Country estates were locked up like fortresses. Many of the rich fled to safe apartment hotels where they could live inconspicuously like the aristocrats of France and England. Mansions on Fifth Avenue were equipped with bulletproof steel shutters. The Manhattan luxury dwelling market was booming, as it does after every stock market panic.

In 1932, Dorothy summered at Newport. Matrons she knew from her childhood were going door-to-door in the heat, urging their neighbors to snub Franklin Roosevelt and not support him. Other bluebloods favored the hot-blooded Cornelius Vanderbilt, whose great-grandfather said "The public be damned," and his run for Congress on the "Forgotten Man" platform.

By nominating Roosevelt in Chicago in 1932, William Randolph Hearst checked the hysteria among upper-class reactionaries, and the flow of gold out of the country subsided somewhat. Although the conservatives still preferred Newton Baker, a Morgan man, and were pessimistic about their future, they decided not to withdraw all of their assets and flee the country like the Russian aristocracy did in 1917. Still, they worried a great deal about Roosevelt and how he would implement the demands of the left wing into his government programs. The country might come back, they predicted gloomily, but the great fortunes were gone forever.

The Tuckerman fortune was one of those that had been vastly reduced in the Crash. Even more than her divorce, the stock market crash had thrown a monkey wrench into Dorothy's scheme of life. The year 1929 had been a watershed: Before that year she had been rich and after it she was "poor." The loss of the lifestyle she had known since childhood made her feel poor indeed. In her childhood her family had been very rich compared to the general population. Before World War I her father had an income of about $80,000 a year. When Henry Ford shocked the industrial world by paying a minimum wage of five dollars a day to his workers—fifteen hundred dollars a year—the Tuxedo Park gentry were outraged, believing Ford would screw up the whole wage economy.

Dorothy was never able to understand how other people could live on piddling amounts of money, and she never pictured herself being in that position. Now there was the need to make money, lots of money, the way her grandfather Lucius had, for suddenly, virtually overnight, she didn't have *it*—the ability to live well without ever thinking of money. One paid someone to think about money; *it* made life so much simpler. Now she thought about money day and night and considered herself poorer than the poorest laid-off auto worker, for the disparity of her income before and after the Crash was so great. She had been born rich and felt it was her birthright to remain rich. Now she faced a future without property or furs or jewelry or the wherewithal to throw grand affairs.

The Crash had also affected her parents, who sold their big house and built a smaller one on Circuit Road, Norman in style, on a wooded hilltop overlooking the lake, which they furnished with their heavy Tudor pieces. In it they would finish out their lives. The new house was still large, but relatively cozy when compared with the others. With a dining room, living room, study, bedroom, dressing room, two guest rooms, plus maids' rooms at the back and a chauffeur's house, it was a far cry from the days of hot- and cold-running maids. That life had vanished forever.

Other than trepidation about the future, life for the privileged class went on much as before. The Crash actually improved the quality of life of the highest echelons by removing some of the chaff. Those who had recently made their bundle lost it just as quickly in the Crash, as empires built on paper and their builders went out the window. Rock-solid old money, on the other hand, had everything to gain. Prices were low, labor was cheap, and the rich got richer with everything at twenty-five cents on the dollar. In fact, the Depression was the "Good Old Days" for the upper classes.

The Depression produced a building boom at White Sulphur Springs, where the Greenbrier was building an entire new wing. Acts of fate had winnowed so many undesirables from the guest roster that Old White was once again where the people from Richmond and Baltimore gathered—real Old South society. The Charles A. Schwabs spent a lot of time there, as well as the Robert Lincoln Lees, the Henry Waters Tafts, the George W. Crawfords, and one of the most noted names in thoroughbreds, Judge Nelson Phillips of Dallas.

Once again, the cream of society, north and south, spent their spring and their fall at the springs; some even stayed the entire summer, as had been the custom in antebellum times. It had been the history of Old White to stay essentially the same as society changed, well steeped in its own history like rare tea. Sooner or later, the Real Thing came back.

Among those who sought refuge there during the Depression were the newly frugal Old Guard, who found it cheaper to close their country houses on Mackinac Island or Bar Harbor and don their summer whites at the Greenbrier. An effort was made to make it more of a year-round colony like Tuxedo Park had been. A children's dining room was built, as well as a clubroom for chauffeurs. A school was established for aristocratic refugees making do. It even had a newspaper, the *Portico*, to give the displaced a feeling of community. Much of it was devoted to the comings and goings of the world elite.

White Sulphur Springs was also preferred over European spas like Baden-Baden and Monticatini, for crossing the Atlantic meant six weeks away, and in that time the stock market could rocket or take a nose dive. The Greenbrier was the prudent choice. There one could obtain the Aix and Vichy douches and the sulphur mud packs of a quality comparable to the therapies of Europe.

Getting to White Sulphur Springs was no longer the trial it had once been, for the elite traveled via "the most wonderful train in the world," the C&O Railroad's *George Washington,* the world's first air-conditioned sleeping car train. The observation car was done in the style of a colonial library, and the dining room was done like a pre-Revolutionary tavern with Duncan Pfyfe design Spode china.

The horse-loving British aristocrats much preferred the Greenbrier to the crowds at Saratoga and the geriatric set at Tuxedo Park. The stalls of its stables were filled with the decendents of Traveller and other prize horses of Greenbrier county. The British were particularly fond of the atmosphere. One could feel absolutely on the frontier and still enjoy the comforts of civilization. On misty summer mornings, the riding stables of the Greenbrier would be filled with the voices of British barristers.

The riding trails wound up the mountain into the clouds at an elevation comparable to Les Avants in the Alps. The horses were treated like belles, given perms, facials, beribboned pigtails, and breakfast in bed.

But the real kings and queens of the newly resurrected society at White Sulphur Springs were from the Old South—the Richmond and Charleston set. Two matrons reigned in particular: Mrs. Henry Waters Taft of the presidential family and Mrs. George W. Crawford, wife of the chairman of Columbia Gas. The Tafts and the Crawfords presided over many gala dinner parties, and they were not necessarily of a frivolous nature. The purpose of one that was held at the elegant club atop Kate's mountain was to "get together in the gloom and discuss the Depression and Prohibition."

Mrs. Crawford was much younger than her sixty-year-old bridegroom. She set fashion trends on the terrace of the cottage where they always stayed through the skeet-shooting season before wintering in Europe. White Sulphur society was overjoyed when they heard the popular couple was expecting a child. Mrs. Crawford, returning to New York early in the fall to have her baby, gave birth prematurely on the train; a porter acted as midwife. Because of this, the golden-haired girl, Martha, was nicknamed "Choo-choo" Crawford, but the child hated it so much it was soon changed to "Sunny," which suited her much better.

During the golden era of the 1930s the *Portico* published many photographs of Sunny Crawford, "Our Greenbrier Baby," sitting in the petunias or dancing down the stairs. It was a blissful time, full of fun and the best of everything. Greenbrier children walked dogs with their governesses, had Cream of Wheat in the children's dining room, and attended classes at Graham-Eckes School, where French conversation and Dalcroze eurhythmics kept them occupied while their parents planned parties, partied, and recovered from partying.

In the North, society remained faithful to Newport, where little Sunny would one day meet a tragic fate as Mrs. Claus von Bulow. The unofficially crowned summer capital was still Bailey's Beach, even though the U.S. Navy used it as a garbage dump, making it one of the filthiest beaches in the country. There the new society matrons still rose from the sea, although no longer wrapped in the obligatory bathing capes of Dorothy Draper's youth, their well-tanned flesh exposed to an astonishing degree.

Nearby, their oxfords incongruous in the sand, detectives still watched the children of the very rich at play. Newport was crowded with them in the 1930s. Most of the Old Guard rented their summer castles for the season, or sold them to one of the many entrepreneurs who made a lot of money during the Depression. It was the same old play with a new cast of characters.

• • •

The scene was just as crowded in New York. In the 1920s New York was a small town. If you knew anybody you knew everybody. That atmosphere disappeared after the Crash. During the 1930s there were more wealthy people living in Manhattan than ever before, more than could be accommodated within the old boundaries. Because of demand, the Depression-devastated luxury hotel business was making a turnaround. Impressed by what Dorothy had done with the lobby of the Carlyle Hotel, hoteliers upgraded their accommodations by attempting to copy what she had done. Some of them even paid lots of money to hire her services.

The Phipps family, members of Dorothy's social circle, had been impressed by her Carlyle job, and had an interesting project for her. They owned a row of tenements on Sutton Place with apartments renting at an average of twenty-five dollars a month. Although the neighborhood was not particularly desirable, the river view was. In 1922, Elsie deWolfe built a house with curved glass windows on Sutton Place. Mrs. William K. Vanderbilt followed, but society did not, and the "high type" tenants the Phipps family wanted to rent to would sooner move to Brooklyn than to the tenements of Sutton Place.

A hundred years earlier, the area had been a neighborhood of coal yards, breweries, and fat-rendering plants. Then a dry goods merchant named Effingham Sutton built a row of houses by the river in an attempt to improve the neighborhood. He went broke doing it. Since then the neighborhood had been déclassé. Could Mrs. Draper help the Phippses exploit the bullish luxury apartment market?

DD's very small budget of fifteen thousand dollars for each of the four buildings didn't allow for much in the way of structural changes, even if they could have been made by slipping around city regulations, as she had done when she secured the garage for her Upside-Down House. She had to do something dramatic with such a small budget, and the only answer that kept recurring was "paint."

For hours Dorothy paced up and down Sutton Place, imagining it in every season. The tenements were a dreary row of cold-water flats without much going for them architecturally. The builder had run out of money before he could supply any nice extras. The only thing to do with such an undistinguished quartet was to make them disappear, and the way to make them disappear was to paint them black.

The Phipps family trusted her and did not make a fuss. They knew her reputation and did not expect her to come up with something timid. It was a small risk. Sooner or later the flats would rent for a good price. Mrs. Draper could just make it sooner rather than later. Nothing was said among the painters who did the job either, and Mrs. Draper remained on-site to supervise just in case someone came along to try to talk them out of it.

All the trim was painted white. Dorothy thought it looked smashing. Then she thought some more. She recalled seeing some paintings in a museum, or perhaps during her travels. Somehow the doors of the four row houses became prominent. She decided to paint each one a different, strong, vibrant color—startling red, grass green, chromium yellow, and cobalt blue. She was excited now. Had she presented such an idea to her society clients, they would have tried to have her quietly put away.

Then Dorothy ordered romantic plantings for the backyards of the row houses—syringa, apple trees, and lilacs. When told regulations prevented her from removing the unsightly fire escapes, she faced them with elaborate white scrollwork. Then she hired a red-cheeked former coachman as a doorman "because he looked like love and security."

Sutton Place was successful in the way that mattered most: the bottom line. Rent before the flats were touched by Mrs. Draper's magic color wand was fifty dollars a floor, with no takers. Afterward it was one hundred eighty dollars and the buildings were sold out.

A small article about the job, plus a picture, was hidden on the inside pages of the real estate section of the *New York Times,* but there it was read by those who mattered: "Four Cold Water Flats Now Showing Reasonable Net Income" was the headline. "For a long time, the buildings had an average vacancy of 33 percent," said Mrs. Tuckerman Draper (Dorothy completely disappeared behind her last names as befitted a divorcée). "After spending sixty thousand dollars these old flats are now bringing in a rental which will amortize the alteration charges in about three years."

The Sutton Place success would bring more success because it was in dollars and cents. Not only that, Dorothy had demonstrated that as a leader she had the power to get society to move east of Third Avenue all the way to unfashionable Sutton Place, previously the address of nobodies.

The smart black-and-white flats got on the wire. Hearst picked up the story. Soon the flaming red doors of Sutton Place were being shown in the ladies' magazines and talked about on the radio. Overnight, black became drop-dead chic. Depression-devastated hotels seeking the lucrative upscale trade began copying the Draper style and a few even hired her; for example, the state of New York asked her to remodel the Gideon Putnam, its ramshackle hotel in Saratoga Springs.

Dorothy Draper discovered to her delight that she was good at sparring. She could really go to battle with the head of a company, and then her height was actually to her advantage. She all but swooped a train behind her when she went into the ring with "Mr. Tycoon," especially if he was "Mr. Tiny Tycoon," of which there seemed to be a disproportionate number. Short or tall, most of them had never even seen the inside of Tuxedo Park, and Dorothy was offering its essence for sale. From her point of view, she was doing them a favor.

And she was shrewd, too. For instance, if they objected to the high cost of laundering her silk-lined casements she said, "Put it into your advertising budget and amortize the cost." After all, her high-contrast colors were selling the place.

And Dorothy sold. Hers was one of those strange successes, like hula hoops, only lasting, because her trade was not fly-by-night. All of a sudden everyone wanted what she had. Her concepts had a way of being translated to the common man in that good old Yankee-Doodle way. She sold good taste at a bargain rate. Paint was cheap and Dorothy provided her magic ingredients: imagination and color. In the women's magazines of the day, Dorothy Draper's name began appearing almost as frequently as Eleanor Roosevelt's name.

Mrs. Draper sold good taste, guaranteed good taste, straight from Tuxedo Park, which in the public's mind had been leading the way since young Griswold Lorillard gave them the tux. And she sold it to absolutely anybody at all. Eleanor Roosevelt had her mission, and Dorothy Draper's was to democratize good style, to make it possible for anyone to live well and in the best of taste—her taste.

Dorothy came along at a time that could not have been more gray and dreary—seven years of Depression—and she set out to banish all that gloom. While all around her were timid she flew a red flag—scarlet red, not the usual toned-down red that was then considered proper. Dorothy's red wasn't the dusty red of plush but the gleaming red of the lips of Hollywood movie stars, the provocative red that is waved in front of the bull. "Now take that red and paint your front door with it," she would say. Shocking as it may seem, across the land a lot of people did just that. And who was to question their taste if Dorothy Draper told them to do it? Not anyone in *their* town.

When Dorothy's predecessor Elsie deWolfe first saw the Parthenon, her biographer reports her as saying, "Oh good—beige, my favorite color." The prevailing fashion pre–Dorothy Draper was a washout of beige, or all white, as favored by Syrie Maugham. Dorothy Draper's colors throbbed in contrast to that stark environment; she burst forth like a rocket.

It was a good thing Dorothy's business was doing so well. Her good fortune and five years with Smiley Blanton enabled her to cope with success as well as certain personal matters. Wedding bells were ringing all over. Diana was in love, and so were Dorothy's former husband and his new lady. Why it should bother her at all was the question, but it did. Fortunately, Dorothy had twofold assistance—her darling Dr. Blanton and Dr. Peale. She followed Dr. Peale now; his words would ring in her ears at moments she didn't think she could stand it all. He was her inspiration in her hour of need.

Dan Draper's choice caused Dorothy a particular kind of pain. His fiancée was also a decorator. Her name was Elisabeth Low, five years divorced from Seth Low, and she would have been called one of DD's competitors had Dorothy recognized any.

After Dr. Draper left Dorothy in 1929, he moved into an apartment at

320 East 72d Street. Dining in the home of friends soon after, he met Elisabeth Low. "I hear you're a decorator," he said.

"Yes, I am," she replied.

"I've just taken an apartment. Would you like to help me with it?"

Saturdays were best for her. She went over and decorated his apartment, thinking he was the most unlikely man to have been married to a decorator. Nevertheless, they fell in love soon after. He was fifty-five, and she was twenty years younger, the perfect match. She was attractive, tall, thin, and elegant. She took pride in saying she was a total nonintellectual. Elisabeth was tremendously orderly and frugal and not at all the dominating type. In fact, people catered to her because she did not pay enough attention to herself; she would forget to eat unless someone came along and fed her. People tended to be fond of Elisabeth. She was highly likeable. Dr. Draper called her "Hap," short for happy, which she was.

Dorothy was awfully good about the wedding, although it tore her to pieces. Only her son was loyal, for whatever reasons he may have had. He sent the new Mrs. Draper roses every Christmas and that was it. Even Penelope was close to Elisabeth. It couldn't be helped. When Diana had emergencies it was Betty she turned to because her mother "wouldn't be able to handle it."

There was also a business angle. Having to share her husband and children was bad enough, but having to share the Draper name in the decorating profession was an awful blow. From the beginning it created confusion.

Dan Draper wed Elisabeth Low at the Madison Avenue Presbyterian Church on April 10, 1935. Both bride and groom dispensed with attendants. At the end of the small announcement in the newspaper it listed their former spouses, reinforcing to the public Dorothy's station as divorcée. She refused to dwell on the matter and was glad she had a business that demanded her full attention day and night.

Diana, now a slim and lovely twenty-two, had been avoiding her mother for years. Through Aunt Dorothea, her father's sister, she had met Nelson Jay. They hit it off from the start and became a Fitzgeraldian couple around town.

When it came to selecting a husband, Diana for once did not rebel. Nelson was one of the flock. His father was hand-picked by Morgan to be one of his men at Guaranty Trust, and early in his career with the company was sent to Paris before World War I to look after Morgan interests there, including investigating reports about the antics of the children of his men as they sowed wild oats on the Left Bank. The motto of J. P. Morgan at Guaranty Trust was "steady as she goes," and he placed it like a mantle on the shoulders of every Morgan man.

Nelson Jay had been yanked out of too many schools at an early age to be steady. He loved Paris, where his mother, who adored him, introduced him to great cultural riches. Then, when he had begun pursuing his artistic, musical, and literary interests, he was sent across the Atlantic to St. Paul's for prepping for Harvard and The Company.

Nelson Jay quit Harvard just six months short of graduation and came to New York City to enjoy the Prohibition life. He found the perfect companion in Diana Draper.

Diana was as lovely as a movie star. Her breeding showed. Her face was as fair as her mother's but softer, without the haughtiness in the eyes. Her body was pencil slim. She did not have the weight problem her mother battled with increasing frustration. But like her mother, she was used to getting her way, and could charm her way around obstacles.

Nelson Jay had an aesthetic quality unlike other St. Paul's/Harvard men, who were being trained to replace Dad as head of the family fiefdom. Having grown up in Paris, he was more sophisticated than the average American man. He and Diana shared an interest in music. There was a wild streak in both of them. They wanted to get out from underneath parental control. Diana saw marriage as the ideal escape, much as her mother had at the same age.

Diana and Nelson were married on Valentine's Day in 1936. Planning a wedding where there were two households to consider on the bride's side of the family was a delicate matter. Dr. and Mrs. Draper attended the wedding at the church, then entertained at their place. Some family members went there instead of to the official reception on 64th Street. It was a big affair, the last Dorothy Draper was to throw in the house she had made famous by turning it upside-down. The bride wore her mother's wedding gown, and Grandmother Tuckerman's train. She looked like a meltingly demure blend of them both, with orange blossoms tucked around her sleek blonde hair, carrying white lilies of the valley and gardenias. Her thirteen-year-old sister, Penelope, was the maid of honor. Penny's cousins, Nancy and Cynthia Tuckerman, were bridesmaids. George came up from the South, where he was working in a steel mill for reasons his mother could not fathom.

It was a sloppy February; a lot of snow and slush was in the street. The young attendants were carried into the church.

"You don't have your mitts," said Cynthia Tuckerman to Penelope.

"That's alright," Penny said, recovering grandly. "I'm the maid of honor."

For years, the house on 64th Street had seemed too big for comfort. When sent downstairs to the living room to practice on the piano, Penelope played as fast as she could; she hated being alone in the big room. Nanny had been gone for three years, and it was just Dorothy and Penny now. It was also a drain on the budget. And then there were the memories. With no fanfare and a minimum of grief, Dorothy put the house on the market and hoped it would bring a good price. She needed the money for something special that had been on her mind for some time.

When 1929 had come crashing in on her, she had been rescued by the philosophies of Dr. Blanton and the persuasive Dr. Peale. Could she sell to the public what she had learned? Her five years on the couch with Dr. Blanton had released her of her color inhibitions in some wonderful and mysterious way she did not understand, because there were no words for it. All she knew was, one fine day after coming three times a week for a year "it" finally happened. Before, she saw the world in brown and beige—dreary, washed-out colors. After the transformation, whatever that had been, she saw the world in different colors—vivid, clear, strong colors minus the earth colors and the murky pastels. The blue she saw through her new eyes was the color of a cloudless sky.

Flowers bloomed joined by beribboned garlands around rooms bathed in sunlight. A fresh breeze was constantly stirring. The depression she had endured for so long was over, and from a marketing standpoint, her timing couldn't have been better. The whole world was tired of being depressed, and she had the remedy. It was simple, so very simple; Dr. Peale had translated what she had no words for. It *was* possible to control your own destiny to a greater extent than anyone thought possible. And enlightenment was possible for the average citizen if Dorothy could somehow market at a reasonable cost what she had learned about living from her two mentors.

The wherewithal came to her with the sale of the house on 64th Street. She invested fifty thousand dollars of her own money in "Learn to Live," a correspondence course that would teach people in twelve easy lessons how to think positively and forge themselves a new destiny: "The first time such a complete and comprehensive course in the fundamentals of successful living [had] ever been prepared or offered, a finishing school in the privacy of your own home."

She paid a good price to have the brochures written by the best experts in the field. So great was the demand for the first installment that a second printing was ordered. Once again, Dorothy Draper seemed to know how to appeal to the public in a way that got them to part with their hard-earned money.

Even members of her family responded positively. Sarah Delano wrote, "I am always interested in everything you do, having been such a close friend of your grandmother's and having known all your family for so many years."

"Time that passed without a plan of action led to loneliness," according to the brochure. No one knew that better than Mrs. Draper. Some of the advice had an ironic twist, such as the need for children to complete one's life: "Every mother will understand her child better if she understands herself first." (Perhaps if Dorothy had understood herself better, her own children would not have flown the coop, Diana all the way to New Mexico.)

Another irony was the guide to successful spending that the course offered: "Make sure the amount allotted is not exceeded by the amount spent!" Her brother, pained to hear how much the course was costing, could now only hope it would turn a profit.

Customers sent away for the course after reading the comprehensive initial brochure that had been so successfully received. The first lesson was also well received. In a series of exercises, it taught the reader how to make use of the power of positive thinking. Readers were to overcome their fears by writing them down and striking them off, for nothing consumed energy like fear. "Mrs. A" was a fearful type. She rushed to wait on everybody and was forever apologizing. She was as tense as a wire and so was everyone around her. Poor Mrs. A. got that way by being dealt with too strictly. She was repressed and made to feel inferior. Advice was offered: "I want you to take time to go into your early years which you've shut off behind the iron barriers of your will and stop fighting. Relax. Aunt Mary is dead. Don't try so hard. Be natural. Be easy."

So much for five years on the couch with Smiley Blanton. Dorothy Draper would will that slow and agonizing process away with a wave of the hand. "Be happy!"

"Mrs. B.," on the other hand, was too confident. She should curb every impulse to boss or excel or inform. She should learn to say phrases like "you're right" or "possibly so" as often as she could in a conversation with a person she didn't like. "Instead of talking, try listening."

An avalanche of letters arrived praising the exercise, but few subscribed beyond the first lesson or two. Most thanked Mrs. Draper for saving their lives so successfully that they didn't have need of further lessons.

Dorothy had been done in by her own success. The business loss was phenomenal. Her expenses had, of course, been considerable for such a serious undertaking. When she began to realize that the first lessons had been *too* helpful, she embarked on a direct-mail campaign, exorting subscribers to join up for the rest of the course. But to no avail. Many may have gone on to read Dr. Peale's *Power of Positive Thinking*. Others may have taken to the couch themselves.

Fortunately, Dorothy could still handle an economic crisis. She knew how to sacrifice with style. There was a vacancy in one of the Sutton Place flats that she had designed with "romance and young couples in mind." They were no longer the bargain they had been before her gentrification, but an apartment there was considerably easier to handle monetarily than living in the enclave between Third Avenue and Central Park. Penelope was going off to school. Nanny was gone. By sleeping on the couch and giving Penelope the one bedroom, the place would do.

Dorothy wrote an article for the magazines on how to make a small apartment look larger; there was a severe housing shortage at the time, particularly in big cities. The article explained everything she had done to her "bandbox by the river," as she romantically called it. To expand tiny space paint everything sky blue, she advised—the walls, molding, ceiling, furniture, picture frames, and even a lovely old-fashioned mahogany secretary. That way, she said, everything melted into the walls. Blue was the color of the draperies, too. Then she recommended painting the floor white and putting down a deep white fur rug.

Even her dog, a black-and-white dalmatian named Dewey, fit into the color scheme. Dewey slept in the bottom bunk of Penelope's double-decker bed while Penelope slept on top. Penny thought the new apartment was much cozier than the house on 64th Street with all its empty open spaces.

Before the photographers from *Vogue* and *Harper's Bazaar* came to photograph Mrs. Draper's bandbox apartment by the river, she removed the personal items, including a stupendous multicolor Chinese mandarin coat that had been displayed on the wall, each color blazing like a brilliant jewel. She called it her diploma.

Fame

Across town, on the west side of 59th Street at 150 Central Park South, destiny was waiting in the form of a thirty-eight-story residential building that had been empty for five years. By 1937, it had earned the nickname "The Ghost of 59th Street." Constructed to be one of Manhattan's first cooperative apartments, it had been a casualty of the Depression and was currently owned by the C-2 Series, a series of bonds with three trustees in charge installed by the state. The trustees importuned Vincent Coyle, with whom DD had worked on the Carlyle Hotel, to manage the Hampshire House, and then called in Dorothy Draper to do for them on a grand scale what she had done for the Phipps family.

The structure had enormous potential. Four setbacks on the park side of the building provided a glorious sweep of Central Park. Made of white Virginia brick, it was French in design, the kind of snow-white building one sees on the Côte D'Azur. Each suite had its own foyer and was in every way like a private home. Could Mrs. Draper, who had lured society east to Sutton Place, now move them west? Even to the "Wild West" bordering on the Seventh Avenue frontier?

A tour was made. It was quite a crowd: the Coyle and the Elliman people, who had the property under management, two or three trustees, Mrs. Draper, Lester Grundy, her new designer, and her secretary.

The decor was the usual sad story: muted colors in the public rooms, small insignificant lamps, and features no one paid much attention to. Dorothy found the lobby "pompous, with kingly theme chairs and pretentious decor." The complete tour held no surprises. But the contract negotiations did. Compared with the sixty-thousand-dollar budget she had on Sutton Place, the Ellimans were talking about a budget of close to four hundred thousand dollars, which boggled even Dorothy's mind. She also got her usual carte blanche. The realtors she had worked with didn't know what they wanted their property to be besides a financial success. The decorating was entirely up to her. But the luxury-dwelling market was booming and the Ellimans wanted to know if she could have the hotel ready by September 15.

Dorothy suppressed a gasp, then said "Yes, and within budget, too." She signed the contract on April 15, 1937, and received the first installment of a fifteen-thousand-dollar fee for a $396,000 renovation of 117 suites. It was the largest decorating contract to date ever given to a woman. The size of her contracts were making quantum leaps. Her fee alone was what she had been allowed to spend on one of the Sutton Place buildings.

She immediately hired two more people, a young buyer named Ted Stewart and Belle Clark, a secretary who turned out to be a marvel, tall and slim and superbly organized. Unlike the others, Belle seemed to understand what Dorothy needed without Dorothy's having to explain.

Seeking inspiration, she went to Hudnut's Salon for a massage. While on the table she emptied her mind as she had learned to do, and an idea came to her. It didn't have words, just features. When she told an interviewer how she got her inspiration for the job, Hudnut's reported that the week following the publishing of the article, someone came in and asked for the same treatment on the same table.

Her idea was simple: Make the public and private rooms of the Hampshire House as intimate and cozy as those back home in Tuxedo Park. It wasn't a revolutionary idea, but she thought it had potential. She discovered she had a treasure in Lester Grundy. He was an art historian with a curator's depth of knowledge, and he also loved the eighteenth century. He was a great admirer of Grinling Gibbons and the white plaster motif with its grand scroll-and-shell motifs. Lester also loved the baroque, and Mrs. Draper's unusual color sense. He admired her haphazard combinations of periods and the way she arranged them to perfection. Their work together would achieve a perfection more lasting than either would ever know, and their association too sacred to share. (When interviewed by telephone by the author shortly before his death in 1985, Mr. Grundy declared, "I have nothing to say. I shall take my fond memories of Mrs. Draper unsullied to the grave." He did.)

When Lester heard of Dorothy's idea of plaster motifs on an expanded scale, combined with art deco and whimsical Victorian styles, he understood immediately the look she was after. No one had done plaster motif appliqués for years. A search was made for a plasterworker. After much investigation, Dorothy discovered the Cinquinnis, a family of artisans who carved marble and were equally skilled with wood. They lived in Brooklyn and could make Lester's overscale plasterwork Grinling Gibbons motifs. The fantastic scroll-and-shell plaster motifs the Cinquinnis produced in their Brooklyn shop were works of art. It was difficult to decide whether they framed the walls of Victorian green or elephant gray or the richly glowing colors framed the stark white of the plasterwork. On other walls, Dorothy abandoned the past and used shiny black patent leather, and wallpaper in a stripe so wide it had to be stenciled on.

The combination of Dorothy Draper and Lester Grundy brewed up more ideas than they could cope with. Mrs. Draper started seeing the job the way her ex-husband used to talk about his patients—in total, as an entity in which each individual part harmonized with another. A thirty-eight-story white elephant was some entity, but Dorothy realized the job had to be done comprehensively, from top to bottom, from the color concepts to the matchbook covers. She would do not only the walls and the floors (in her enormous 2′ × 2′ black-and-white marble tiles) but also the patterns on the china, the liveries, the stationery, and everything that was displayed, right down to the swizzle sticks in the cocktail bar and the buttons on the vests of the busboys!

Having grown up in Tuxedo Park, where liveried servants were part of daily life and eating in the club was merely a larger version of eating at the family manor, Dorothy knew exactly what was required: a larger version of home-sweet-home with a punched-up color wheel. She could practically do the job with her eyes closed.

The entire hotel would be done like a princely flat on Hyde Park, its public spaces no different from the quality private home. Walls were hung with linen and painted by her newly hired artist, Glenn Boyles, with enormous clusters of huge cabbage roses. The same cabbage rose motif was printed in the glazed chintz with a white ground that covered the chairs and sofas. The colors in the chintz were strong and clear; the combination was surreal—grass green and scarlet, wine, watermelon, and coral, with turquoise and mustard yellow. Never before had such colors been used in a commercial job.

When Dorothy presented her color sketches to her fabric suppliers, she was told they were all "special order." At that time there were only two colors in the hotel decorating trade—shades of brown and black. Because the fabric suppliers were eager for her business, they went out of their way to find special dyers who would try to give her exactly what she wanted in color. Other specialists were needed to fill the job, unique people who, being artists, didn't like to make more than a dozen of anything because it bored them. Dorothy kept the names of these special jobbers in a notebook that Belle kept in Dorothy's traveling bag. DD's "sources" were carefully cultivated, their names not shared even with her dearest friends. In return, her jobbers were fiercely loyal to her.

It was in the lobby and the public rooms of the Hampshire House that Dorothy Draper really let loose with her fantasy. The big chic black-and-white marble tiles were laid out under a pink ceiling. White iron trees lit from the inside were set against vast mirrors in the restaurant. And everywhere she mixed periods and styles as she pleased: Modern touches of chromium and black lacquerware were combined with amusing Victorian harp-styled chaises covered in rich rose-colored satin. Elaborately swagged Victorian draperies, ever so slightly tongue-in-cheek with their gaudy, extra big ball fringes, were used with ultra-lux venetian blinds.

Dorothy was also getting on-the-job training in the hotel business. She designed a wonderful creamy gray envelope that turned out to be too large to go down the mail chute. Little mistakes like that cost hundreds of dollars. One of the highlights of the job was a big chandelier with long prisms that people insisted used to hang in a palace in imperial Russia. But Mrs. Draper had designed it herself, just made it up in her head, she told the press. Unfortunately, when the workmen hung the chandelier it was too low. People couldn't walk under it. She instructed them to bevel a huge hole in the ceiling and fit the chandelier up into it. She was never afraid to make architectural changes.

Dorothy was the first to disguise beds in an effort to make the hotel's bedrooms look more like suites. She ordered practical twin-size mattresses and box springs that served as free-standing sofas and flanked them with large coffee tables and scaled-up furniture. The rooms lost their bedroom look and could serve as meeting places.

The average hotel room circa 1935 was decorated in practical, durable fabric in colors that didn't fade or draw attention to themselves. The Hampshire House changed all that. Mrs. Draper really believed the whole world should live as well as possible, and her secret was as simple as homemade pie: You don't draw the distinction between what you like for yourself and what you give the customer. It was how she had done business since she sold her first house with all its contents to a persuasive friend fifteen years earlier.

In the thick of getting the Hampshire House ready, rushing to meet all her deadlines, her son George appeared one day and told her he was going to Spain to fight the Fascists.

"Oh, really, dear?" she said, deep within a cloud of distraction. "I hear the soldiers wear overalls over there."

Dr. Draper was furious. He saw his son's plans to fight the dictator Franco as a form of adolescent rebellion that had gone too far.

George was twenty-one at the time and attending Columbia University, where he met Nancy Guggenheim, the dark-haired young woman who eventually became his wife and the mother of his two children. She was the daughter of Harry Guggenheim, a member of the prominent New York Jewish family. This relationship caused young George Draper to be particularly sensitive to the actions Hitler was taking toward the

Jews in Germany. He knew that Hitler and Mussolini were going to combine their air arsenals to assist Franco in destroying the democratically elected government of Spain, and France and Great Britain were doing nothing to help. In the United States, virtually no protest could be heard beyond Union Square or the Columbia enclaves about what was happening in Europe.

George decided to join the Lincoln Brigade. In spite of her lack of enthusiasm for her son's decision for reasons of chic, Dorothy was concerned about it. She introduced him to Billy Chilton, the English ambassador to Spain, whom Dorothy had met when Chilton was stationed in Washington, D.C., during World War I. Unfortunately, the ambassador couldn't be of much help, since he had moved out of Madrid when the fighting started and set up his embassy in Biarritz, France, across the Spanish border. George shipped out, and DD hoped for the best.

Grandmotherhood was imminent. When Diana became pregnant, the Paul Tuckermans paid for her to be flown to the Doctor's Hospital in New York from her home in New Mexico, because they were concerned about the sanitary conditions of the Southwest hospitals. Six weeks before delivery, Diana had made the long and difficult flight in unpressurized airplanes.

Delivery was also difficult; forceps were used and a hole was punctured in the infant's right upper skullcap. Dr. Burns, the family obstetrician, had given Diana a new painkiller called Twilight Sleep, which didn't do a thing for the pain; it just made her forget about it afterward like a dimly remembered nightmare. The proud papa didn't make the situation any better when he took off with his Harvard buddies for Tuckerman's Ravine and skiing while Diana was still recuperating in the hospital.

The new parents and infant George stayed for the next few months with the Tuckermans, who were thrilled to be great-grandparents. If DD was less than thrilled to be a grandmother at that point she didn't let on.

Between the ages of twelve and thirteen, Penelope had gained thirty pounds and had grown six inches. Her mother took her to a neurologist, a very small man named Dr. Davidoff, at Columbia Presbyterian Hospital. Mrs. Draper informed the doctor that when Penelope was a small child, her nanny had fallen down the stairs with Penny in her arms. Although Nanny had tried to protect the infant in the fall, Penny landed on her head and was knocked out for twenty-four hours. A similar accident had happened to Penelope's father at the age of seventeen. While riding a bike, he fell on his head, and in the next four years grew to a height of 6′2″. Dr. Draper was of the opinion that the injury might have shook up her pituitary gland.

Dr. Davidoff tested Penelope and said, "This is a very healthy young woman. I'm afraid, Mrs. Draper, you have a very tall daughter." From that time on, Dorothy took extra pains to make sure that her daughter did not slump but stood proudly erect, with chin thrown back "like a stag at bay," as she herself had been taught.

Dorothy wanted Penelope to go to Foxcroft. In fact, she insisted upon it. Dr. Draper was very unhappy that the school they had had so many misgivings about when Diana had attended had also been chosen for Penelope. She was obviously a gifted child and should not be going to a finishing school but to a college preparatory. Garrison Forest was his choice, where 80 percent of the students went on to college.

Dr. Draper sent Elisabeth to discuss the matter with Dorothy. They met for tea. It was all very civil. Elisabeth presented the argument for Garrison Forest, Dorothy agreed that it was the better choice, and the meeting was quickly over. There was a clock tower outside the window directly behind the second Mrs. Draper's head upon which the first Mrs. Draper focused through the entire conversation, never once meeting her replacement's eyes.

Penelope was sent at once to Garrison Forest, where a Miss Offutt, the head mistress, reintroduced the voracious reader to the English language. Dorothy was happy about her daughter's success; she had never forgotten her own misery at Brearley.

With Penelope tucked away at Garrison Forest, Diana nursing her infant back in New Mexico, and George off fighting in Spain, DD was able to turn her attention 100 percent to the transformation of the Hampshire House. It opened on time and under budget, as DD had promised.

The press pronounced the new Hampshire House "veddy swell" and "ultra swank," unlike anything they had ever seen. Dorothy Draper had turned the cooperative's common and private rooms into something grandly British but still homey. They reported that the rooms looked as if the lord and lady of the house had just stepped out. They looked lived in and comfortable, with flowers, magazines on the table, and a real fire in the fireplace.

But it was the chintz that was most talked about—cabbage roses of heroic size in enormous clusters, like rain-drenched blooms in a Tuxedo Park garden on a sparkling white ground. The colors were vivid coral, turquoise and mustard yellow, strong pink and magenta, emerald green and scarlet. She said she disdained the usual "tiny, fidgety" chintz pattern and touted the oversize scale.

Photographs of the Hampshire House rooms began appearing in *Vogue, Harper's Bazaar,* and even in "housewife" magazines, where Schumacher ran advertisements of its line of Dorothy Draper designer fabrics. So popular was the large-scale cabbage rose design from the Hampshire House that Schumacher launched a million yards of chintz on the market. Her cabbage rose print became one of its all-time best sellers. As one of her envious competitors said, "It used to be very difficult to get the kind of fabrics she first popularized. Now it's rather difficult to avoid them."

Shortly after the gala opening, the Hampshire House was filled to capacity with socialites, wealthy social climbers, the international set, and high-class artists like the well-known diva, Madame Lucrezia Bori of the Metropolitan Opera Company. Then Mrs. Draper herself moved in, to an airy duplex on the thirty-fourth floor with a park view, where she got everything at 30 percent off from the well-pleased Ellimans.

It was quite a change from her two-room Sutton Place flat with a view of the East River. The duplex was a jewel, with high ceilings, well laid out rooms, and windows overlooking the panorama of Central Park. Upstairs there were two bedrooms. Downstairs there was a dining room, drawing room, and small kitchen.

Dorothy's beloved Auntie Mee had died in 1924 and had left her house, "The Old Place" at Stockbridge, to Dorothy, along with Wolcott,

Gibbs, and Tuckerman heirlooms. She placed these few precious family heirlooms throughout the gorgeous Hampshire House rooms, including Oliver Wolcott's desk, her favorite, and many vases of fresh flowers. Nowhere in the rooms was there a feeling of anything garishly new. She felt at home again.

The Essex House, next door to the Hampshire House on Central Park South, was another early project. Once again, Dorothy worked with Vincent Coyle. The hotel was terribly run down when Dorothy first saw it; for example, one floor was a jumble of maid's rooms. She decided to do a garden restaurant that looked as if it were outdoors. The color of the room was to be pale blue, "like the sky in springtime." She wanted bricks in the room painted blue as well, but she didn't like the way they looked painted at all. As the workers began removing the paint from the bricks, the resulting finish was, she decided, a "lovely soft pink," and they were left like that.

Two columns were made to look like trees; the branches rose surreally up the wall and then to the ceiling. One end of the indoor garden was made to look as if it were the front of a house with windows and a flower box of geraniums. The fantasy atmosphere made the room a favorite for private parties.

It was obvious that hotel managers were fascinated by Mrs. Draper. When she addressed them they were spellbound. She invited them to dinner and regaled them until they were ready to promise her anything. She charmed her way into nearly every big hotel job in New York City.

Dorothy Draper's time of relative poverty was over. She had come a long way in a very short time. For some, success is interspersed with a series of setbacks, but not for Mrs. Draper. She had the Midas touch. During the next few years, she enjoyed one success after another, launching as many column inches in the press as yards of chintz upon the decorating public, and soon her roses were blooming in Depression living rooms across America.

Dorothy's sudden fame was no flash in the pan. In 1960, more than two decades later, The Center for Research in Marketing conducted a survey in which both housewives and professional decorators responded to the same questionnaire. They rated in order of importance their answers to the question, "What do you think the average homemaker today wants her house to express?" The professionals rated good taste first, abundance of possessions second, high social position third, happy family life fourth, and virtue as good housekeepers fifth. The housewives were diametrically opposed, and rated social position last and happy family life first. Given a list of George Nelson, Dorothy Draper, Russel Wright, Paul McCobb, and T. H. Robsjoin-Gibbings, the pros picked Wright as the most familiar name, but the housewives picked Dorothy Draper.

She was once interviewed by Mary Margaret McBride about a furniture exhibit she had done where everything lay on the bias. McBride complained, "It's like the furniture is going downhill." Mrs. Draper laughed and said, "Well, you know, anything to attract attention." She had a natural flair for quick comebacks, and the provocative statement. "Begin by thinking of your rooms in the nude," she said.

From the beginning of her career, DD achieved long-lasting fame by remaining utterly herself, by abiding by none of the rules, and by joining none of the professional organizations. She was a natural publicist. Some people call Ben Sonnenberg the best publicist that ever was and give him the credit for all the publicity she got, but others said it was all her own doing, with Ben going along for the ride and lots of free refurbishing.

Ben Sonnenberg got his start doing public relations for Bergdorf Goodman with the Grand Duchess Marie, but it was "Johnny" and the "Call for Philip Morris" campaign for American Tobacco that made him famous.

Sonnenberg lived on Gramercy Park in a fabulous house the Draper office decorated many times without charge, including his roof-top motion picture theater. He kept telling Dorothy what great things he was going to do for her. The man who wrote the book *Always Live Better Than Your Clients* and whose character is said to be the model of Sammy in *What Makes Sammy Run* practiced what he preached, but not too many people liked him for it. "A complete bastard who never thought of anybody but himself" was a typical comment. Sonnenberg himself admitted he was no saint.

Nevertheless, Ben Sonnenberg was as high-placed in the realm of public relations as Dorothy was in the decorating business. Justice Fortas was his close friend, and Sonnenberg used him to the hilt as he did everyone. Even his admirers said Sonnenberg was terrible to people, but he did a lot for them if he felt like it.

A great collector of English Georgian antiques, he was very tough on English antique dealers and thought nothing of keeping things for a year without paying for them, and maybe keeping them for good and not paying at all. Dorothy was treated similarly. He liked the Draper touch and her scale. A small man, he preferred the overscale and always the best quality.

Sonnenberg's parties in the Gramercy Park house were famous, too. He brought together the politicos, the literati, the theater crowd, a few aristocrats from abroad, members of the café society circuit, the most flashy current movie stars, and his nouveaux riches clients from Chicago, Minnesota, and Indiana, and mixed them all up. People stood and ate rare roast beef on crusty bread and drank champagne (which was all he ever served) while the out-of-towners tried not to ogle the famous people.

Mrs. Draper was often invited to fill her double role of thoroughbred and celebrity. She didn't like to go to the parties nor did she need the exposure. She really preferred to stick with her old crowd. There were always a lot of shenanigans going on at Sonnenberg's, a lot of noise and politics. It wasn't her milieu.

Contributing to her rocket ride to fame was the fact that she was high born. "She knew someone on the board of nearly everything, and with her connections there wasn't anybody she couldn't ring up, don't you know," said one of her competitors. A lot of people had to struggle for years just to knock on the door. Dorothy merely opened the door and went in.

But from that point on, she took all the credit.

She enjoyed literary success as well. Employing Betty Thornley, one of *Vanity Fair*'s writers and a member of Dorothy's crowd, she wrote

Decorating Is Fun. It sold forty-seven thousand copies in 1939, and she immediately wrote another, *Entertaining Can Be Fun.* She got her good friend, Mrs. Theodore Roosevelt, who once played with Dorothy in the Alexander girls' mock Tudor playhouse in Tuxedo, to write the fore-word.

Around that time Dorothy had a radio show on WOR called "Lines About Living." She gave advice on how to live a fuller, richer life. "A timid person can change to a more aggressive thinker by stopping being so nervous about living with color," she said, and warned that a popular woman had to be clever enough not to seem as clever as she was.

"Write down all the things you were afraid of today," she would urge her listeners. "What made you worried and anxious? What did you find difficult to accept? If you are afraid, you are wasting energy which should go into your creative life."

Then she was hired by William Randolph Hearst to write a daily syndicated column, "Ask Dorothy Draper," which made her famous in little burgs across America. She adored having her face in the papers three days a week in the New York *Journal American* along with Dorothy Kilgallen and Louella Parsons. The great triumvirate was featured on the Grand Central Kodak board surrounded by lights. Dorothy was very excited about it and liked to go down the steps to the Grand Central Terminal watching her face and name shining down on the commuters. She was a real star in the firmament, just like her darling father had always told her she would be.

Although DD loved the publicity, she didn't love writing the column. Answering all those dreary letters bored her to tears. She turned it over to another writer, Bosco Knoll, and then didn't see eye-to-eye with the answers she put in. Finally Bosco told her, "Mrs. Draper, you're going to have to write it yourself."

The column became the orphan of the office. Someone was always having to write it. Dorothy didn't even read it in the paper, and then complained to her staff when people brought up things mentioned in the column and she didn't know what they were talking about. But the column was worth it. It made her a national celebrity. Her name even appeared in a *New Yorker* cartoon: A man in his newly decorated living room reads a newspaper with the caption, "And Dorothy Draper says, add a little green parrot, too."

Her name was one of the few in the society news that was not mentioned because of what she had worn to a party, or what scandal she had been involved in or absolved of, or because of a party she had just thrown for a charitable cause. She got into the society news because of the incredible things that went on in her head.

"I always put in one controversial item," DD declared. "It makes people talk." She had a natural proclivity for high-power publicity. Decorating was ideal for her because she had to be center stage. There she could build set after set with her in the middle of all the drama. Although a lot of information did not get through to Dorothy (she did not receive on some wavelengths at all and she seemed to miss innuendo entirely), she was great at being bigger than life. It may have helped that she was already big and had very good taste, which entitled her to be as big and as grand as she wished. Her ideas may have been derivative as her competition claimed, but no one else executed them on the scale she did. When faced with doing a dining room that seated five hundred people, she had the ability to do it as if it were a dining room in a cozy cottage in the English countryside.

Fame brought her the sweetest gift of all. Years ago, when she realized she had married into a family of geniuses who left her not even a small corner of the limelight, she had vowed to outshine them all. She had finally achieved that goal. She had made the Draper name more famous than the well-known Doctor, certainly more famous than the second Mrs. Draper, more famous than Muriel's son Paul, the dancer, and more famous than Muriel, too. Most of all, she was even more famous than Ruth. If a man or a woman on the street were asked which Draper they knew, nine times out of ten he or she would answer "Dorothy."

During the 1930s, Ruth Draper had enjoyed her second decade of success and was still performing her monologues to sold-out houses on both sides of the Atlantic. One of her most well received was "Italian Lesson," about a silly society matron being tutored in Italian while on the telephone. Visited briefly by her well-starched children and paying not the slightest attention to their replies, the woman calls Nanny to take them away. The other was "Three Women and Mr. Clifford," about a man, his secretary, his mistress, and his wife, the latter bored beyond belief with her husband. During one of the runs of her Broadway appearances, Ted Stewart gave Dorothy's confidant, Jean Gordon, two tickets. "You and Freddy should go see Ruth Draper," he said.

Unprepared by Ted, Jean and her husband sat in the seventh row. As Ruth Draper launched into "Italian Lesson," Jean grabbed her husband's arm. It was a brilliant depiction of their well-known employer. So was Mrs. Clifford, although she was a bit more wicked. Did Dorothy know? She never let on.

Muriel Draper had also gone into decorating, so three women in the business shared the Draper name. However, Muriel was not the kind to run a company, as gypsies are not the kind to sleep in houses. After she divorced Paul, who eventually drank himself to death, Muriel could not get a job, so she decided to be a decorator. She would rent houses to live in while she fixed up others, and was forever calling up her friends and telling them, "You know, James, dear, I've got a leak . . ." Muriel required a lot from her friends, but they willingly gave because she was so much fun. Muriel was cared for by society matrons. Lincoln Kirstein's mother was one who regularly clothed her.

"We all had fun with Muriel," remembered James Amster, "but nobody had fun with Dorothy. She never left her family, really. Never left Tuxedo Park."

But it was not true that Dorothy Draper didn't have fun—she just had it elsewhere.

Before Dorothy Draper, professional decorating was primarily a field for "ladies in business," not businesswomen, who "did" the homes of polite society. Dorothy was not interested in such work or in associating herself professionally with her competitors. They worked in a milieu she found too restricting for her revolutionary ideas. Besides, she had nothing to gain by ingratiating herself to polite society, which was the motivation of many of her social-climbing competitors. She already was where they clamored to be.

Nor was Dorothy's presence missed. Her competitors, men and women alike, driven to near madness by the fact that Dorothy didn't care what they thought, spoke spitefully of her among themselves, and some did amusing imitations of her Edwardian manner, but they had a hard time criticizing her work. It was like criticizing Cecil B. De Mille. There was no other criterion for spectacle in the decorating profession in those days.

Dorothy had one idea, they said—roses. When it came time for a new idea, she just expanded the old one and came up with bigger and bigger roses. That she did commercial work better than any of them was not a point in her favor. They shunned the commercial. Polite society work was much safer than what she did.

After the Hampshire House job, Dorothy Draper earned the increasing enmity of her competition, for her fame quickly grew. The society pages were filled with news of her every opening. Even more odious to her competitors was the fact that in the process she had become the official voice of the decorating profession, speaking for all, and they hated her for that. They also hated her because she got all the big contracts, and because their offices were puny by comparison. They hated her because she hired the cream of the crop, first Lester Grundy and then Glenn Boyles. They hated her because behind her every decision, right or wrong, was the imprimatur of Tuxedo Park. In the comfort of Dorothy's great security, the recently arrived, dizzyingly insecure, basked in her absolute authority. The relief of that was great, so great that they were willing to pay her a very high price.

The vast majority of her competition bid among themselves for the residential jobs, usually through old school ties. Mrs. Brown at McMillan, the original Biedermeier girl, did the Ford house and other homes of the super-nouveaux. She was more important than Dorothy Draper in retail decorating. Polly Jessup had Palm Beach sewed up. Miss Buel and Mary Dunn worked for Katie Tyson at Wanamakers and were also well known and influential. Then there was Sister Parrish, a double cousin of Dorothy's who had once been brought by her mother, Mae Kinnicutt, to Dr. Draper's office when Sister had been naughty at school. Now Sister was making a name for herself as someone who could show the rich how to live comfortably. Dorothy didn't like what Sister

Parrish did, calling her chintz fussy and her colors boring. She put Elisabeth Draper in the same category as Sister Parrish. They both did safe things.

Actually, DD didn't care for what any of her competition did. She thought their work was piddling, with no drama or scale. Although she was to become a good friend of Elsie deWolfe, she thought her decorating was faddish and too occult. Syrie Maugham's all-white rooms were impractical and made her yearn to throw around some splashes of her own fabulous color. Even Melanie Kahane did not interest her. Dorothy saw her competition more as students than as peers. Sooner or later they all came to her office and sat in her chic little waiting room with its wall full of plants to get some of Dorothy's fabrics. Great efforts were made to locate her jobbers. Her competitors even stooped so low as to hire spies to work in her office.

Over the years, Dorothy's black leather-bound sourcebook became as soft and worn as a Bible. The names and telephone numbers of her precious jobbers were neatly typed and updated by the efficient Belle Clark. Its front page was marked PRIVATE in large red letters. REWARD IF FOUND appeared in smaller letters. Over the years her secretaries and traveling companions like Jean Gordon became keepers of the "Black Book," keeping it safe in DD's big, chic, black traveling bag. Business was war, and Dorothy Draper was no fool. Surrounded by loyal employees, she actually enjoyed the intrigue. Besides, her jobbers were intensely devoted to her. If anyone did manage to secure the names of her sources by snooping around the accounting department, they were given a frosty brush-off.

Dorothy was hard on secretaries, which was why she was so grateful when Belle finally came along. Mrs. Draper was extremely meticulous. It was the real secret of her success. No detail escaped her cataloging mind. She labeled everything and kept inventories of what she had and who it belonged to, what she served at parties, and who sat next to whom. She liked to have everything indexed, cross-referenced, and kept neatly up to date. Taking notes on Dorothy as she dropped and picked up ideas was an acquired skill. She had a mind like a computer, but did not want to retrieve the information. That was the job of her secretary, and many who were hired were not equipped to handle it. They came and went with great frequency. "My dear, we're just not getting on, are we?" she would often cheerfully declare on Friday mornings, and part on good terms with yet another secretary, who would leave with a generous severance check in hand.

One day one of Dorothy's new secretaries approached Jean and said, "There's a woman out front who says she's a duchess."

"Well then, she probably is, so send her in," said Jean.

And so she was. Even the duchess of Windsor made a personal call on Mrs. Draper when she and her decorator, Boudin, were doing an old mill in France. Although Boudin, being French, probably got paid by the duke and duchess of Windsor, nobody else ever did, and a lot of decorators, including their great friend Elsie deWolfe, did jobs for them. They didn't pay because they knew the connection would be exploited to the fullest and considered they were doing a favor to those who gave them service.

But the first lady of decorating dismissed them all, including Boudin, with a wave of her hand. Not one of them would know the first thing to do with a dining room for five hundred. Their minds thought small scale, and hers thought large scale. It was as simple as that.

Dorothy had taken on residential jobs when she needed money, but she usually let her employees take them over after the initial visit. From the beginning she had had difficulty with the necessity when doing a residential job to consider the client's opinions; her commercial clients were not allowed to have opinions. Mrs. Winston Guest was one residential client with whom Mrs. Draper had trouble. Dorothy visited Mrs. Guest with Ted Stewart and walked through her living room. "It's so dreary," Mrs. Draper said. "We must put some red in here somewhere." Then her eyes lit on Mrs. Guest's collection of Braque abstracts.

"We could put a red margin around these paintings," she said. Mrs. Guest drew Ted aside and told him quietly, "Get that woman out of here. *You* look after me."

Mary Lasker recalled when DD did her house in 1932. "She was very definite about what she wanted and not at all interested in what I wanted."

The more timid residential clients were swept away by her emphatic attitude. Mrs. George Blumenthal wrote of the screen that Mrs. Draper had suggested, "It is so extreme I fear it. I would also like a bit of coral velvet in this room if you can see fit to put it in." Mrs. Draper thought nothing of destroying something a client had already approved of. If DD changed her mind about a piece, she took it out no matter how much it cost and absorbed the loss.

Mrs. Draper lost her famous cool on only two occasions. One time was with Mrs. Walter Winchell. DD liked her husband because he was always giving her a plug, and in gratitude for his kind words (fawning would best describe them), she wanted to do something nice for him. One day Dorothy called him up and asked him whether she could do something for his house at cost plus expenses. She would charge him no fee because he'd been so sweet. Walter enthusiastically agreed.

The Winchells lived in Scarsdale, New York. Dorothy went up there with Jean Gordon. After they had seen the rooms, DD thought she had nothing much to work with, aside from buying some new things that would help spruce up the place. Lamps, coffee and end tables, and a few accessories were purchased and installed, and a few pieces of furniture were reupholstered. Mrs. Winchell then went to her friends, who gave her advice that made her change her mind until soon there wasn't a thing the office had done that was right. Everything was wrong, she complained. Mrs. Draper tried to remain calm as the complaints went on, but finally lost her temper and let Mrs. Winchell know her opinion of her taste. Those who heard the put-down said it was more like a squash.

Several days later the office received a two-page, single-spaced, typewritten letter from Mrs. Winchell. Dorothy took one look and gave it to Jean to read.

"Terrible," said Jean, "the worst thing I've ever read."

Walter Winchell had a reputation for flying off the handle. Everybody in the office worried that his wife's ire would inflame him to take revenge on Dorothy in his column, and he had a way of lashing out that was brutal. Mrs. Draper attempted to track him down, calling all over New York: Walter never stayed more than one night in any one place because he was always afraid someone would kill him.

Finally she located him, and immediately took the initiative. "Your apartment is never going to be completed unless you do as I ask," she told him. Mr. Winchell was far from angry. He was a pussycat. "I'll do anything you want," he said.

"Take your wife for a cruise. Be gone at least two months. When you come back it will all be ready." He did as she bid, and when the Winchells came back from their cruise the job was finished down to the flowers in the vases and the latest magazines on the coffee table. It looked as if the couple had just stepped out. Mrs. Winchell loved it.

Worse than any one client was a group of clients, Mrs. Draper believed, and the worst of them was a group of *society* clients. The Tuxedo Club had not been redecorated in many years. Although the members in charge of hiring a decorator didn't want Mrs. Draper to do it, they could hardly not hire her to do it. From the beginning Dorothy's heart wasn't in it: All the society matrons stood around and took turns saying, "Oh, I don't like that." She would rather take on a couple of cigar-smoking mafiosi than demur to the wishes of a group of stuffy matrons who still longed for the grandeur of their past youth. Although the fence was gone and she had fond memories of her childhood, Dorothy still hated Tuxedo Park as much as she had when she escaped it by marrying Dan Draper. Soon after the initial visit she turned the job over to her employees and didn't give it another thought. When word got back to her that the matrons were not terribly happy with the finished product, she didn't give that another thought either.

After her divorce, Dorothy began attending social functions, always bringing her own escort. In fact, she often brought two, both of them invariably tall, young, and good-looking. She was still a beautiful woman, and lots of fun. DD often attended professional functions with matching escorts also, and always wore a commanding hat. At the opening of Amster Yard, a group photo was taken: It shows Mrs. Draper wearing such a hat, in the prime of her life, surrounded by the luminaries of the decorating profession—Nancy McClellan, Billy Baldwin, Bill Pauhlmann, Ruby Ross Wood, Marian Hall, and Muriel Draper. None of them commanded the attention Mrs. Draper did, even without the hat. She was so much more stylish, more aware of how to handle herself.

"You've got to be born rich to know that," said Jimmy Amster, without a hint of envy in his voice during an interview given shortly before his death. "She knew just how to do things from a chic lady's point of view. She had more style than anyone else in the room. She had it her way."

"She wanted to do it her way and she did," said another of her competitors ruefully. "Basically in our business it's [done] the client's way. You take them as far as they'll go and then you shut up. At least then you have a down payment and can get started. But Dorothy was right there doing what she wanted to do and her clients would put up with her. The rest of us just weren't offering what she did."

Dorothy offered her clients something that was 99 percent herself because she was her main source. She didn't read. She didn't even listen. She cut off people mid-sentence with any nonsequitur she chose. One associate called her attention, "the little man who wasn't there."

"As soon as someone says an expert says something I shut my ears," Dorothy said in an interview. From the beginning of her career Dorothy Draper did it her way and was rewarded for it. Janet Flanner expressed her admiration for Dorothy in *Harper's Bazaar* in 1940, describing her as "brisk, iconoclastic, inventive, unapologetic, and successful."

"Tall, tailored, as telling and decisive in her manner as a man might be" was how columnist Barbara E. Scott Fisher of the *Christian Science Monitor* described Dorothy in 1941. Very few women who did audacious things in business got by; even fewer got rewarded for it. Dorothy Draper's audacity, however, was bankable. In fact, the more outrageous she became, the more publicity she got, the more sales she made. And no matter how iconoclastic her ideas were, she could never be accused of being in bad taste. Because of the Tuxedo connection, her taste was beyond criticism, and objecting to it would be like objecting to the size of the pyramids.

Dorothy had the nerve to do audacious things because she didn't care what people said. Once, sitting at a table in a fashionable restaurant with members of her staff, she was approached by a man she didn't know who confided, "I don't care what they say, Mrs. Draper. You should go right ahead and wear that hat." Dorothy simply thanked him.

She got along with men in business. They said she thought like a man. Successful men in particular found her interesting and amusing. They got a kick out of the way she got her way. And because they didn't know what she was talking about half the time, they let her have her way. When they wound up with something truly strange, like eight-foot wrought-iron camellias in the hall, they still didn't complain because at the opening the columnists came to write about Dorothy Draper and her crowd and inevitably gushed over the wrought-iron camellias.

"Either a prospective client hears my ideas and has an attack of apoplexy or he gives me carte blanche," Dorothy said. Some of her qualities that grated on people socially were a valuable asset in business, such as her extreme self-possession. She never went into battle in a mimsey way. There was no negotiation. She did not discuss money. The only numbers she concerned herself with were telephone numbers. Her clients quickly learned that her famous permissive decorating dictum, "If it looks right, it is right," had a different meaning when she was there. Then it meant "If it looks right to *Dorothy Draper,* it is right, and if it does not, it is wrong."

And everything she did, she did as the *grande dame.* When signing a contract with an important client, she invariably brought the entire office with her. She never traveled with less than an entourage. When prospective clients heard what she required in the way of special amenities, they were known to pound the table and shout, "My God, who's hiring whom?"

No adulation is unanimous. Dorothy had her detractors. She was a country girl. She didn't have the sophistication for New York. She knew Tuxedo people but not the newer element, and it was the newer element that generated the excitement taking place in the visual arts. Since 1912, there had been a veritable explosion of new art on the New York scene. Georgia O'Keeffe took the art world by storm in 1916 with a one-woman show of her paintings in the gallery of Alfred Stieglitz. Her colors were brilliant and astonishing, her flowers outsized. Dorothy may have been influenced by O'Keeffe when she did the same in fabric and was surely influenced by Matisse and Gauguin in her use of color, for she admired their work very much.

On the whole, however, Mrs. Draper was not one to venture into the avante-garde. She was the rear guard. Her favorite period was the eighteenth century, the "Golden Age of Democracy." She left the trailblazing to the café society crowd, preferring to sail her large ship through the deep channels of past glory. No Picassos hung in her lobbies. She preferred the imperial plaster bust of an unknown dignitary.

Dorothy did not celebrate a particular fashion as much as display a terrific sense of style—which is different from fashion because it lasts longer—and with it a rare sense of scale. Things couldn't get too grand for her. Coming from a time when everything was itty-bitty, she thought big. She thought like a Roman emperor copying the classical Greek: She wished to display a majestic feeling of manifest destiny.

More than anything else, she brought color into the home; her own home could always be recognized by its clear, strong statement. Other decorators simply did not have that unique signature. Her colors were as definite as she was—cerulean and sky blue, lime and poison green, shocking and hunting pink, scarlet, and lipstick red. She didn't like orange or apricot or any kind of earthy color and couldn't stand pastels. Too demure for the grand scale she worked on, they didn't ring with the thinness of good china but made a thud like a thick, opaque diner coffee mug.

Most of all, she couldn't stand brown. She didn't even like wood finishes. She never did a paneled room that wasn't painted, except in the face of strong objection from the rare private client. When she had her way, the wood—no matter how intricately carved or molded—got coated with many coats of base and one coat of gleaming, boiled frostinglike high-gloss enamel.

"Loads of other decorators had painted woodwork white before Dorothy did, but she sold it," explained a competitor. "Then she tied it up with the paint manufacturers, who loved her. Elsie deWolfe was really more important, but Dorothy got the credit. Elsie wanted to make contacts, but there was no one to show her how to do it. She didn't have Ben Sonnenberg."

But two Ben Sonnenbergs couldn't have promoted the lady as well as she promoted herself. "Be critical, never humble" was one of her many catchy dictums. "Birds are so much wiser than we" was another. "A robin builds a nest for robins. A seagull builds a nest for seagulls. They don't copy each other or build themselves nests as described in the *Birds Decorating Magazine*." In her superpermissive approach ("jumble periods cheerfully"), she was to home decorating what Dr. Benjamin Spock was to baby and child care.

Dorothy knew exactly what she was doing. She once described her mission as "creating display on a large scale aimed to awaken emotion on the part of the public." She accomplished that mission so well that projecting her vision upon the emotional consciousness of the 1930s and 1940s in hindsight is difficult. The modern eye is jaded by the familiarity of her once revolutionary ideas.

Although California had never appealed to her much, Dorothy eventually turned her sights to the West, with two of her three children living there—Diana in New Mexico and George, back from Spain, in San Francisco, working as a reporter for the *Chronicle*. When she got the Arrowhead Springs contract in 1939, her imagination caught fire. She would show Hollywood a thing or two about style.

Arrowhead Springs was located sixty-five miles from Los Angeles in the foothills of the San Bernardino Mountains. It was a rugged atmosphere, and the hotel was Georgian in style, an interesting combination. She decided to do the hotel in an adaptation of English Regency typical of the British West Indies. She put it in rhapsodic terms: "A mythical Georgian mansion on an imaginary island in the Caribbean sea." Never again would an entire hotel take on the look of an English country house in Barbados.

The California reporters loved the fact that she was a member of the Daughters of the American Revolution, "probably the only Colonial Dame of America with a union card." They wrote that she suffered from writer's cramp after adding up her bank balance (untrue). They described her as someone who a decade before was an "idle society butterfly" filled with resentment against architects who never put in enough closets and designed convenience kitchens that were decidedly inconvenient. They loved the fact that she had given up her superior social position to mingle with "plasterers and paperhangers," and were mollified somewhat by the fact that, although outlanders had come in to do the decorating, most of the furnishings came from California. Only the drapery fabrics were purchased back East.

Marshall Kester of the *Los Angeles Examiner* wrote, "Dorothy Draper, noted Eastern artist-decorator who's being brought out at great expense to do the interiors, is listed socially as Mrs. Tuckerman Draper. That'll lend tone to the deal." Another westerner noted: "The new AHS jernt is so swanky that the ski jumpers will feel like bums unless they wear soup-and-fish [tie and tails]."

Arrowhead Springs was where tired movie stars came to put themselves back together in the mineral springs and on the golf course. Rita Hayworth could be seen eating her lunch—wheat wafers—at the edge of the swimming pool. "I eat them in foot-high stacks," she confided.

The year before, a fire had started in the kitchen of the hotel, and in a matter of minutes the entire building had been ashes. With a million-and-a-half dollars and the magic of Dorothy Draper a new superspa was to rise from the site like a giant tropical phoenix. Mrs. Draper modestly called her budget "limited."

One of the reasons for doing the project at Arrowhead Springs was the fitful situation in Europe; Hollywood was so alarmed that a movement began among song writers not to write any songs that would stir up war sentiments. It was better to take the cure at home than to risk getting caught up in the fighting going on in Europe, and Arrowhead Springs was the next best thing to Carlsbad. The new spa was a three million-dollar project: 150 suites, a theater, shops, a cure house, steam caves, mud baths, and massage rooms. On the board of governors were Jay Paley, Darryl Zanuck, Constance Bennett, Claudette Colbert, and Al Jolson—an all-star cast.

The look Dorothy gave Arrowhead Springs was the most modern thing she had done, with gleaming marble columns and curved, graceful lines. It looked like a present-day postmodern art deco showroom, but the colors were brilliant and the scale was massive—huge tables and flocked lamp shades, as well as sensational superwide chenille. The marble was particularly distinctive, its pattern resembling a magnified Rorschach test. The rugs were black and had big floral patterns. The bedspreads were satin with a double bolster.

The opening of Arrowhead Springs may have been the most memorable of all. Everybody was there: Edgar Bergen, William Powell, Loretta Young, the Sam Goldwyns, the Louis B. Mayers, the Gary Coopers, Dolores del Rio, Irving Berlin, and Esther Williams. Groucho and Harpo Marx starred. They did a pantomime burlesque of an ardent decorator dismantling a room. At a press conference and cocktail party, Alice Faye asked Mrs. Draper if she had visited a movie set, and Dorothy replied that she hadn't had time. "Motion pictures, however, have taught us much in scale and value of the dramatic," she said. "I've learned that a single geranium on a kitchen windowsill may sometimes lend dramatic note."

Dorothy's style really impressed the Hollywood crowd. "For vivacity and gusto, few of our film stars can match DD," wrote columnist Ella Wichersham. "When Constance Bennett, Virginia Zanuck, and the Jay Paleys found her at a cocktail party at the sumptuous Paley home, Mrs. Draper brought along her candid camera and in practically no time at all had a million dollars worth of movie stars posing for her all over the place. Unlike the artists in most other fields, she would talk shop like everything, even at parties."

Asked at the opening if she believed in creating a mood in the home, Dorothy answered with an emphatic no: "No one is constantly in the same mood. If there is to be a set mood, I'm usually for gaiety with restraint and always for a basis of solid comfort." Upon hearing that, he-men Gary Cooper, young Doug Fairbanks, and Errol Flynn were almost inspired to cheer. Although Dorothy said she was fascinated by the spontaneity of the architecture, the eucalyptus trees, and the hibiscus blossoms, she was surprised at the lack of color in the California home.

"I don't mean strong color, but to me, California suggests clear, crisp colors."

And California thought she was wonderful. The press outdid itself in finding ways to describe the glamor of her touch: "The sky takes on a firey hue which seems to blend with the red bands on the wall of the crystal room. The entire scene takes on an unreal quality of beauty reminiscent of Wagner's *Gotterdämmerung.*"

In charge of the opening ceremonies were Rudy Vallee and Al Jolson. The gossip columnists roved, looking for copy. They heard Judy Garland had to have long nails attached to her bitten ones when she had had her hand prints taken at Graumann's Chinese Theatre. "Cement got between the legit and the fake and had to be cut, resulting in terrific pain," crowed Louella Parsons. Hedda Hopper also roamed, picking up news that a nightclub on Hollywood Boulevard had found a real carbon copy—"I mean literally a carbon copy"—of Garbo. "The gal is billed as 'the Creole Garbo.' " William Saroyan had spent his *Time of Your Life* profits on the horses. Groucho Marx had won a medal from Arthur Murray in a rhumba contest. Hitler had seen a print of Universal's *Flash Gordon Conquers the Universe.* Hollywood was in the dither about the press preview of the blockbuster novel, *Gone With the Wind.*

No one of consequence was left in Hollywood because of the Arrow-head Springs opening. With his familiar, "Heigh-ho, everybody," Rudy Vallee took his turn and described the new Arrowhead as "the place where the stars of Hollywood meet the bright lights of the night." Judy Garland sang "Comes Love."

Lana Turner arrived in an evening dress slashed to the knee and a daring headdress, emulating the late Jean Harlow. Sonja Henie and Edgar Bergen talked about how they, Jean Hersholt, and Garbo were the first stars to contribute more than one thousand dollars to Finnish relief. Arturo Toscanini and Edward G. Robinson were deep in conversation at an outdoor lunch. Not even at Edith Grove had so many luminaries come together in one place. Dorothy Draper's parties now surpassed those of Muriel Draper and got reviewed as well.

Even Eleanor Roosevelt had something to say about Dorothy's job on Arrowhead Springs, in her column, "My Day" (October 28, 1940): "I was very much interested in the hotel, for they tell me it was decorated by my friend, Mrs. Draper. She has done some bold and almost startling things. While I feel that her work here is somewhat in the nature of the little boy who is showing off and says, 'See what I can do?' in a spirit of bravado, still it is charming and restful."

After the opening of the Hampshire House, Dorothy Draper enjoyed one success after the other. That success really began, however, in 1933, when the Gideon Putnam Hotel in Saratoga Springs, which she had redone for the state of New York, netted $10,000 in its first year after being "Draperized." When the owners of Chicago's venerable Drake Hotel heard about the profits hotels were earning after being given the Draper touch, they hired her to do a room for them in 1940. One of the basic tenets of interior decoration is that the atmosphere should be appropriate to the surrounding environment. Dorothy broke that rule, too, and for the room in the Windy City she decided on a tropical motif—massive camellias and light fixtures that looked like spun sugar. It would look, she said, "like a great English house in the Tropics." The room's size, however, worked well with her flamboyance. In a town where rooms on the whole were larger than those back East (and even the portions of food were bigger), Dorothy's oversize features fit right in.

Dorothy didn't like the modern style on the whole. Like many, she found it cold. But she liked to combine modern elements with other styles. Red brocade, black patent leather, gold trim, wrought iron lanterns, footmen garbed in cerulean blue livery, walls covered in rich red felt, Padova chenille, and a specially designed damask in an Italian Renaissance Gothic design gave the Camellia House an elegance that Chicago had not seen since the great private residences of the early twentieth century. The tropical effect was painted on; a mural above the bar depicted a Caribbean blue harbor rimmed with mountains. A tropical midnight sky sprinkled with diamondlike stars twinkled overhead. On the floor was a black carpet with huge pink camellias.

The society press raved once more about the color scheme applied with "utter abandon," the mirrored columns that reflected fold after fold of flaming draperies, and the sugar frosting candelabra chandeliers—"architectural atavism at its most lavish." "Absolutely the most exquisite thing you can imagine," they cried. "Devastating richness." "Veddy elaborate, veddy swell," said Lucius Beebee of the *New York Herald Tribune.*

The job was not only an aesthetic success but also a financial one. The Drake Hotel's largest dining room operated at a loss as high as seven thousand dollars a month. The smaller Camellia House showed a profit of fifteen thousand dollars a month. Within a year, increased profits had paid for its renovation.

The room soon became a place to be seen; society news photographers worked the room, providing grist for the columnists' mills. Mr. and Mrs. Henry Ford II, for instance, were told by the handwriting expert who worked the room that Mr. Ford had two years of travel in store. The heir to the Ford millions replied, "That's true. I'm in the navy now."

The Camellia House became the playground of opera stars; it was also a favorite for theater groups, debutantes' coming out parties, fashion shows, and fund-raisers for British war relief and ambulance corps and the Free France effort. *Vogue* loved to pose its mannequins in front of the famous green double door. The place was usually packed. Dorothy Kilgallen advised, "It's wise to know the head waiter before you try to get a table."

After the Camellia House was finished, another job in the Chicago area came up that intrigued her. The Charles Morrises asked her to decorate a thirty-two-bed hospital in St. Charles, Illinois. It was a new experience for Mrs. Draper, who had never been in a hospital in her life. To prepare, she took a room at the Harkness Pavilion and went to bed for four days, having her secretary come to her bedside for dictation. In bed she saw mostly the ceiling, which she decided should definitely be included in a hospital decorating scheme. In bed she envisioned ruffly curtains on the windows, dancing bouquets of pink roses tied in blue ribbon, and red apples with bright green leaves.

Never before had a hospital been done with such style. Instead of the usual sickly green walls, roses and daisies covered the halls. The wallpaper in the children's ward featured songbirds in cages. Emerald green taffeta curtains and organdy were featured in the nurses' rooms, and heavy fringed tweed in the doctors' quarters.

Dorothy objected to the dedication of the hospital. It was going to be to the "relief of suffering." That, she said, was entirely the wrong approach. "I had them dedicate it to health and happiness." She believed that people who go to a hospital to get well should not be surrounded with an atmosphere of sickness. There were hunting prints on the walls leading to the operating room. Some rooms had wallpaper featuring stenciled red apples and musical scales that read "Health and Happiness." She renamed the maternity ward the nursery and did the bassinets in pink-and-blue dotted Swiss. (That fabric didn't last long. Upkeep was too costly.)

Dorothy Draper had taken the entire office to the Arrowhead Springs opening and foot the bill. Her generosity was an integral part of her style, but she and money did not understand one another. A lot of money came in and a lot of money went right out—straight through the office like water through a sieve. Mrs. Draper's inherited wealth could not continue to underwrite her lavish way of living, for it was drowning quickly in the sands of a sinking business. There was the Tuckerman well to draw from between windfall contracts, but her brother was getting more and more crotchety about the amounts she was drawing on her trust fund. It was something to fall back on should she lose too much money in the business.

Dorothy's problem was she wanted what money bought but didn't realize she couldn't throw out a marble staircase that the owner had put in just because she didn't like it. Dorothy believed you couldn't change what had been done when the client was perfectly happy with it just because you didn't think it reflected correctly on you. Instead, you simply threw it out and didn't charge for it.

Mrs. Draper's inherited wealth could no longer continue to be used to underwrite her lavish manner. In 1939, the year of the disastrous "Learn to Live" course, the company lost eighty-six thousand dollars. In 1940, it lost nearly fifty thousand dollars. The following year, in spite of the big splash of the Coty remodeling and a hefty ten-thousand-dollar fee followed by the Mayflower Hotel job in Washington (another ten-thousand-dollar fee), she could not make a profit. The few big commercial contracts in the field all went to her, and they were generous, but not as generous as she was.

One good thing did happen in 1939. She became the head of *Good Housekeeping's* "Studio for Living" and had the opportunity to fill its dozen pages with decorating ideas each month. Dorothy saw it as a platform from which to wage war against dullness and boredom, from which to lead the fight for a good life for all. Quickly she learned that the publishing business was not run for her convenience, however, and from her first day on the job she had trouble due to wanting things her way. But she was thrilled to be a journalist for a magazine that had been in existence since 1885 and whose slogan was the rousing "conducted in the interests of the higher life of the household."

By 1940, the decorating business was in dire straits. In September of that year DD had cocktails in the Camellia House with Lady Mendl, who told her about an experience she had had with the German espionage system. Leaving France, her party stopped at Biarritz, where the duke and duchess of Windsor had also stopped on their way to Lisbon. While dining together, someone turned on the radio and heard the voice of Lord Haw Haw declare, "You may laugh at the German espionage system, but to prove its competence let me tell you that at this moment the duke and duchess of Windsor are in the————Hotel, in Biarritz, dining in room————with Sir Charles and Lady Mendl." The war in Europe had become an everyday concern, even though it was half a continent and an ocean away.

Patriotism was on Dorothy's mind when she chose red, white, and blue as the colors for the Coty Salon on the corner of Fifth Avenue and the Rockefeller Promenade. They also happened to be the French national colors. The opening in the summer of 1941 was also intruded upon by the war. The opening gala was touted to be the most lavish since the World's Fair. It included the Rockettes and a squadron of Radio City Music Hall ushers. Thousands watched Mr. and Mrs. Al Smith dance to the "Sidewalks of New York." A bottle of perfume was broken on the steps of the salon, a Coty tradition, and the doors opened to reveal Dorothy Draper's latest fantasy: Tall lacquered black screens with exotic red roses and mother-of-pearl leaves, a smoky blue carpet, tall white plaster trees, walls covered with massive roses, tulips, and lilacs. The columnists found a new name to describe it: "Modern Baroque."

Then several people walked up to the president of Coty during a lull in the ceremonies and demanded to know whether one hundred twenty thousand dollars worth of essential oils produced in occupied France and brought across the Atlantic by a Coty courier were going to enrich the Nazis. The president of Coty said, "Of course not. They haven't been paid for yet," but columnist Emmet Maun wondered whether the perfumes that had been heavily misted around the sunken garden were "just as fragrant to the Nazis as they [were] to the shop girls." By then, the world situation was such that no industry, not even one as seemingly innocent and frivolous as the perfume business, could operate on a business-as-usual basis.

As the end of 1941 approached, Paris had fallen to the Nazis and Russia had been invaded. The war that had been in Europe was rapidly becoming global. Many standard materials were no longer available. Although the United States was still neutral, all industries had been organized under the National Defense Advisory Commission, which now administered production, and there would be little to spare for chintz. Thoughts of the future kept Dorothy up nights in her duplex overlooking Central Park. Unless a substantial contract appeared from somewhere, she would go under like dozens of other decorating firms, closing shop for the duration of the troubles, which hopefully would not last long.

The War Years

On a quiet Sunday afternoon, on December 7, 1941, while people across the United States listened to Toscanini on CBS or to a baseball game between the Giants and the Dodgers on the Mutual network, the war struck home. A bulletin from the White House interrupted all programming. The Japanese had attacked Pearl Harbor. Three days later, Germany and Italy declared they were at war with the United States.

New York City had three air raid warnings in the next two days, one at the height of the rush hour. Mass confusion resulted during the first drill, but by the second, New Yorkers merely looked at the sky, saw no planes, and ignored the whole thing. Citizens were ordered to darken their windows at night to deny the enemy a target in case the Fascists started bombing the United States the way they were bombing England.

Dorothy Draper came to the rescue. The December 16, 1941, *New York Times* published an article on the necessity to cover New York's estimated seven square miles of window with heavy fabric. Macy's was already running out of percale at twenty-seven cents a yard, and at the fancier yard goods stores drapery fabric at fifteen dollars a yard was marked down to a bargain $7.50. The *Times* advised: "Mrs. George

Draper suggested that blacking out could be done inconspicuously and decoratively by stenciling or painting with designs on opaque roller shades and inserting them between the venetian blinds and the windows. To do away with the necessity to sew on linings or make new draperies, she suggested using decorative adhesive cloth that could be ironed on the back of a dark fabric to provide a proper shield against light. Thin curtains would not do, and one tiny window left unblackened would be all the Luftwaffe needed for a perfect target."

The call went out to every able-bodied man from age twenty to forty-four to meet a draft of 12 million to defend the United States and the Allies against the Axis powers. Winston Churchill gave the United States this bellicose Christmas message: "The United States, united as ever before, has drawn the sword for freedom and cast away the scabbard."

Still in shock from the sudden curtailment of their ordinary lives and the transition to the new state called "unlimited national emergency," people celebrated the holiday season with a frenzy. The office party at Dorothy Draper Inc. was no exception, although the news was particularly bleak for the interior decorating business. There would be very little building in the private sector for a long time, no silk from Japan, no china from Dresden or Beijing, no Irish linen or English chintz. As purveyors of nonessentials, the decorating business was so low on the War Production Board's priority list that it virtually fell off.

The staff made a special effort to cheer themselves up and to honor Mrs. Draper, who had kept eighteen people on the payroll through another year of hard times. Someone had bought a Sound Scriber, one of the early Dictaphone-type machines, and on it they recorded jingles they had made up about every client on the roster. Then, while everyone was having drinks and celebrating, John Wisner, one of her new designers, made a gesture to turn on the radio and told Mrs. Draper to come to listen because there was going to be a special program on about them. Everyone crowded around the radio; Mrs. Draper was in her glory. Then out of the radio came the voice of Ted Stewart talking about Schlitz beer, "with just a kiss of the slops," followed by a similar mock commercial for every client on the roster. Mrs. Draper laughed uproariously, for she had detested the slogan Schlitz had chosen for its big campaign and had tried to talk the company out of it.

At *Good Housekeeping,* where each month Mrs. Draper advised the American housewife how to be chic on a budget, she joined the "Victory Campaign," the national effort to support the war. In the 1940s there were far fewer mass media outlets; the largest were the radio, the movie newsreels, and the popular magazines, especially the Hearst press. William Randolph Hearst was the Rupert Murdoch of his day. *Good Housekeeping* was one of the largest magazines, and immediately after the bombing of Pearl Harbor it went to work promoting the war effort.

The January 1942 issue was full of appeals to remain calm and pull together to meet the needs of the national emergency. Leading the way was Eleanor Roosevelt. She told people to "remain calm, voices down and chin up." This was no time to change jobs, nor should fear turn people into amateur G-men. Most of all, she urged people to "respect aliens. Do not discriminate against foreign children in our schools. They are part of tomorrow."

The magazine also addressed the problem of shortages. Panic buying was already breaking out at hosiery counters. Women were afraid they'd never see another pair of stockings. *Good Housekeeping* insisted: "We must sacrifice our personal vanity for parachutes and powder pouches. That shimmering dancing dress is made of rayon. Its base of cellulose goes into powder to shoot with. Lipstick comes in a pretty metal container."

Also at the ramparts was Dorothy Draper with her usual gusto: "Here's a brand new year, and it's time that we, the women of the United States, resolved—in times none too auspicious—to make our homes so cheerful and pretty that not only our own families but the chance passerby will draw courage from the sight of them. A hand-polished brass knocker on a freshly painted front door, shining windows with clean, newly washed curtains and a bowl of flowering bulbs will help you live through the difficult times ahead. And morale is in your hands. So let's stop dreaming and begin doing. Let's reach out in the independent way that is the American birthright. Let's be daring, courageous, and unregimented at home, reflecting in every inward and outward aspect the free spirit of our country."

Following that rousing admonition were instructions to war brides on how to live well out of a trunk. Those lucky enough to be accompanying their military husbands (as she had been back in her Washington days during World War I) were told to travel with a large trunk, the contents of which would allow them to turn the dreary hotel room or temporary living quarters into something grand and homelike. Included in the "magic trunk" were flowered chintz curtains, many yards of brilliant red corduroy to drape over the windows for a valence effect, matching bed-covers, and chintz slipcovers for the upholstered chairs. Even the trunk was lined in gay chintz. Then, out came a cocktail shaker, backgammon board, tea cloth and napkins, electric grill, blanket covers, appliances, a silver tea set, and four large prints of birds with green matting! "Wherever these traveling wives go, home goes with them," she said.

Other members of the design industry did their share of cheerleading, too. *Interiors* magazine ran an editorial in its January 1942 issue that predicted soldiers would want recreation buildings that didn't look like "abandoned tobacco barns" and ride trains that "didn't smell like a menagerie." "These are great days," they cheered, "and great days for the interior designer, too."

But *Interiors* was whistling in the dark. By the end of January, the war had spread like a terrible disease all over Southeast Asia. Rommel was storm-trooping across the African desert, and the Germans were advancing on Moscow, causing huge civilian casualties. India was caught in a double vise between the Eastern and Western fronts, and England was a horror scene of charred cathedral towers and naked girders.

There was no more business as usual. Roosevelt's State of the Union address in January of 1942 set goals of 125,000 planes, 75,000 tanks, 35,000 guns, and 10 million dead-weight tons of ships by the end of the year. That was a plane every four minutes, a tank every seven, and two ships a day. In order to meet a quota of 160,000 parachutes, nylon for hosiery and underwear was cut 20 percent. Deliveries to woven fabric makers were slashed 40 percent.

Fashion designers fell right in line, relishing the need for the sudden change in fall fashions: no more patch pockets or vests with double-breasted suits. Lapels would be tiny, trousers narrow. The short coat for women would be the hot fall item. Everyone was doing their patriotic best to free up cotton and wool to fight the Nazis.

Out in Fort Washington, Private First Class George Draper (who would later become a field artillery commander) had just been released from the guardhouse when Pearl Harbor was bombed. He had been given ten days for going AWOL to San Francisco to say good-bye to his wife Nancy and their son, Dana. He had made the trip because it was rumored his outfit was about to be shipped out to the South Pacific. George had been drafted nine months before Pearl Harbor.

Out in New Mexico Nelson Jay didn't wait to be drafted. He joined the RAF, as did Saunders Draper. Diana closed down the New Mexico house and came East with her two children to stay in the Hampshire House with Dorothy, who rehired Frances Somson to take care of the little ones. Fortunately, Penelope had her own apartment by then and a war job working in a factory as a draftsman.

Of Dorothy's staff, Ted Stewart was drafted right away and several others were put on notice that they could be called up at any time. Among the suppliers, Scalamandre had a large cache of silk fiber that he put aside for special customers like Mrs. Draper, but it would be only a matter of time before luxury fabrics would have to be made out of something else. There were even those who gloomily predicted that as purveyors of nonessentials, the entire interior decorating business would soon be forced into hibernation for the duration of the war.

In such circumstances, not even Mrs. Draper could hope to hold her business together for long. Fortunately, she was still getting 30 percent off her expenses at the Hampshire House. There she spent a lot of time late at night suffering from unusual bouts of insomnia as she wondered how long she could keep meeting her $2,000-a-month payroll. Unless some kind of miracle came along, she too would have to consider the idea of temporary hibernation, or at least cutting back on her entourage. But what would her poor staff do?

True to Dorothy's business luck, the miracle occurred, right on sched-

ule. One morning late in January 1942, she received an unusual visitor,
a tall, striking woman, exquisitely groomed and impressive, the sort of
woman she enjoyed working with. Her name was Elena Cavalcanti. A
former concert pianist who had once lived in Paris, she was now
divorced from her dilettante architect husband and living in Rio de
Janeiro. What Elena Cavalcanti pulled out of her briefcase boggled Mrs.
Draper's mind: blueprints that had been drawn up in Brazil for the
biggest hotel ever built in South America, a gambling resort to rival
Monte Carlo with its towers, turrets, and amazing Bavarian touches.

The resort was to be built in the mountains above Rio near Petropolis,
the summer capital of Brazil, by a man named Joachim Rolla. He also
owned the Urca casino and two other popular gambling palaces in Rio
and was frequently photographed with the international elite in *Town
and Country*. According to Mrs. Cavalcanti, Rolla had prepared for the
construction of his dream resort by journeying to Hollywood to "learn
about splendor." Then he had sent her on a mission to find Mrs. Draper
because he knew Dorothy would deliver his dream.

Money was apparently no object. Rolla had hired fifty-two architects
just to draw up the plans and then put his favorite parts of each together:
The result was an exhibition hall as large as a football field, a domed
gambling room with a circumference eighty feet larger than that of St.
Peter's Basilica, five hundred guest rooms with fifteen-foot ceilings and
mountain view balconies overlooking three thousand soon-to-be-land-
scaped acres, a vast swimming pool shaped like a map of Brazil, and
even an ice-skating grotto.

The estimated cost of the project was a cool ten million in 1942
dollars. Dorothy's fee would be $30,500. It would be the largest commer-
cial decorating contract signed to date, and the first contract of any kind
for a North American man or woman with a South American firm.

"Of course, there is the problem of the war," said Mrs. Cavalcanti.
However, all materials for the project would be made in Brazil by
Brazilians with Brazilian products. Mr. Rolla was adamant about that.
The only thing Mrs. Draper need supply was her famous touch that Mr.
Rolla had seen with his own eyes at Arrowhead Springs. However, she
warned, Mr. Rolla would insist that Dorothy herself or one of her staff be

on the site if he wished, but he would pay all traveling expenses. No problems were anticipated. The United States and the government of Brazil had been on the best of terms under the Good Neighbor policy, and with Mrs. Draper involved in the project, how could it not receive State Department approval?

A pleased Mrs. Draper called in her staff, which now included an architect, an engineer, and three designers, to see the blueprints of the wonderful project that would keep everyone's paychecks coming for a few more months.

"Is this a joke?" asked Ted Muller, the new engineer.

"Astounding," said John Wisner, one of her recent additions, a talented designer fresh out of Parsons. "It looks like one of those monster hotels on the Channel."

"It's got to be a joke," said Glenn Boyles. "What are these exterior details supposed to be?"

"Cast concrete painted brown to look like lumber!" cried Ted.

"Well," said Mrs. Draper briskly, "we'll just not think about the outside as there isn't anything we can do about that."

"But, oh, the basilica, DD," said Dick Kent, another designer. "What you can do to this!"

Dorothy was all smiles: That was the power of positive thinking. Aside from the encouraging financial aspect, which would keep her ship and its crew afloat for the estimated six months it would take to do the job, there was also the romance of it. Even the name was romantic— Quitandinha! And the romantic locale—half-jungle, half-mountaintop—was especially appealing on a blustery January afternoon on 57th Street. Suddenly her future was coming up roses.

The office prepared a large model of the Quitandinha and shipped it down to Rio. They even full-sized each piece of furniture to be designed for the project. Ted, not long out of MIT, was selected to make the initial visit to Rolla in May prior to Mrs. Draper's visit in July for the usual news event.

Muller was typical of the kind of professional Mrs. Draper hired—top drawer. She was comfortable with people of his background. This was not to say that Muller was comfortable with her. He had recently married and had spent his honeymoon at Virginia Beach, one of the few resorts where one could still vacation. He had welcomed the respite from Mrs. Draper, who sometimes drove him crazy, and he was worn out like the rest from implementing her steady stream of money-making ideas.

On the beach, he had started a conversation with another exhausted man, an executive in the Hearst empire, in magazines, Muller gathered. The man had said he had been sent to Virginia Beach because he was on the verge of a nervous breakdown. It seemed this woman, Dorothy Draper, was driving everybody nuts at *Good Housekeeping*. . . .

"Never heard of her," Muller had said and had listened with the sympathetic ear one gives to a stranger's tale of woe. The photographers were tearing out their hair, the man had continued. When she didn't like the photos the editors had found perfectly satisfactory, she tore them up and demanded they shoot the job all over again. And then there was her budget. He couldn't even talk about that. He'd get the palpitations again.

For days the troubled man had looked around for Muller to talk to, but Muller had started avoiding him, tired of hearing about Dorothy Draper for hours a day on his honeymoon.

Consequently, Muller looked forward to flying down to Rio in May 1942. It was likely to be a trip away from DD for a week or more. Under normal circumstances, a flight to Rio took three days, but with the world at war, even with full State Department approval and priorities, he thought the trip might take somewhat longer.

Even though a lot of Brazilian ships were being torpedoed by the Axis powers, Brazil had not yet entered the war. A considerable number of Nazi sympathizers lived there; however, the majority of the population was against the Axis. The dictator, Getúlio Vargas, continually shifted his support. A lot of important people in Brazil were wary about getting into the troubles that had been going on in Europe for so long.

Fights in the streets were breaking out all over Brazil as people put pressure on Vargas to declare war. But still Vargas kept stalling. Vargas did amend the constitution to allow him to seize Axis property in the country, but skimmed off one-third for himself. The cream was thick: A million Germans lived in Brazil, a million-and-a-half Italians, and

250,000 Japanese. Vargas's one-third included many banks, businesses, and the German Condor airline.

Vargas decided to embark on a massive public building project, as pharaohs have done since time immemorial. With Brazil's rich untapped resources in such demand around the world, there was a killing to be made in products like rubber, sugar, chocolate, coffee, and tungsten and other suddenly extremely important trace minerals. Because Vargas could also be assured of a juicy cut of future profits, his building projects were comfortably underwritten for some time to come.

Getúlio Vargas had ruled Brazil since 1930, when he led a revolution in the southern provinces. He was the popular conquering hero at first and did a lot for local businesses with his policy of "Brazil for Brazilians" to the exclusion of the rest of the world. That was one reason its resources remained undeveloped going into World War II. But after awhile Vargas got greedy. By 1935, he had more or less declared himself king. In fact, short, fat, and silly-looking, he was often compared with Napoléon. After 1935, Brazil was run as a police state, and by 1942 a lot of the officials were Nazis. Muller assumed that dealing with the state of Brazil was not going to be exactly the same as dealing with Nick and Dom down at the bistro.

Like Vargas, Joachim Rolla was from the Rio Grande do Sul (the equivalent of Texas), where homesteaders farmed and gauchos tended enormous herds of cattle on the pampas. Eugenia Sheppard called Rolla the Billy Rose of South America. There were a lot of conflicting stories about Rolla's origins. One was that he was an ex-gaucho who had parlayed one cow and a borrowed bull into a huge gambling empire. Another was that he was a peasant who started out as a butcher peddling meat door-to-door. His press releases described him as starting his career as a sheepherder from the hinterlands, "a dreamer who saw mirages above his herds on the grassy slopes beneath the mountain ridges." The most likely story was the one he told Ted Muller: He had lost all his money one night in a casino in the interior and decided that gambling was the way to make a living.

However Rolla got started, he apparently had little difficulty getting into the casino business and soon ended up one of the richest men in

Brazil. The crème de la crème of international society flocked to his casinos in Rio. Should such a man, still dreaming of mirages in the sky, desire to build a gambling Valhalla high in the mountains above Rio, it seemed likely that he should have it, and being the good friend of Vargas didn't hurt.

The great harbor of Rio de Janeiro was in the middle of an enormous boom in May 1942, full of ships, for the whole world was clamoring for Brazilian goods. Coffee was needed for the millions working overtime at munitions plants, cacao beans for the chocolate bars Yanks were giving out to children in war-torn countries in both hemispheres, cotton for millions of uniforms, hides for combat boots, rubber for tires, and cattle for C-ration stew.

So many cranes were visible from the air that the scene below looked like a convention of praying mantises. Buildings in other countries were being blitzed around the clock, but in Rio the government claimed they were going up at the rate of one every fifteen minutes, of which the Quitandinha was merely the biggest.

Muller got a taxi to the Copacabana, one of Rolla's casinos, where he was to meet the man himself. Rolla was a charming, good-looking man, still hard-muscled like a cowboy. He had a charming smile and a charming wife. Exhausted from his five-day flight, Muller soon excused himself from Rolla's convivial salon to check into the Icari, a hotel also owned by Rolla, where he went straight to bed. In the morning he was driven immediately to Petropolis, where he saw the Quitandinha with his own eyes.

Although the structure was only in the elementary stages of construction, Muller could already tell it was going to look just like the monster castle they had seen in the blueprints. The interiors were a challenge, with spaces so vast even Mrs. Draper would have trouble finding gestures grand enough to fill them.

Muller needed not only to negotiate a complicated contract with Rolla but also to get a feeling for how long the project would take, and what he could discern about the ability of Rolla to deliver the goods and services. It was clear to Muller that mountains would have to be moved if the Quitandinha was going to open by Christmas 1942.

Every evening of his four-day stay, Muller took the ferry across the street from his hotel to have dinner with Rolla and company in one or another of the three casinos he owned. Rolla remained a very nice guy, very pleased with his well-made Yankee connections. Elena Cavalcanti, who served as Mrs. Draper's representative, was also pleased. Even the State Department was pleased. Large as it was, the Quintandinha was but a small part of a massive assistance project in the works between the two countries, hands clasped across the hemispheres to fight the Nazis, and everything they did had full State Department approval. Brazil's undeveloped resources were desperately needed by the Allies, who were grateful Brazil had not fallen under Axis influence as had its neighbor, Argentina, and other South American countries. Although Vargas continued to balk at declaring war, at least he was cooperating with the Allies. Germany used to buy one-third of Brazil's coffee crop. Now the United States bought 90 percent. A lot of Nazis had to switch to tea.

Obviously, the Roosevelt administration wanted to do everything possible to cultivate the goodwill of Mr. Vargas, but it was a tricky situation. On the one hand, Brazilians were eager to receive the enormous influx of American technology and technicians that was to come. On the other, they wanted to keep out undue Yankee influence while reaping their rewards. Had Muller known what that situation was going to mean in personal terms, he would have been chilled by all the smiling. As it was, he was cheered by their enthusiasm and another major publicity event for the company in the making.

Muller's enthusiasm disappeared by the second week of trying to get back to New York. On the ninth day of taxi rides to and from Panair, shipside, the U.S. consulate, the censor, BWIA, and several rather desperate cables to New York, he took yet another taxi to a seaplane base, where after discharging the usual "diplomatic expenses" he finally boarded a plane to Miami. If every trip down took two weeks of traveling time, and if the casino took as long to construct as he estimated, there was no doubt in his mind that the project would be finished by Christmas—Christmas of 1943, that is.

Mrs. Draper was undaunted by the report of his traveling hardships.

She never had any trouble traveling and could sleep as soundly sitting up in a train or plane as she could at home in her monarchial canopy bed. She relished the trip down to romantic Rio. In preparation for the Camellia House job in 1940, she had booked passage to Martinique, where she wished to see the foliage and get inspired. Then she canceled, deciding to rely on her imagination instead. Now, war or no war, she would see tropical splendor for real.

Wherever she went, Dorothy Draper went well swathed in her imagination. Fantasy and myth were her constant companions. As merchant ships bearing Brazilian flags were torpedoed in numbers so great even Vargas would soon have to declare war, and as the shops and homes of Germans and Italians were ransacked throughout the country, Dorothy blissfully prepared for departure. Shortly before she left, she sat for a photo session and interview with Patricia Coffin of the *World Telegram and Sun*, perched jauntily on the edge of one of the large-scale over-stuffed English chairs covered in her large-scale chintz in her Hampshire House apartment, wearing a hat of the maid Marian variety with a jaunty feather, her large hands crossed primly in their white gloves.

"Imagination being on no priority list," wrote Patricia Coffin, "the war has not restrained Dorothy Draper from slapping her clean, brilliant colors on the walls of a Bridgeport factory worker's home or putting blue baize on the roulette table of a 200-foot circular gambling room in Brazil. The lush look, as characteristic of herself as of her decor, will not be scrapped."

" 'I think a red rose is my trademark,' " said Mrs. Draper. " 'I launched rose-patterned chintz, rhododendron leaves instead of flowers, apartment house halls that look like home, unlined curtains and mirrors. I started lacquer furniture in hotels, bright touches of Irish green and stripes.' "

As for her latest achievement, the capturing of the largest decorating contract ever to be awarded, Dorothy was not unduly modest about it, describing it as "the talk of South America." Sweepingly she described her plans for the biggest hotel ever to be built in Brazil. The walls would be lined in white native tiles with blue, pink, and green Portuguese designs like those seen in the fabled tiled sidewalks of Rio. She would employ the light and dark South American woods which she found "heavenly. We will use of lot of dynamic parquetry."

All materials in the hotel were to be made locally because of the war. Fabrics would be specially woven. "The only thing we lack is sheet mirrors," she said, and described the ice-skating grotto she was planning for the hotel with white plaster icicles dripping from the ceiling. Instead of the traditional red of gambling casino decor, used deliberately to incite passions, Dorothy chose blue baize "to sooth the nerves." (She did not approve of gambling.) An immense bird cage so large it would virtually disappear would contain live tropical birds that would fly above the winter garden's black-and-white marble floor.

A reporter asked her to comment on the war, and Mrs. Draper described how after her marriage to Dr. Draper, they had gone to Washington, which had been much more colorful at the start of the last war. "Diplomats wore sweeping capes and you were more conscious of uniforms." Beyond the visual aspects, it was obvious that once again Dorothy Draper simply wasn't terribly conscious about what was going on.

However, by July even she must have been unable to ignore the war that was raging practically at her doorstep. There were rumors that Nazi submarines had deposited spies on the beaches of Long Island and Florida. Yale was sandbagging its walls. For the first time women as well as men were going to war. The need for soldiers was so great that those traditionally opposed to the idea of recruiting women for noncombat duty had been overruled. Thousands of women went into the service. The corset and bra industries were booming; they were part of the WAC uniforms designed by Lord and Taylor. Madison Avenue and the government had cranked up the Victory Campaign to high gear.

Because Brazil was being cheered as a loyal ally, Dorothy saw her trip as a morale booster as well as a business venture and prepared for it with gusto. As for the kind of people she would be dealing with, Mrs. Draper had done business with casino people before. One expected a lot of underhandedness, but rarely did one receive arguments from them on matters of taste; the casino types trusted her judgment on taste matters. Even more than other clients, they tended to give her carte blanche. She might have thought (if she gave it any thought at all) that dealing with Rolla and company would be much like dealing with the boys at Fefe's Monte Carlo. However, there was a difference she failed to understand. In Brazil "the boys" owned the entire country.

Although Rolla was a small man, Dorothy was charmed by him and he by her. She was enthusiastic about Brazil. It was grand and gaudy. "On all sides I found fluent expressions of the baroque in architecture," she told the press, "a period of which I am very fond, with its plain spaces and ornate carvings, its irregularities and power. It is the kind of decoration I have always loved and used, and I shall use it again in connection with this new hotel."

She was impressed by the hair-raising ride to Petropolis and the feeling of having been swallowed up by the jungle on the winding mountain road that led to it. "I found myself in the midst of gorgeous, gleaming foliage, alive with chattering monkeys, flocks of gaily plumed parrots and other birds dramatized by the flaming colors of tropical, unbelievable flowers."

She was in ecstasy surrounded by the large-scale floral environment. Petropolis was also a little town to her liking. It was once the home of the Portuguese emperor who each year had sailed to Brazil for the summer in a grand way, complete with his entire court, servants, trunks of belongings, and musicians.

"A nostalgic atmosphere pervades the gentle little town," remarked Dorothy to the press. "Few of the glories of the emperor's days remain, save the botanical gardens where the gardeners continue to prune, never to plant, so luxurious is their growth. There is the quaint look of a sleepy Bavarian village about the place today. Small colored houses with gingerbread trim reminded me a bit of Baden-Baden."

With the thrill of challenge she walked with Rolla and his retinue through what would be the halls of the Quitandinha. Rolla wanted marble to be used as extensively as in the ancient buildings of Rome. Everything would be done with an eye to luxury. Mrs. Draper enthusiastically agreed.

She was thrilled with the prospects of the Quitandinha. After all, she had had no trouble creating a Caribbean jungle atmosphere in Chicago or a Louis XV atmosphere in mafia bistros; here in South America she would be able to have her work gloriously reflect its environment, instead of be incongruous to it.

"We shall steal straight from the irresistible magnificence of the jungle, with its great splashy leaves," she reported to the press. "South American colors will predominate—sharp yellows, limes, cochineal, and a galaxy of greens."

For weeks Mrs. Draper endured the inconvenience of Brazilian transportation, taking the buses and taxis on those death-defying hairpin turns up the crumbling road high above Rio to Petropolis, careening through fog and kudzu, seeing to purchases and painting, dining with Rolla at his many hotels and casinos, cavorting with Mrs. Cavalcanti, and generally enjoying herself. "I love the Brazilians," she cried. "They are the most friendly and cooperative people I have ever worked with."

As Dorothy was preparing for her return home, the war she had managed to ignore entered her consciousness quite literally under her bedroom window.

"It was about nine in the evening," she told the press. "I heard singing—serious, quiet singing. I stepped to the balcony and looked out. There were people marching through the streets converging on the president's palace. They were nice-looking young people in groups of twenty or thirty, mostly men, all carrying the Brazilian flag. It gave you no sense of fear. You felt they were people well in control of themselves, and as I watched them I thought how terrible that peace-loving nations should be forced into war!"

There was a reason why the nice-looking men were marching on the palace. Nine more Brazilian ships had been sunk. This time it was suspected that the Nazi sympathizers in Rio Grande do Sul, Vargas's home province, had reported their positions to Nazi U-boats.

Mrs. Draper then speculated on the immediate future: "The Brazilians were planning a tremendous tourist development," she said. "Hotels, cooperative apartments, skyscrapers going up over night. Now I guess they'll have to wait until the war is over."

The casinos were closed immediately. "I had the feeling that the populace was worried about how exposed it was, but it wasn't discussed," Dorothy reported. "You discuss very little politics in the open."

At Fortaleza, their first stop en route to the states, she and Muller saw heavy bars in front of German and Italian shops and banks. All their windows had been broken by angry Brazilians. Six hundred more lives had been lost aboard the coastal vessels sunk by German submarines.

The people Mrs. Draper had watched marching on the palace were going to make Vargas declare war; he finally did, but his doing so made little difference. There was no major military call-up. Life went on as before. The casinos reopened. The building did not stop. In fact, it increased as Vargas confiscated more Axis assets and put interred Fascists to work improving the country's roads, including the crumbling highway that led to Petropolis.

The situation for those in power was too lucrative to be curtailed by entry into the war. Along with every other wheeler-dealer in Brazil, Joachim Rolla was going to maximize the situation of being courted by the Allies. Like blushing brides they invited the Yankees down to Rio to talk development, and then did everything to keep Brazil pure. It was treacherous for both sides.

Once Mrs. Draper got stateside, she thought no more about the Quitandinha, turning the job over to her underlings and turning her attention to the Victory Campaign, which she would wage from her helm at *Good Housekeeping*. The shortage situation was approaching crisis. Even goods from Brazil were suddenly unavailable because the aim of the Nazi submarines was too good. The sight of empty shelves in stores sent shock waves through the public, making the war more real than did any gory newsreel. At many places not even nylon hosiery was available. Hosiery manufacturers were using rayon with decidedly unchic cotton tops and feet. It was troublesome. Betty Grable was the number-one pinup girl of World War II, and she certainly didn't wear cotton hose.

One of the great dilemmas of the stocking crisis was how to wash rayon, a nylon substitute which was very fragile when wet. *Good Housekeeping* economists recommended drying them a full twenty-four hours.

Demand was high for new nylon stockings made by Du Pont in combination with cotton or rayon. At least they were not as difficult to care for as rayon. The problem soon solved itself, however. Rayon was converted to war use and became almost as rare as silk and nylon.

Unlike European civilians, who often endured wars on their own soil, Americans had been much more fortunate. Several generations had lived without that experience, and so the shortages hit hard, creating panic buying and hoarding. It was as if people had suddenly been denied a right they thought had been inalienable.

Regarding the stocking panic, readers of *Good Housekeeping* were told to pledge to "resolve to wear stockings made of cotton or anything else my government prescribes and if they are not sheer enough to flatter my legs, I'll thin down my legs to flatter *them.*"

"Women mean more to men than ever now," advised Marian Corey at *McCall's.* "Mothers, wives, sisters, girlfriends have become in these few months more precious. We are part of what they are fighting for and they have put us on pedestals. We better arrange to be worth it! Let's be sweet if it kills us."

Lacking any American role models for *joie de guerre,* the style-setters emulated the English women who had been enduring bombardment for two years in the typical chin-up fashion. The circulation of British *Vogue* was higher than ever, and hats (often an old one retrimmed) had never been more important. Echoing the British, fashion columnists in American mass magazines recommended, "A hat is one small bit of peacetime status quo that does no one any good to do without." The new hats were not at all influenced by the military look as was the rest of fashion, but were "transparent, limpid, vaporous mists of chiffon and net."

But down below it was all hup-two-three-four. Skirts were slimmer. The redingote was the big fall statement, and there was a new suit, minus cuffs and vest, called the Victory suit. Handbags were smaller to save leather. Fashion was now "smart, economical, and patriotic."

Beauty was also patriotic. "Beauty Is Your Duty" was the slogan of Dubarry's new lipstick, *Emblem Red.* Revlon's new lipstick color was called *1942*—"a wonderful blue-toned red as gallant as courage." Tussy came out with a lipstick called *Fighting Red.* Ads and articles pointed out that the taxes on beauty products contributed to the war effort. One hundred forty thousand boxes of face powder would pay for a Curtiss P-40; seventy thousand jars of face cream yielded enough tax to pay for an army transport truck.

There was no olive oil from Europe, no nut oils from the Pacific. Magazine economists instructed their readers on how to render and clean bacon fat for lard: "If each of *McCall's* three-and-one-half million readers saved a cup of bacon drippings a week and used them in cooking, you would release enough edible fats to triple the ration quota of the people of Birmingham, England."

Canned goods in tin were scarce. Sugar was rationed to three-quarters of a pound per week per person. Candy manufacturers stopped making chocolates with rich cream centers because they were 96 percent sugar. The same was true for certain flavors of ice cream like strawberry and cherry. Many sweets now bore the message "Contains saccharine—a war product." Even the sugar content of sugar-coated pills was reduced.

Rubber was the number-one scarcity. There was talk of making car owners sell all the tires they owned over five per auto. It was hard to get chlorine bleach because it was used to produce chemical munitions. There were no aspirin, no spices, no paints on many shelves. Dyes were limited in their colors because of the rationing of chlorine. Dusty colors would take the place of the clear strong tones promoted by Dorothy Draper, and her stark white wasn't available either. About the only color that was readily available was black.

Out in Oklahoma, Ted Muller and Mrs. Draper's coordinator, Isabel Berringer, were handling the job for Kerr's Department Store. They had been lucky enough to find a local craftsman who could do gold leaf, but there was no more plaster. Mrs. Draper would have to settle for wood, which she didn't like. Her reply to their urgent telegram was succinct: BLACK LACQUER. Black lacquer became the look.

By the summer of 1942, there was no more quinine, no lawn mowers, jewelry made of precious metals, caraway or poppy seeds, slide fasteners, hooks and eyes, paper clips, brass cuspidors, lead foil in cigarette packs, or licorice.

Dorothy Draper was bred for the crisis. Morale building was what she had based her career on, starting with her own morale, which was occasionally devastated. Like her friend Eleanor Roosevelt, Dorothy believed in salvation. As she once expressed it, "I wish there were forty-eight hours in each day. Perhaps then I could give more time to those people who need advice so desperately."

Choosing a typical five thousand-dollar home from a group of houses built for defense workers in Bridgeport, Connecticut, Dorothy did it from top to bottom for nine hundred dollars: "We selected 320 Burnsford Avenue in preference to others because it had simple lines, a black roof, an attractive front door, no wasted space inside—living room, kitchen big enough to eat in, bedroom and bath both of good size, another smaller bedroom, and an attic that could be finished later as an extra."

Thousands of defense houses like the one at 320 Burnsford Avenue were being built across the country as munitions plants expanded. (Many still exist today in older suburbs.) Taking the builder's allowance for the money usually spent on stock wallpapers, she added forty-five dollars of her own "which bought heavenly papers that quite made the house." Then she and her retinue went to the Howland Dry Goods company in Bridgeport and bought "quality at a low price" furniture, and used her favorite double-hung crisp organdy curtains on all the windows. Not content to limit her furbishing to the house, she proceeded to the yard, where she recommended the planting of a defense vegetable garden, a grape arbor, and even a beehive "if you're not afraid."

All over the United States, wherever the paint was available, people started painting their front doors watermelon pink, and the clear, strong hues of red, yellow, green, and blue which she celebrated. They also followed her orders to arrange the shrubbery along the side of those brightly colored doors in a less regimented way, and laid a curve in the sidewalk. When she recommended painting the gravel in their driveways bright yellow, they even did that, for if Dorothy Draper said it was in good taste, who was going to argue?

She taught war brides how to buy a house full of furniture for $500. Sharing rooms was the patriotic solution in a housing shortage. "In almost every home in the country today readjustments must be made," she chided. "Let's not be downed by it. Let's make something fine and new with the situation. And let's get started!"

"Don't throw it away!" she cautioned readers in an article full of suggestions for using remnants and leftover wallpaper. Looking forward to the end of the war, she decorated a thrifty little house with a big picture window that might be a prototype for the one people would soon spend their war bonds buying. Like the Bridgeport house, it was in the five thousand-dollar range. If a house wasn't available, Mrs. Draper suggested furnishing barns. She found one in New Jersey and furnished it with plaid covers that were "honest-to-goodness horse blankets." Old horse stalls were turned into a dining hall. Bunks were built around a central fireplace. The hayloft was outfitted with cots and a Ping-Pong table so that there was room enough to sleep a whole family or "a large group of soldiers from a nearby camp." A barn turned into living quarters became an ideal recreation spot for entertaining servicemen. "Or with traveling out, have your friends walk over, bringing their food ration books, to share a barnful of fun!"

Once she was asked for her secret of selling and said, "Give people what they really want translated into one's own terms, even though they may not be quite conscious of this themselves." What she gave them was an intangible—quality—complete with the *Good Housekeeping* Seal of Approval. Her instantly recognized pages were splashed with pink roses and green leaves, a magazine graphic never done before. Before the wartime shortages, she had blithely encouraged her readers to paint their front doors watermelon pink and all their dark, gloomy Victorian woodwork white. If Dorothy Draper said to cover their dreary, dusty, upholstered furniture in bright red roses and hydrangea leaves, they did that, too. People emulated her ideas in their homes not only because her style was undisputably in good taste but because it made them feel grand and expansive and secure in a worry-filled time. She sold them beauty at a bargain price.

In the summer of 1942, DD offered advice for a fun war vacation spent at home. That Christmas, she suggested celebrating the holiday in a hotel room by going first to the local five-and-dime: "Dash out and buy eight folds of red crepe paper, fifteen cents each, and twenty-five white bells, five cents each, for a Merry Christmas window. Buy two bright red crepe paper tablecloths at thirty-five cents and two folds of white crepe paper at fifteen cents. You'll have to cut the fringe yourself and pin it round the table. Use six boxes of star stickers at ten cents a box. Stick two stars together and hang it on your little table top tree. All this for only $4.05!"

For people who couldn't get a real tree during that grim Christmas of 1942, she suggested hanging their ornaments on a rubber plant, or cutting a tree from a large blotter and tacking it to the wall over the mantle and pasting on paper ornaments ("Looks real!"). Or dried branches could be painted white and placed in a bean pot, or a big bright green umbrella could be stuck in a pail of sand. Christmas presents could be wrapped in the funny pages. Christmas gifts could be homemade, such as a closet door umbrella holder made of two bits of oilcloth sewed with a pocket at the top. . . .

Back at the office, the focus was hardly on money-saving homemade items. It was on executing the Quitandinha, which was still months from opening in spite of the contract's projected Christmas 1942 completion date. Even Rolla could not manage to deliver the goods on time, given the situation. Communication between Brazil and New York was difficult, but the telegrams that got through all spelled out the same message: Rolla wanted his technicians on site. Someone—Mrs. Draper or an emissary—would have to go down to Petropolis and help. The contract gave him that right.

"There's a lot of coffee in Brazil" went a popular song that year. There was coffee rationing in the United States, although there was none yet in Brazil. The situation in Brazil was more calm. No Victory Campaign was blaring. Nevertheless, normal routines in the country were badly disrupted by war despite the general attitude of business as usual. Life on the high seas continued to be risky business for merchant ships. There were severe gasoline shortages. Of all the problems that existed for the Yankees who did business with Brazil, the greatest was transportation. Getting down there was a big headache. Getting from one part of the country to another was a major migraine. It could take two days to get from Rio to São Paulo by train, a distance equivalent to the run between New York and Washington, D.C. The express run, a top priority diesel train, took twelve hours. The airlines were handling freight as well as mail and passengers who usually went by ship. When a technical mission went down to Brazil to see what could be done to maximize the amount of goods that could be exported, the technocrats were discouraged by what they found. Brazil simply had no uniform standards. It was every man for himself, a truly lawless frontier. Although raw materials and the labor were plentiful, it would be impossible to streamline production given the individualistic attitudes of local businessmen.

When Ted Muller went down to Rio for the third time in July 1943, it took him eleven days to get there. The situation he found there was just short of chaos. The Quitandinha, now six months behind schedule, was still only in the construction phase, despite the strings Rolla pulled. When cement became unavailable in the vast amounts he needed, he took sand and gravel from his own land and went into the cement business. When he could not get his paneling, plastering, and hardware orders filled, Rolla set himself up in those businesses. But still construction lagged. The problems lay beyond Rolla's control. There was a gasoline shortage, which made shipment of goods a nightmare. There was plenty of oil in Venezuela, but no way to get it across the Amazon jungle to the coast of Brazil. Lumber from Pôrto Alegre had to be shipped overland because no Brazilian merchant ships were allowed on the high seas. The ships under camouflage in the great harbor of Rio de Janeiro were carrying war materials. Worst of all, it was almost impossible to get anything manufactured in America, not so much as a lampshade, and absolutely nothing with a metal frame.

Nevertheless, Rolla went on with his plans, not only for the Quitandinha but also for an entire town around it. The Urca casino would be renovated as well; money was no object. (In the end, the Urca cost close to fifty million dollars.) All these grandiloquent plans required the best Yankee technocrats he could get his hands on, and Rolla intended to make full use of whomever he could lure to Rio.

167

With no standardization of machinery, everything had to be custom-made, and more than the usual supervision of labor was needed. The pace in Petropolis had not quickened, even though Rolla was now six months past the opening date as specified in the contract. However, Mrs. Draper was so eager for more of Rolla's business that she met his demands and did not complain too much about the extension. But she was too busy to go down to Rio herself, in spite of her enthusiasm following her visit the previous summer.

"And think!" she had exclaimed then to Barbara E. Scott Fisher of the *Christian Science Monitor*, "This great country, as large as the United States, is now only three fourteen-hour flying days from New York. I can't wait to go back!"

That was not much comfort to Ted as he calculated how much time it would take him to return to New York. He was still borderline in the draft and subject to call-up at any time. The entire Allied transport system was on military priority now, and even Mrs. Draper's connections at the State Department could not get him back on the three-day corridor she so effortlessly took, flying from Miami to Trinidad and then to Rio with one stop in between. Ted would have to fly back the way he came, taking the back corridors where all nonmilitary transportation now went, and it worried him to think how long that would be.

Getting down had been nightmarish enough. On his sixth day of being stranded in Lima, he had contacted a man known only as "O" who would aid him in getting to La Paz. Ted gave him the gratuities necessary to continue his trip. Then he spent another week in hotels in La Paz, Santa Cruz, and São Paulo before finally arriving in Rio, grateful to be there at all. Day by day his nervousness grew.

At Petropolis, he surveyed the construction site and realized with a sinking feeling that the project was still months from completion. Day after day he made the torturous journey from the Grand Hotel in Rio to Petropolis and the Quitandinha site, taking extra trips to the shops where the furniture was being made. Every few days he had to visit the police for the enormous amount of paperwork and picture taking they required, plus, of course, paying the mandatory "contributions." Then there were the taxi rides all over town for a visa and more paper chasing. Getting out of Brazil was obviously going to be even more of a problem than getting in had been.

Ted had been engaged for a fifteen-day stay and had already been away from his draft board for nearly a month. Although he had sent many cables from Rio, there was never a guarantee that they got through, and he heard nothing from New York.

His job at the Quitandinha was finished to his satisfaction, and Ted decided to leave four days ahead of schedule, on July 26. The afternoon before his flight had been taken up with more paper-chasing between the police station and the consulates. Finally late that afternoon he paid a whopping fee for a Bolivian visa, settled his hotel bill, and was packing when he got an urgent message from the Urca casino. Rolla was looking for him.

It was only then that Muller remembered the appointment he had with Rolla that afternoon. He took a taxi at once to Urca and was ushered into Rolla's office. The man's usually calm demeanor and cool smile were gone.

"What's the idea, trying to leave behind my back?" he asked.

"The job is done," said Muller, "and I've got to get back to my draft board."

"I've got you for fifteen days and you've been here eleven," Rolla roared.

"But it took me twelve days just to get here and—"

"Four more days, by God," he said and pounded the table. "I'll get fifteen days out of you or you're a dead man!"

"No way," said Ted.

"Fifteen days or I'll kill you myself!"

In a fury, Ted went to Richard Momsen, a Rio attorney who had been involved in the contracts from the beginning and was familiar with the problems involved in working with Rolla. Ted told Momsen he was leaving and that was that, because Rolla had threatened to kill him. Momsen tried to placate him in lawyerly fashion.

"Rolla is easily upset," he said. "You've got a clause in your contract, and he'll use it to the hilt, and he was promised fifteen days. I strongly advise you to stay to avoid any complications."

Ted stayed. In fact, Rolla made so much trouble he stayed an extra ten days. Fortunately, the trip back took only half the time of the trip down.

He did not dwell long on his harrowing story when he briefed Mrs. Draper. She was more interested in maintaining cordial relationships with Rolla, who was now talking about needing a decorator for the Tyrolean town he was going to build once the Quitandinha was finished. Ted told her that he was not going down to Rio again and that was that. She could fire him first.

By December 1943 the contract was one year overdue and the Quitandinha was still nowhere near completion. The final payment of $8,125 due in June 1943 was still outstanding. Hopes of ever seeing it became increasingly dim. Rolla's fabled hotel, dreamed up in his shepherd days, whose golden domes were to rise above the mountain mists, seemed less and less of a possibility. It was not domes that seemed to rise in the mists above Petropolis but the back of a big white elephant.

Shortly after Ted returned, the situation in Brazil got even worse. Riots broke out in the streets as opposition to the dictator grew, caused by massive inflation, shortages, and graft. Excess wartime profits hit 1,500 percent, all of it tax-free. Vargas was on the brink of his economic waterloo, and the population was split into two groups, both of which opposed him. The larger group was clamoring for Vargas to go to war against the Nazis and hold elections. The smaller but disproportionately powerful group was made up of Brazil's native Nazis, who were in an uproar over the way Vargas was cozying up to the Allies.

Vargas responded by unleashing his police. Censorship by the fall of 1943 was worse than it was in Argentina, which was openly pro-Nazi. Presses were closed all over town. Students rioted. General strikes were called. Coriolano ("Goestapo") de Goes was made the chief of police of Rio. He was closely associated with Vargas's minister of defense, General Enrico Dutra, a man openly associated with Hitler's representative in Brazil. As the democratic opposition rose against Vargas, the extremists in the army became more extreme.

While the populace fomented, business boomed. Thousands of

wealthy Europeans had expatriated to Rio, where they languished in exile clamoring for more luxurious accommodations. American vacations to Europe and the Pacific had been rerouted to South America. Consequently, the luxury hotels of Argentina and Brazil were booked to capacity. Vargas had offered big tax advantages to anyone who built more. He had appointed a committee to plan how to spend ten million dollars on "hotels, theaters, botanical and zoological gardens, and entertainment centers." *Business Week* carried an article on the situation which Mrs. Draper read with interest. As difficult a man as Rolla was, he was part of a group of businessmen who needed her as much as she needed them. The only other major client on the roster in 1943 had been the Savoy Plaza Hotel, small peanuts compared to what was going on in Rio.

On December 8, 1943, a phone call came in from Dr. Guilherme of the Quitandinha office. Mr. Rolla demanded that a *technico* come to Brazil and stay until the hotel was finished, once again citing the wretched clause six of their contract. Hearing that Ted Muller refused to go, Dr. Guilherme requested John Wisner.

As the first step was taken regarding Wisner's application for release from his draft board, Dorothy sent a cable to Richard Momsen, her attorney in Rio.

WHY FOR WHAT AND HOW LONG IS HE NEEDED? ARE THEY ACCEPTING PROPOSITION TO PAY HIS SALARY MADE BY MULLER? MAXIMUM TIME WE CAN SPARE WISNER OR OTHER APPROPRIATE PERSON WOULD BE THREE MONTHS. CONTRACT SO FAR EXCEEDS ORIGINAL EXPECTATION. CAN WE BE ASSURED OF FOURTH PAYMENT ON WISNER'S RETURN?

The mildly phrased "original expectation" of the completion date of the Quitandinha was by then a year overdue and still the project was less than half finished. So far Rolla had adamantly refused to pay salary, stating that he was responsible for nothing beyond the traveling expenses of Dorothy Draper and staff.

A flurry of telegrams were exchanged between New York and Rio that Christmas that foretold all the troubles that were to come. Obviously Dorothy did not want to get Rolla perturbed again. There was no luxury hotel building going on in the United States, going into the third year of the Victory Campaign, to say nothing of the lavish MGM magnitude of Rolla's plans. It would be a tragic loss if she didn't sell him the spectacle that she did so well.

WISNER REQUIRED TO INTERPRET AND COMPLETE YOUR PLANS came Momsen's reply shortly before the office closed for the holiday.

BELIEVE CAN BE PERSUADED MAXIMUM THREE MONTHS STOP.

On the other points, Momsen got Rolla to agree to nothing, and Rolla wanted Wisner to come right away.

Dorothy wired a cordial New Year's telegram to Rolla and Dr. Guilherme and received an equally cordial reply:

WISHING ALL LUCKY [sic] AND BEST SUCCESS TO YOU AND MR. MULLER.

Reading the telegram, Muller laughed out loud.

"Watch out for him," he told young Wisner.

John Wisner had come to Dorothy Draper from Sloans and did great sketches. He was already a valued employee. Dorothy was actually going to pay Wisner to work for Rolla for an indeterminate time. That was not at all auspicious in Muller's opinion, and he began thinking of changing jobs. He saw disaster coming.

On December 27, Momsen sent a long letter detailing the situation, including excerpts from his correspondence with the Quitandinha people. Skillfully Dr. Guilherme had appealed to Mrs. Draper's vanity: "I gathered from Guilherme's statements that they are very pleased with the character of your work but they are afraid that unless you have someone here to carry it out, the local people may distort some of your work producing unsatisfactory results."

Dorothy wrote back reiterating only her demand that her name be acknowledged on the selvege of the fabric that was being made in Brazil—one signature per each repeat—as it was in the United States.

Muller's cable to Momsen was more to the point:

NO MENTION FOURTH PAYMENT STOP UNLESS WISNER GUARANTEED THREE MONTHS MAXIMUM STAY WILL SEND ANOTHER REPRESENTATIVE AS PER CONTRACT.

Momsen contacted Quitandinha and was told that Mr. Wisner could call at the Brazilian consulate in New York for his visa. They could not guarantee the length of time of his stay, although they believed three months would be sufficient, and that was that. Finally they agreed to three months maximum. The situation, he cabled Momsen, was "absurd." A less expensive representative would be sent. But there wasn't anybody else. There was the job at Kerr's Department store, Schumacher's South American line, featuring the Quitandinha fabrics Glenn Boyles had just designed, and Gimbel's in Philadelphia. There was a tantalizing offer from Dorothy Gray to design a package and theme for a new fragrance they were introducing. There was also a rumor that the Fairmont Hotel on San Francisco's Nob Hill (often called the Old Ladies' Home) was going to get a big do-over, and DD was determined to get the job. In addition, the design studio at *Good Housekeeping* took half of her time. Besides Muller, no one else in the company had the experience and the wiles of John Wisner. Ted Stewart had been drafted and was serving in Germany. She could hardly send someone like the highly emotional Dick Kent or gentle Glenn to deal with Rolla.

Fortunately, Wisner was familiar with the Quitandinha job, having been in on the planning stages with Muller and having worked with him on the big sketches. He also knew how to interpret Dorothy's aesthetic down in Brazil. Wisner actually thought it might be easier to do it there than in New York because everything in Rio was being custom-made.

Wisner had been drafted in 1941 and rejected for a heart murmur, but he still could not leave the country without permission. He wasn't unhappy about going to Brazil. Only in his mid-twenties, there was a lot he hadn't seen of the world. However, he knew of Muller's experience in Rio. Although it wasn't talked about much around the office, it was impossible to cover up the fact that Muller had been gone much longer than planned.

Wisner did not have all the necessary papers ready until the middle of March. The flight in a DC-3 took him out of the lanes of military traffic down the west coast of South America, crossing the Amazon and the Andes. Lacking travel priorities, he was wait-listed at every stop until there was a flight that wasn't already filled up with government priorities.

The sky was like a giant grill in Panama. Days went by, each the same, with frequent taxi rides to and from the Hotel Tivoli to Panair to see whether he could get wait-listed. The planes were small and didn't hold a lot of people. Afternoon meant another hot ride back to the hotel and another hot night in the Canal Zone.

His stay in Lima was even longer. Wisner's life had been reduced to a routine of checking out of a hotel, taking a sweltering taxi to the airport, spending a day in long lines of desperate travelers, taking another taxi back to the hotel, and checking in again. There were few civilian priority flights down the east coast corridor at all because soldiers and supplies were being transported to Europe and the war in the Pacific had been sharply escalated.

Life in Lima became unreal in the thin dry air. Then Wisner got sick. Feeling cut off from the world forever, he lay in the dispensary in the British-American hospital in Lima and wondered whether he would ever get out of Peru.

Brazil did not make Wisner feel any better. Checked into his room at last in Petropolis, he lay weakly on his bed and got such a severe bout of chest pains that he was taken to Rio, where a doctor put him into a hospital at once. He had pleurisy.

When he finally got to see the Quitandinha with his own eyes, it was with some relief. It didn't look to him like the monster castle that had appeared in the original drawings. It was almost charming. Like many anachronisms of large size, it took command and declared itself. It was a Cecil B. De Mille Gothic, a Tyrolean Wonderland molded from thousands of cubic feet of cement made and all but poured by Rolla himself.

Only one hundred of the five hundred rooms were open that April, and no restaurant facilities were completed. The rest of the hotel was still under construction. The spaces were enormous indeed. Even the corridors were vast. The Quitandinha corporation had set up a large drafting room in the hotel. Unfortunately, it too was under construction. Dozens of people, many more than necessary, worked at drafting tables under the supervision of Pierre Walco, a decorator from Rio. His job was to expedite the execution by draftsmen of all the items that were being made for the hotel in Brazil. Wisner's function was to interpret the Draper office's drawings to Walco's legion of draftsmen. Rolla's office

The queen of Sutton Place. Dorothy Draper made the neighborhood chic in
1940 by painting the since demolished Sutton Place row houses black with
dead white trim and brilliant colored doors.

The Garden Room at the Greenbrier, featuring baroque plasterwork eagle-and-swag by the master artisan Cinquinni. Fresh azaleas massed in clay pots were an unusual indoor touch in 1947.

Dorothy Draper in the Presidential Suite at the Greenbrier with Mr. and Mrs. Robert Young and Greenbrier executives, 1947.

So popular was the Camellia House in Chicago's Drake Hotel that when it was redone in 1957 it retained many of its original features, such as the black carpet with giant pink camellias and green leaves.

Mrs. Draper's version of the Greenbrier Southern Belle, modeled by Mrs. Robert Case, is presented at the New York Junior League's Mardi Gras Ball in 1952.

Kerr's Department Store in Oklahoma City gets the royal Draper touch, but with painted graphics due to wartime shortages, 1944.

The International Hotel at JFK Airport, New York City, 1957. Dorothy's entry into the jet age was one of her last major jobs. The spindliness of it all didn't thrill her.

The Fazenda lily screen (hand painted with plenty of roses), at the Quitandinha, Petropolis, Brazil. The sculptured rug, massive coffee table, and bold leaf pattern side chair were all innovative features of her forties decor.

The Dorotheum cafeteria in The Metropolitan Museum of Art in New York City, 1954, where patrons could dine cheaply while enjoying the Carl Millais sculptures in the fountain (not shown). Birdcage chandeliers are still in use today, but the Roman pool has been replaced by a high-priced restaurant.

The Ben Sonnenberg house on Gramercy Park, ca. 1952: Dorothy Draper's rendition of what a man should have who saw his house as society's crossroads.

Mrs. Draper's apartment in the Carlyle in New York City. The portrait is of Anna Mary
Wendell (Mrs. Robert Bown Minturn), DD's great-great-grandmother. The eighteenth-
century mantle clock with two lions couchant is French.

Proof that what was good enough for the masses was also good enough for the queen of decorating: Mrs. Draper's bedroom in the Carlyle lavishly features her most famous print, the Hampshire House cabbage rose.

Baroque to the tenth power: The Coty Showroom on Fifth Avenue, 1941.

Cabbage roses cling to the walls and ceilings, complimented by Christmas-green satin chairs and red silk draperies in the Hampshire House, 1938.

Mrs. Draper's ultra-baroque treatment of the Camellia House in Chicago's Drake Hotel, 1940, features oversize black-and-white marble tiles, baronial doors, and lavish use of plasterwork.

Aqua and white leather chairs, china, and menu cover for the Camellia House, the Drake Hotel, 1940, all designed by Mrs. Draper.

New 1952 Packard '300'—one of eight new models in four price ranges

Overnight......it's one of the Packard immortals!

Throughout the fashion world, the achievements of Mrs. Dorothy Draper have long been legendary. Now, for the first time, she has brought her talents to the field of motoring . . . in the magnificent new 1952 Packard.

Consistently, up through the years, Packard has dominated motordom's roster of never-to-be forgotten cars.

And now, here in your time, is the greatest Packard of them all.

The *smartest*—with exclusive new beauty that reflects all the daring originality . . . and comfortable practicality . . . of talented Dorothy Draper.

The *finest performing*—with the incredible smoothness of Packard Thunderbolt engines, America's highest-compression eights . . .

the unequalled simplicity and efficiency of Packard's exclusive Ultramatic Drive . . . and the most restful riding and driving ease you've ever known!

The best *long-range buy*—with deep-down, precision-built goodness that mellows with mileage . . . stays silently new, year after year after year.

Definitely—never has a Packard so clearly deserved to be called an "immortal." And never has a Packard been so practical to own!

ASK THE MAN WHO OWNS ONE

PACKARD for 1952

FASHION-KEYED by DOROTHY DRAPER

The car Packard custom-designed for Mrs. Draper in gratitude for this successful campaign was white with red leather upholstery. Note Tuxedo Park–like background.

"In the Pink" cosmetics line for Dorothy Gray, designed by Dorothy Draper and bought by reunited war brides and grooms by the tens of millions in 1945.

The 46th Street Theater survived the era of Broadway theater demolition, but has been redecorated since Dorothy Draper did the interior in 1948. The curtain is black-and-white damask, the walls ruby red.

Decorating greats of three decades all assemble in one room in this photo taken at a party given by James Amster (second from left) in the late 1930s. To the right from Amster are Muriel Draper, Ruby Ross Wood, Billy Baldwin, William Pohlman, Dorothy Draper (wearing a hat as always), and Eleanor Brown.

One of Mrs. Draper's rare jobs remodeling private residences; this one for Mr. and Mrs. Charles Geisenheimer of Middletown, New York, early 1940s.

Mrs. Draper is all smiles over the safe arrival of bales of English chintz despite shortages during World War II.

Mrs. Draper in her office at 38 East 57th Street, 1953.

Dorothy Draper at her desk in 1953: twenty-five years in the decorating business and still on top.

then handled the work Walco passed on and coordinated the manufacturing.

Wisner got along well with the people working on the Quitandinha. Occasionally he had reason to go down to Rio and report to Rolla himself, and they became friendly. Wisner found Rolla a dynamic man who was used to getting his way about everything, but had given him no trouble. The construction was moving forward at a snail's pace but moving nevertheless. The fabric-making equipment followed no uniform standard like American machinery. Wisner had to design it all from the nuts and bolts. With some help from Schumacher, who had more than a little interest in the success of the project at that point, workmen were soon inking the strongly punched up Draper colors on the rollers. Brazilian lumber for the furniture was hard to come by and cost a fortune, but Rolla found both the money and the means. He obviously had the power to get a lot of people to cooperate with him.

Weeks went by, then months. Winter came to the summer resort, where the seasons are reversed. Occasionally Wisner would get down to Rio on the torturous road with its hairpin turns that was always under construction, but transportation to anywhere was difficult. Even the buses required reservations two or three days in advance. They were run by charcoal burners instead of gas, and were fitted out with little tanks that trailed along behind the vehicles. Transportation by private car was virtually nonexistent because of the gasoline shortage. The few cars on the road were also equipped with charcoal converters. Although there was an old relic of a railroad that also went from Petropolis down to Rio, it hardly ever ran.

Just getting from the Quitandinha to Petropolis was difficult, which meant that Wisner was almost totally isolated. Even making a local telephone call was hard. Telephoning the United States could occupy an entire day. Weeks had gone by with no contact from the office. During the week Wisner was very often the only customer in the restaurant that had finally opened, with a kitchen big enough for seventy chefs. After dinner, the three chefs on skeleton duty came out to sit at Wisner's table and talk the evening away, also in need of company.

As soon as the roof of the casino was finished, it opened. Rolla invited many people up at his own expense because he knew he'd recoup the cost at the gambling tables. Strays came up from Petropolis and people filled the buses from Rio. Pretty soon the casino was crowded day and night, even during the week, and the profits from it began to help pay some of the project's mountain of bills. King Carol of Romania was Rolla's major attraction. He was a standard feature around the world's royal gaming tables and provided conversation material because of his henna-haired consort Madame Lupescieu, whom he finally married.

King Carol was one of the first displaced European monarchs to settle in Brazil. Mrs. Draper had decorated a room for the couple with Madame Lupescieu's hair color in mind. Other would-be royals would follow, with faint hope of ever returning to their thrones. The royal Romanian couple were inveterate card players and would stay up all night. Their presence gave the Quitandinha the international panache it needed.

By July Wisner's three months were up. For weeks he had been trying to correspond with the office but had never heard a word. He sometimes wondered whether the letters had disappeared or been censored. The next time he went into Rio to consult with Rolla, he gently brought up the matter of his departure. Instead of addressing that, Rolla told Wisner excitedly about his building plans. He was going to build hotels in cities up and down the Brazilian coast, some with casinos and some without, to meet the influx of postwar tourists and displaced aristocrats who might be lured to Brazil. Millions would be spent to turn Brazil into the playground of the western world. "Already I run the largest and most successful casinos in Rio. Why limit myself to just one city?"

And all he needed to complete his plans was John Wisner. "I will pay you handsomely," he said. "You know your accommodations will be the best. Have we not treated you well so far?"

As Wisner had to agree, Rolla urged him to wire Mrs. Draper and tell her he was now working for Joachim Rolla.

Wisner thought for awhile and then said, "It's an interesting offer but I have a family. First I would have to go back and take care of certain matters." Wisner left the office without getting an answer about when he could return, and as travel was being paid for by the Quitandinha office, he was a captive. There were lots of reasons Rolla could give for an indefinite delay. He had no idea if his messages to the Draper office ever reached them, and Mrs. Draper's Brazilian attorney Momsen said he could do nothing. Finally, Wisner resigned himself to the fact that he was being kept hostage until the job was done, which was exactly what Muller had said would happen all along. There was nothing to do but be philosophical about the situation.

Fortunately, the resort was nearly finished. Management began talking about a fall opening, and Wisner took comfort in that. When he couldn't stand the solitude another minute, he would take a bus to Petropolis and walk around the gardens of the summer palace of the Portuguese Braganças. It was run like a small museum. There he meditated on how little the situation in Brazil had changed since the time of the Portuguese emperors. The only difference now was the dictators were local instead of imported.

Meanwhile, unbeknownst to Wisner because of his isolation, the political situation all over Latin America was in a state of upheaval. Fascist tyrants were falling right and left. In May, Hernandez Martinez of El Salvador bit the dust by a national strike. That summer, Guatemala's dictator, Jorge Ubico, was swept from office the same way. Meanwhile in Argentina, the United States and Britain had recalled their ambassadors because of the growth of Nazi influence. Both sides of the political spectrum were moving to the extreme, and Vargas had to follow suit. In August, giving in to pressure from the Fascists in the military, Vargas removed all the pro-American members of the ruling elite. Friends of the United States resigned or were removed from office.

Meeting halls of the opposition were padlocked. Members of the press were attacked by hoodlums on the street. Underground activity spread like wildfire. Strikes and protests took place every week. Discontent was further inflamed by inflation, shortages, and the outrageous profiteering of the Vargas regime. Construction at the Quitandinha was decryed as a scandal that had used up millions of man-hours, consumed tons of scarce materials, and cost $15 million.

A popular street song went as follows:

> *Rio de Janeiro, city of delights*
> *By day there is no water*
> *At night there are no lights*

The Fascists among the military then pressed for an end to the Good Neighbor policy altogether and nullified all existing American contracts.

An August issue of *Time* magazine carried a piece called "Rough Stuff in Rio," which revealed what was happening to pro-American factions in the government. The future of Vargas could not have looked more ominous. Still no word came from the Draper office, although by that time she too had been briefed. But the telegram sent by the Draper office never reached Wisner. Fortunately for Wisner's state of mind, he didn't know about the severity of the political situation until he got home.

Suddenly one morning, he was told he could go. His journey back up the spine of the Americas took him exactly one month. Once again he became overly familiar with the Hotel Bolivar in Lima, Peru, where he spent half his time trying to get to Colombia. Reading magazines to pass the time, he could not help but react to the ads showing disconsolate soldiers waiting in passenger terminals pleading, "Have a heart, pal. Go easy on the traveling and leave some room for us." If there was a scarcity of room for soldiers, there was none at all for civilians that fall, and the political unrest throughout South America did not speed up travel.

At last Wisner returned to the office. The situation he found there was only slightly less tumultuous than the one he had just left. Mrs. Draper was not her usual cool self.

"Thank heavens you're back," she said. "Mr. Muller and Miss Berringer are gone. I'm making you a vice-president of the firm and want you to take Mr. Muller's place." It seemed the pair had left to open their own decorating business. The circumstances surrounding their sudden departure had been very unpleasant.

Obviously, Mrs. Draper was in no mood to hear about Wisner's troubles. In his mind, the trip to Brazil quickly faded and with the entire period of the war took on the bizarre dimensions of a bad dream. France was liberated, the Allies were closing in on Germany, and the war in Europe that had once seemed would go on forever was drawing to a close.

In September 1944, the Quitandinha opened at last. Press coverage was the usual big splash. Brazil was going to be the vacation spot to which everyone would be flocking, carefree dancing the *carioca*, at the war's end. Rio was advertised as "a golden promise, headquarters of the world's greatest era of opportunity." The exotic Quitandinha was a taste of the near future which tantalized a populace weary of austerity and self-denial. How lavish it must have seemed at the time, when even paper clips were hard to come by. Syndicated columnists had difficulty describing the splendor and reached new heights of hyperbole: "To imagine the Quitandinha," wrote syndicated columnist Dave Roberts, "close your eyes and recall the most super-duper, ultramodern, hanky-swanky movie set you've ever seen. Multiply by six and add ten."

Like the story of Rolla's origins, the actual meaning of *Quitandinha* in Portuguese was in doubt. Some columnists said it meant "little farm," others, "little marketplace," still others, "fruit and vegetable stand." In every way the place was hard to describe.

"A Busby Berkeley movie set," wrote Eugenia Sheppard. "Something out of the 'Arabian Nights,' a dream of the 'Wizard of Oz,'" wrote Cholly Knickerbocker of the *Journal American*. "Dorothy Draper was given carte blanche in the matter of imagination and expenditure and she went right to town with a color scheme of chartreuse and shocking pink, etc., that would knock your eyes out."

Although the entire project was still incomplete, two out of three of the gambling halls were finished in time for the opening; each was three stories high with three-story marble columns and wall-to-wall mirrors. The kitchen had eighty-four chefs who served nine-course meals. There were eight hundred employees, one for each guest. Rare Brazilian woods, such as jacaranda, an ebony like wood, and cerejeira, a bleached oak, were lavishly used throughout, even for entire walls and closets, mixed with antique Portuguese furniture, black lacquer, and gorgeously fringed upholstery. Rare eighteenth-century prints of Brazilian birds and conquistadors adorned the walls. The Venetian mosaic floors rivaled those of the sidewalks of Rio de Janeiro.

But the frolickers came to Quitandinha not to observe the paintings but to play roulette, baccarat, and chemin de fer in the two hundred-foot circular gambling room with its domed ceiling covered in midnight blue velvet.

A man like Cholly Knickerbocker could scarcely be relied upon to describe the colors Dorothy Draper chose ("chartreuse and shocking pink, etc."). The main color was Draper green, clear, intense, three-dimensional, and vibrant like shiny jungle foliage. Riotous red, pink, and lavender were used all together, in the way they grow on the maniana tree. Poinsettias, orchids, hydrangeas, bougainvillea, and fazenda lilies bloomed inside the Quitandinha as well as outside. Prints were splashed with enormous banana leaves in three greens. Eyes thirsting for color after so many years of wartime drab were satiated, then overwhelmed; the hues used were in the brilliant part of the spectrum. Cochineal was used with dead-white walls. The carpet in the reading room was hunting pink, and the walls were dark, shiny green. A stenciled wallcovering used three shades of pink. Bedrooms had pale yellow walls and bright green carpet, which was especially effective— during the war, green and yellow were the most difficult colors to get. Visitors received a visual jolt similar to watching the *Wizard of Oz* when suddenly black-and-white Kansas bursts into the technicolor of Oz.

Reporters paid a great deal of attention to the most gorgeous of the "presidential" apartments, that King Carol, and Madame Lupescieu. The press gushed over the exiled couple as they did over the duke and duchess of Windsor, except the Romanian couple was much more scandalous. Not only was Madame Lupescieu a "commoner lady" but also the former king took his time tying the knot. Ruth Montgomery of "Capitol Circus," a Washington, D.C., syndicated column, cooed, "The exiled lovers are first occupants of the suite Dorothy Draper splashed with spectacular greens to set off the fading beauty of the henna-haired consort." Madame Lupescieu was indeed a beauty, as Wisner had already concurred when he observed her at the gaming tables early in the morning when he rose as she was departing for her boudoir, although wan under the hennaed hair from so many nights at the gaming tables.

Children swam in a seahorse-shaped swimming pool that floated on an artificial lake. They ate in a dining room decorated in a circus motif complete with a movie projector. Waiters of small stature were employed to serve them. After eating, the children voted on which movie they wished to see while their parents entertained themselves in the adult game rooms.

There were telephones along the bridle paths. The Quitandinha had its own daily newspaper and a post office. There was a beauty salon that offered radium therapy. There was, in short, everything but the skating grotto to make the Quitandinha fully qualify as the first fantasy resort in South America. As for the skating rink, the Draper office was already in negotiations with Rolla to do that job for an additional two thousand dollars. So eager was Mrs. Draper to avail herself of business opportunities south of the border, she was willing to overlook the fact that Rolla had held Wisner captive for weeks while she paid his salary. As for getting payments from Rolla, his bills were at that point years overdue.

On the home front, the euphoria of the Quitandinha faded, and the Victory Campaign dragged on into its fourth year. "We're weary. And lonesome," read a magazine ad for Cannon sheets. "And we get the old feminine reaction: 'I wanna buy something new and unnecessary!' Any time but war time that's a swell idea. Today—unh-unh. If we want to get our men back quicker (*do* we!) we'll clutch our purses tighter and get along with things we already have."

"You can't say I'm not patriotic about 'making do,'" read another ad. "This nightie's three years old." Consumer patience was wearing thin about doing without the things they had taken for granted before December 7, 1941, but the war seemed far from over. Although the Allies had crossed the Rhine, the Pacific fleet needed more insecticide, more nylon hammocks, insect netting, landing craft, and lightweight cotton clothing.

The new material demands further reduced civilian allowances for lightweight fabrics, and shortages would continue for a long time to

181

come. Citizens were told to be ready for a protracted fight with the Japanese. Continued sacrifice was required. *Life* promoted the "friendship skirt" made out of shared scraps of fabric. Wool and other heavier fabrics were now available as the war in the northern hemisphere came to an end, but estimates of a protracted war in the Pacific created further havoc in the fashion industry. The new rayon stockings still gave women the same trouble, even if Dorothy Lamour posed for the new rayon stocking ads and, of course, looked great. The only reasonable solution was to bare the leg. Helena Rubenstein called for "hairfree, carefree legs and arms." Yes, fashion styles were to be bare all over in 1945—bare back and shoulder as well as legs and arms. Skirts were short. The skimpy cut also eliminated the need for zippers. They were more scarce than ever because the army was using them in jungle uniforms and flying suits. The head was also bared. Hats were no longer important. The bare look had its consequences: It could not help but also be the sexy look.

Sex was definitely in style during the spring of 1945. The nudity featured in the magazine ads would never be allowed in motion picture films by the Hays office. More soldiers pinned a photo of Betty Grable in short shorts to the inside of their lockers than any other MGM publicity release. The movie industry continued to do its part in boosting morale, as did Mum deodorant. "Be the thrill in his furlough," its ads read. Even conservative *McCall's* patterns echoed the call to be alluring. "All out for Becomingness" was the slogan.

The housing shortage was so great that Cary Grant and Barbara Hutton patriotically continued to live in the same house after their separation. A lot of doubling up was being endured. Money went into war bonds every week instead of being spent on unnecessary purchases. It hurt, but not as much as the wounded coming home in numbers four times greater than the year before.

"Food fights for freedom" was the wartime message from Frigidaire. Refrigerators were no longer on the market, and so the refrigerator companies promoted conservation of food and refrigerating equipment. Appliance repair was one of the few booming domestic businesses in the spring of 1945. Still, Americans were reminded that they didn't have it half as bad at the British, who had been living with rationing for six years by then. Paper shortages were so great in Britain that people thought nothing of taking an unwrapped butcher knife out of the store. It was considered the "chin-up" thing to do to use the same brown paper bag for five trips to the store.

There was no business to speak of in home furnishings. The uphol-stery shortage lead to form-fitting wood furniture. Finnish chairs with modern lines, exposed laminated wood frames, and interwoven webbing in place of upholstery became popular. Chairs designed by Hans Knoll of Knoll Associates or the Danish designer Jens Risom, as well as the sensational "womb" chair of the Finnish designer Eero Saarinen, were particularly coveted. Saarinen also collaborated with another designer, Charles Eames, who had discovered how to mold laminated plywood.

An exhibit of antique Chinese furniture at the Brooklyn Museum got widespread attention. New Yorkers found the style of the "real thing" and not the cheap replica "surprisingly unornate." But most of what was happening in Oriental home furnishings and household goods was the stuff of dreams. China was in the throes of revolution and Japan was being bombed.

Patriotic American homemakers made do with what they had or cheerfully put up with the inferior wartime product. Schumacher put out a drapery fabric called *aralac,* which was made from milk. That and bedsheets were all there was to print on. Wire was still so scarce secretaries used common pins instead of paper clips. People still wore shoes made of pigskin or "bacon rind" instead of leather. Mirrors were now available, however, as shipments of mercury came in from Spain. Paint was once again plentiful, although clear greens and yellows were still in short supply. Walnut and mahogany were reaching American ports from the south again, although much of the stock was still used for the manufacture of gun stocks and airplane parts.

Pretty soon, however, there would be a wealth of new products born of necessity during the war years. There was talk of new textiles like washable corduroy, waterproof house dresses, nonshrink wool, table linens made from aluminum yarn, and something called "drip-dry," a fabric that did not have to be ironed. There was talk that the postwar period would bring razor blades that only needed to be sharpened once in five years, nylons that did not run, synthetic plastic adhesive tape, home insulation made of ground-up chicken feathers, fruit juice concentrated into tablets or candy, puffed banana flakes, mass-market walkietalkies, and radios so tiny they would fit into a pocket. War glue used domestically would mean better bicycles. Tantalum from Brazil, a metal heavier than lead, would make surgical tools so fine they could mend severed nerves and leave no scar.

"Come the peace" promised the magazines, there would be cushioned socks and brighter shoes, and a featherweight line of goods from lawn mowers to bikes to typewriters to valises, and something called television that would turn the home living room into a motion picture theater. On a tiny screen people would actually be able to see what happened when Fibber McGee opened his crowded closet at Wistful Vista.

The home of tomorrow would include the wizardry of television in the living room and the magic of the pressure cooker in the kitchen—food would be steamed in the wink of an eye. All across America, magazine readers dreamed of the day they could spend their savings bonds on the dream house of their future, which would be full of the wonderful gadgets of the future.

Savings dollars would be spent lavishly on such home conveniences. Government statistics estimated that it would take fifteen years to fulfill the housing needs of the citizenry. "Come the peace" there would be a building boom in the United States the likes of which had never been seen before. In the meantime, people could only dream of the home they would one day build after they cashed in their liberty bonds.

"If I just close my eyes . . ." breathed a housewife in a Kelvinator ad, "I see it now . . . the house we'll build together . . . the house we'll have breakfast in . . . Sunday—some day . . . when victory is won."

Mrs. Draper, as usual, had definite opinions about the future of housing in America. She told Virginia Rowe of the *New York World Telegram*, "The boys returning from war will be keenly interested in new houses based on delightful living. They'll not be influenced by the countries where they've been, but will want their homes distinctly American. They'll desire fresh colors and bright interiors." Prefabricated homes that cost between two thousand and three thousand dollars would be the wave of the future, she predicted. "I am progressively interested in the problems of the postwar world. I firmly believe that peace will find people hungry for beauty. My dream is that everyone will be able to live in a delightful place."

During the war years at *Good Housekeeping* she had had a chance to illustrate her world view. The housing crisis in particular afforded her many opportunities to be helpful. In "Share Your Home—Cut Your Rent!" young "Mrs. S." converts her extra room into a separate wartime apartment for a little extra financial security while her husband is in the marines. "Mr. M.," whose business has been frozen for the duration, builds a basement apartment with a double-decker bed. "Mr. and Mrs. B.," with both sons in the service, create a room out of their extra space for "an ideal apartment for two girls in the war industry."

Dorothy also tackled the problem of the room that served as dining room by day and guest room by night. "The dining room table has been whisked into the kitchen. The night table and lamp have been brought from the living room, and the bed unfolded out of a window seat."

The government encouraged remodeling as the patriotic approach. "Use your wits and you'll never want," Dorothy urged. If you have to make do with old furniture, then cut the legs off that old-fashioned oak table in the attic and use it as a coffee table in the living room. It was also big and accommodating, the way Mrs. Draper liked things. "There are many people who have excellent furniture and accessories, who need only apply little touches of ingenuity to give new life and verve to them," she said. And if they lacked the necessary verve, she would lend them some of hers.

Dorothy Draper taught her readers how to make a handsome chair out of a barrel, padded with cotton batting and her favorite knock-out chintz. Given the job of promoting pressed cellulose, one of the dreary wartime substitutes ("Transform your room with 89-cent draperies"), she bought extra sets and used it flamboyantly on the windows, dressing table, lamps, and even the wastebasket, making the decidedly tacky and tissue-thin material look almost chic. Shadows cost nothing. She showed her readers how to create big plant reflections on bare walls.

When curtailing travel except for emergency was the patriotic thing to do, Dorothy Draper taught her readers how to have fun at home. "Outdoors used to mean some faraway place that was hard to get to—and expensive. But the same sun, the same blue sky, the same bright stars are waiting for you right in your own backyard." She gave instructions for building tables and benches around shade trees, and stocking the fireplace area with "two husky cabinets," big low tables, and a corner aviary.

Can't buy a rug? Sew six white string bathmats together for a soft shaggy texture. On it stand the cut-down old round table painted with black lacquer. Lamps, which had not been available since before the war, were "tin wastebaskets mounted on square wooden blocks, black lacquered all over, and topped with white parchment shades painted black outside." If there was no drapery cotton, there was plenty of white organdy in stock. Mrs. Draper told her readers to hang it double for a luxuriously full window treatment. "Then the curtains have graceful frills down the middle as well as at the edges."

She also ran articles on the decorating of average Americans: An eighteen-year-old made lamps out of inverted washtubs for his bedroom and draperies out of sheeting for only $41.53. Mrs. Trum, from a Yonkers family of "moderate circumstances," took a year to braid her room-size rug and another to quilt her "Harrison Rose" bedspread.

Lacking other supplies, DD told her readers to redecorate their homes with color if that was all there was, for paint was available once again. She ran pictures of walls papered with enormous red roses on a dead-white background and of entire living rooms done in her Quitandinha flowers, including tables all in the neo-Victorian-American-Queen Anne style that was becoming her trademark.

There was no place for the timid gesture in her studio. Either one made the big statement or turned the pages. "The wider the curtain and the bigger the cushion," she declared, "the smarter the effect." And her readers believed. Builders also believed. When DD applied her bigness to living room windows to "let nature in," builders began including something called the "picture window" in the family tract house of the near future.

Dorothy urged home owners to give up the symmetrical approach to landscaping. Instead of using two privet hedges side by side at the front door, she encouraged using a meandering sidewalk and planting shrubs of varying sizes and shapes with "studied casualness, to make just the right effect."

There was something comforting about doing what Dorothy Draper told you to do. Following her dictates eliminated all doubt. Her motto, "If it looks right it is right," was becoming as firmly established in the minds of her readership as "In God We Trust."

As the hotel and entertainment businesses got ready for the postwar splurge, Dorothy Draper landed two big contracts, the first major projects in America since before the war: redoing the Fairmont Hotel in San Francisco and the Versailles, New York's most expensive supper club. The former would bring her lasting fame (and stands today as she decorated it in 1945), and the latter would be her economic Waterloo.

In the Tuckerman celebrity gallery there was a Minturn who, as a member of the firm of Grenell-Minturn, designed and built clipperships that sailed around South America during the California Gold Rush. One of the ships was the *Flying Cloud*. For that reason, Dorothy took the romance that was San Francisco to heart. It made the era a matter of personal pride. The Fairmount would cry Gold Rush the way the Greenbrier would later cry Tara.

Located at the very top of Nob Hill, the Fairmount was the center jewel in the crown of the Golden Age of San Francisco. The building had been nearly completed at the time of the earthquake of 1906, which had reduced it to a charred granite shell. Julia Morgan took on the task of its architectural restoration. She was Quakerish and severely dressed. Miss Morgan had to buttress the shell and rebuild the great staircase. She went on to design San Simeon to accommodate Mr. Hearst's art collection.

For forty years the restored hotel became the official residence for San Francisco grande dames, its decor still reflecting the personality of Julia Morgan. It was then bought by the Swigs of Boston, who were known as tightwads in that extremely tight-fisted community. They planned to modernize and glamorize the hotel, but did not know exactly how to do it. Newly hired in Dorothy's Possible New Business Department was Joan Vandemaele, sister to Nancy Guggenheim, who was married to George Draper. She was assigned to land the Fairmount contract, and she began courting the Swigs.

A man who could squeeze a dollar until the eagle croaked was not going to do business with someone who demanded carte blanche. Negotiating the Fairmount contract with Joan Vandemaele was John Wisner, who assured Mr. Swig that Dorothy's need for carte blanche did not include the budget, only the aesthetics. In fact, Mrs. Draper had a reputation for bringing jobs in *under* budget. After doing some checking of his own, Mr. Swig was satisfied to that effect and hired Dorothy Draper to remodel the entire hotel however she saw fit.

Swig was willing to spend a half-million dollars to turn the hotel into a replica of something fine. Mr. Swig wanted something vaguely out of an Edith Wharton novel. He wanted afternoon tea to be served in the court while harpists played, and he wanted beautiful bedrooms fit for kings, queens, and presidents. He also wanted the hotel completed in time for the United Nations conference so it could be the meeting's headquarters. The fee was a hefty $20,000.

The present lobby was terribly depressing. It didn't look like an old ladies home, Dorothy said, but like the catacombs. Standing in the middle of all the dust and frippery, Mrs. Draper began to conjure. That night she dreamed. The vision was still in its gossamer stage—delicate and ready to burst into flight. At the inevitable press conference she described the project: "an enlarged copy of a grand Venetian palace." Standing by her side, Ernest Drury, manager of the Fairmont, told the press that no expense would be spared.

"That's the first time I've heard that," chortled Mrs. Draper.

Working in such an environment had apparently mummified the minds of the hotel staff. They talked about the awful things that high-and-mighty Mrs. Draper was doing—brown-and-black walls, black-and-red carpeting. It sounded like she was doing a funeral parlor.

What Mrs. Draper planned was one of her most surreal projects, a vision of the Gold Rush era, where grubstakers went wild in the rooms upstairs and the madam strode grandly through the hall, parading her ladies, while in the back room the sounds of breaking furniture could be heard. DD would fly to Versailles and back on the butterfly wings of her most colorful vision yet.

At the point when the paint went on—wild geranium and strawberry, gold and black lacquer—she turned the project over to Ted Stewart. He spent the next two years on it, managing to finish the hotel in time for it to become the birthplace of the United Nations.

Dorothy's cheerful advice was one of the few upbeat notes in the April 1945 issue of *Good Housekeeping*. The Easter ham of processed "parts" that were better not to speculate upon did little to cheer anyone's spirit. Yet, eating canned ham was a small sacrifice to make when compared with the sacrifices others were making. By that spring the war that had gone on for so long had taken the lives of nearly two hundred thousand Americans. Weekly casualties were higher than ever, more than six thousand the week the marines invaded Okinawa in the bloodiest battle of the Pacific to date. "Home Alive in Forty-Five" was the slogan that year, as Allies closed in on Hitler in his bunker. Meanwhile, Tokyo was being raided from the air day and night. It was not a happy Easter anywhere.

On the home front, the condition of the president had become a national concern. It was rumored no one had any influence over FDR and he was literally killing himself. The presidency was turning him into a specter, ashen and ghostly. Two weeks after Easter, the news came from Warm Springs, Georgia, that he was dead. Eleanor wasn't with him at the end, but Lucy Mercer was; showing her thoroughbred breeding (at a time it counted most, when the chips were down), however, she revealed nothing and kept busy at her post.

Truman was suddenly commander in chief, and the war went on. The Victory Campaign kept up the message that it was far from over. More food and medicine were needed for the displaced European population; more rationing at home loomed ahead.

In August the war was suddenly over, and the world entered the nuclear age. Although the war in Europe was also over, the effigy of Hitler still hung between two buildings on 35th Street between Seventh and Eighth Avenues. By December 1945, with the strains of "I'll be Home for Christmas" and "When the Lights Go On All Over the World," most of the enlisted were back home.

It was the first hopeful Christmas in many years. The Dorothy Gray "In the Pink" cosmetics campaign that was featured in the Christmas issues of magazines threw a rosy glow over the future for Dorothy. It featured her now famous rose motif. Daring ads featured a naked woman bathing in bathtubs overflowing with roses. The scent was "lifting, lilting, to put wings to your spirit." It was in keeping with the new feeling of exhilaration "so prevalent everywhere." Nor did Mrs. Draper forget the men. For them there was a nifty verbena soap wrapped in a "rough-house" gunnysack.

So much gratification had been delayed for so long, and so many savings accounts had reached figures never seen before that enduring all the strikes that followed V-J Day was hard, for it meant delaying purchases even more. One industry after another went on strike, creating more shortages and longer delays in finally buying the new car, house, or appliance. A tidal wave of spending was being delayed yet another year. Of course, black markets flourished. If "bonuses" were generous enough, goods could be bought, and were, by a great number of people who had delayed gratification longer than they could endure.

The urge to buy and beautify was so great it made the public nearly salivate. It was a time of golden opportunity for anyone who knew how to create desire in the buyer, and that was what Dorothy Draper based her creed on. She knew just how to do that and had been waiting for the economy to catch up with her ideas.

Following the big splash of the Quitandinha opening, anticipating an end to war in the not-too-foreseeable future, she had signed a contract with Schumacher for a line of fabric based on the designs that had been created for the Brazilian resort. Many of them had to be drastically scaled down for domestic use, but otherwise they replicated what had been created for the luxury hotel. "All the important decorating trends have started in the big hotels," Dorothy Draper told the press, "followed up by department stores and filter their way into the individual's home."

Packaging cosmetics may have been a challenge, but it was not grand enough in scope for Mrs. Draper. She wanted to do more hotels on the gargantuan scale. Consequently, she remained interested in courting Rolla, who was still planning to do an entire town of casinos around Petropolis. The situation in South America was more hopeful after the war, and there was a lot of talk about mutual trade and defense agreements. Plans were in the making for President Truman to attend an inter-American peace conference to be held not in Rio, where such conferences often took place, but at the Quitandinha. That excited Dorothy very much.

Night life had resumed with a vengeance in Brazil. Every room in the Quitandinha had been occupied for Carnival that year, despite prices that were astronomical, even for Brazil. "The bank did most of the winning," reported the society press. "From the way the croupiers kept raking in the chips it was easy to see how a large part of the resort's tremendous overhead was met."

Late in 1945, Mrs. Draper was again doing business with Rolla, doing the skating rink he wanted so much, although she had to cut her fee in half before the contract was signed. The political situation in Brazil was uncertain as usual, but she gave that little thought as she turned the project over to her assistants for completion.

It seemed, however, that the skating grotto was on hold for the moment. Little correspondence passed between the Rolla people and the Draper office. During the two months that the Urca casino had been closed, Rolla had poured fifty million dollars into its renovation, a staggering amount even for Dorothy to contemplate. Did he cover the walls with real gold leaf? What she could have given him for fifty million dollars! Reports were that local people had to do the job, for anti-American sentiment was high. Nevertheless, Dorothy wrote Rolla a letter offering to work for no fee if he would consider her for his future projects. She would regard it as her contribution to the furtherance of good relations between the Americas.

The month after Dorothy Draper signed her new contract for the long-awaited skating grotto, Brazil reached the brink of economic collapse. The world at war had been willing to pay any price for Brazil's goods. Now it was not. Because of wartime inflation, a can of Campbell's soup that cost six cents in the United States cost sixty-five cents in Rio. Citizens were now overwhelmingly against the government. Vargas had been in power too long.

In September of 1945, Vargas lost control of the military and was forced to resign when Eurico Dutra, his minister of war, and other officials staged a coup. The future seemed uncertain. The new president had swastikas in his past. How he would change the direction of Brazil was uncertain; it was said Dutra was still chummy with the Nazis in power in Argentina.

At first the Draper office took the change in government in stride. Plans had been finalized for the inter-American peace conference to be held at the Quitandinha, making it a showplace for hemispheric neighborliness. And a group of geologists from both hemispheres had also sat in the Petropolitan splendor and discussed paleontology. That also pleased Mrs. Draper very much. The Fairmount was to be the set for the first United Nations conference. Could a Nobel Prize be in her future? She had always planned her public rooms to inspire elevated thought more than lucre. The Quitandinha would get free publicity every time a prestigious group posed for photographs among the three-story marble pillars.

Then, without warning, the Dutra government outlawed gambling in Brazil and its national territories. Rolla was suddenly persona non grata. The Vargas government had made a contract with the Quitandinha, stipulating that should gambling be outlawed, Rolla would receive about $6 million to cover his losses, but the new government said it did not recognize contracts made under the previous regime. The Urca casino, open only four days after its $50 million facelift, closed. None of the contractors had been paid, or knew if they would be. A discouraging letter came from Richard Momsen: "At the Quitandinha, they have let practically everyone go, and in the hotel proper, they have let go about 80 percent of the personnel. It has been terrible to see this take place after such a great effort on Rolla's part."

Nevertheless, Momsen reported that Rolla was *still* planning to go ahead with his plans for ten more hotels on either side of the Quitandinha. They would house ten thousand guests. Instead of gambling, he would transform the town into a great commercial fair like the one at Leipzig. "The gambling rooms, the grill, and the skating rink will be remodeled into exhibition halls. Mr. Rolla has even thought of calling on Dorothy Draper to design the halls."

As Dorothy read, her heart skipped a beat. She was terribly fond of the Quitandinha, especially because it had generated so many royalties in fabric, furniture, and wallpaper; however, John Wisner had more recent knowledge of the local situation and harbored grave doubts. A thousand dollars was still owed to the firm for the skating grotto. If Rolla was planning to build ten more hotels, then he should be made to uphold his promises to pay. It was all too much like the rerun of a bad movie, and Wisner tried to discourage Mrs. Draper from getting her hopes up, as did Momsen, who wrote, "The country becomes more and more disorganized, and it is necessary to wait in line for everything, including coffee." How could anything be forthcoming from the new government if its citizenry had to stand in line to buy its own coffee?

Nothing came of the final payment on the skating grotto, or the great Leipziglike commercial fair, or even the completion of the third casino. The Quitandinha office was acting elusive, which was understandable. Finally, a very formal letter came from the long-suffering Momsen that sounded like the end of the party. Momsen was of the strong opinion that Rolla would *not* be building any more hotels in the near future, nor was it likely that gambling would be allowed for some time. "Concerning your proposal to come here at no fee on the understanding that your traveling expenses were paid, we regret that we are not in a position to give a definite opinion on the matter, although we are inclined to think that the present would not be a very propitious occasion for such a visit, since we are under the impression that as regards his hotel activities, Mr. Rolla's financial situation is somewhat uncertain."

Dorothy Draper did not need to hear more. The lure of the jungle quite suddenly left her. A man who had lost his credit was not for her.

The Quitandinha project had dragged on for four years, becoming an economic albatross. It had been a slow bloodletting, but the Versailles project was a hit-and-run affair. It was a one hundred thousand-dollar remodeling of the popular nightclub, whose owners boasted about having the largest average check in town. Its reopening in 1945 was a symbolic relighting of Manhattan cabaret nightlife. Edith Piaf had gotten her start at the Versailles and had created its international flavor. It had always been one of the most sophisticated spots on the nightclub circuit.

But Mrs. Draper did not like the owners. She said Mr. Prounis acted "like a gangster," and she complained about Mr. Rossfield's big cigar. She was continually waving smoke out of her eyes when she talked to him. Unlike most of the cabaret owners she had worked with, they even tried to interfere with her work. Dorothy insisted that the lighting be pink, and Prounis insisted it had to be white. Every time she came to the place he had changed the light bulbs back to white.

Her jobbers worked through weekends for her, glad for some business at last. Dorothy also hired extra people to get the nightclub finished on time. She camped out on opening night to make sure Prounis didn't change all the light bulbs back to white. That night the club was packed to the rafters. Carl Brisson, billed as "the older girl's Sinatra" as well as "the Great Dane of Song," sang thirty-eight love songs and still the audience cried for more.

The columnists described the decor as "delicate and tasteful opulence unsurpassed in New York." Especially praised were Dorothy's murals by Frederick Buck, which depicted the vista of the gardens of Versailles. "Marshmallow and chartreuse [a color Dorothy never used—it was more like lime green], mauve and vermillion are admirably juxtaposed," wrote the café society columnists. "One inhales elegance," commented Esquire, "and after straightening one's tie, exhales it, too."

With the Versailles opening its doors to postwar fun seekers, the columnists predicted that "Nick and Arnold will have nothing to do all season but count their profits."

But Mrs. Draper wasn't counting hers. Shortly after the opening, the restaurant owners declared bankruptcy, apparently knowing it was coming all along. Dorothy paid off all the people who had been working for her, and all her jobbers, and when she had cleared her accounts her little nest egg was gone, swallowed whole by one job, one mistake she didn't see coming. Her days of big spending, like having jolly dinners for all the staff at the St. Regis, were over. The little buffer between her and disaster was gone for good.

Still, she couldn't complain. The jobs were coming in, more than her office could handle, and so she hired more people, which she would use any excuse to do. Business was booming and Dorothy was full of ideas for how to get the world to laugh, dance, and be gay again. If there ever were an aesthetic that fit the times, Dorothy Draper's big blooming roses fit 1945.

Her New Family

After World War II, the Draper family was scattered once more across the continent. George Draper, by then a field artillery first lieutenant, returned home from Germany to his family in San Francisco. He had flown a light artillery spotter plane in Germany. Four of the original ten pilots he flew with had been killed, and he had been awarded the Silver Star for gallantry in action. His cousin Saunders Draper was not so fortunate. He was killed in an RAF plane crash. Diana and her children, George, Dean, and baby Susan, returned to New Mexico when Nelson Jay was discharged from the RAF. Penelope took a teaching job in Cleveland.

World War II also brought an end to the American career of Ruth Draper. Times had changed, said Saul Hurock. He couldn't sell her anymore. Youth, glamour, and novelty was what sold now. She continued to be successful in Europe, however.

With Penelope gone and the Jays back in New Mexico, the Hampshire House was suddenly very quiet. But Dorothy's life had been filled with new interests, new people, several lovers, and her office staff, which had become a kind of second family. Of course, she chose this family and had the proprietary right to pick the kind of people who interested her and made her feel comfortable.

Dorothy liked to be surrounded by tall, good-looking people of similar background—interesting, fun people. Tall, model-thin Jean Gordon was all that and a stabilizing factor as well. She developed into the office house mother. Jean's ancestry was also pre-Revolutionary War, although, as she put it, "on the other team." They were United Empire Loyalists who fled to Canada one night, their path lit by the light of their burning barn.

Jean was a niece of sorts of Betty Thornley, who wrote Mrs. Draper's books. There was an opening for a secretary at the office, and Jean was interviewed, although her skills were moot. When asked by Mrs. Draper whether she could run a switchboard, Jean told her she could, and then got Belle Clark to show her how because she'd never seen one before. Jean became the expediter, a title she found for herself. One of her jobs was to go through newspapers and magazines and mark interesting articles with strips of paper to draw their attention to Mrs. Draper, who never had enough time to read all her periodicals.

Jean's more-or-less Aunt Betty also lived on the periphery of Mrs. Draper's world. Betty had been involved in *Liberty Magazine* and had published in *Saturday Evening Post*. She had retired from *Vogue; Condé Nast* wrote a rhyme about her in one of his books, as bright and witty as she was.

Betty was big and jolly, a large Dorothy Parker type, and she polished off a bottle of Scotch a day. Men found her attractive, particularly gay men, and she was attracted to them. In fact, she was married to one, Ted Stewart.

Ted was a great deal younger than Betty. He looked like an actor out of the Old Vic, which was undoubtedly what initially attracted Mrs. Draper to him. She did like her employees to look the part. Ted was a six-foot tall, blue-eyed blond, in every way extremely good-looking. He was also funny, one of those cynics who cover up their despair with acid jokes and lots of laughter. Ted was everybody's beloved, especially Glenn's. Ted was only nineteen when he came to work for Mrs. Draper, and he had developed good taste, she said, which is as far as Mrs. Draper went with compliments. She said he was that good because she had gotten him young enough.

At night Ted was what was known at that time as a "Greenwich Village" decorator. He could be outrageous. High-strung, wild, a big boozer and, at times, extremely gay, Ted himself was a guaranteed party. Had he not been so talented and charming, Mrs. Draper would never have put up with him. In fact, he had cross words with her and got away with it. "Oh, DD," he would scream, "you don't know what you're talking about!" In reply she would fix him with her disinterested glare.

Ted was one of those beautiful young men who needed to be taken care of, and Betty did that very well. While he drove around in a white Cadillac with a chauffeur, Betty wrote day and night, on several jobs at once. Fortunately, she said, she needed only about four hours of sleep a night.

Ted and Betty lived in a house in Rosemont so large she could barely keep it warm in the wintertime. The repair bills were terrific. Something was always going wrong with the roof or the boiler or the copper plumbing. She had been trying to sell it for years and finally did, to a railway tycoon named Patrick McGinnis.

The situation had not been good between Betty and Ted since he came back from Germany. During the war, he had met Jim Roebottom, a talented young man who did beautiful sketches. When Ted returned to the office after his discharge, Jim Roebottom was at his side. He got Mrs. Draper to put him on the payroll, because she was expanding her office for the Greenbrier job and other projects.

Running her staff was complicated. Some of her employees were sensitive and difficult. They were jealous of each other and jealous for Dorothy's attention. But she kept her attention on the road and they usually managed to settle down and listen to what she wanted them to do; as soon as they heard her thoughts they were usually happy, because they loved her big, surreal ideas. Dorothy at play was great fun.

Dorothy hired several decorators in those postwar days who were members of her social class. George Steel was one. She had met him at a dinner party and hired him soon afterward. He was very handsome and had spent two years as a monk in Tibet. He was also a Greek and Roman scholar, and there was a book in his hand at all times. Dorothy was fascinated by him, but he didn't stay long.

Another director she hired who wore the right school tie was John Willam. He was tall, good-looking, and married, but he liked to escort society women around town. He also had a good sense of humor, and Mrs. Draper liked to go to dinner parties with him and his wife. But the office decorators didn't like him. Dick Kent couldn't stand John Willam. He couldn't stand that Willam was closer to DD than he was. Willam was also aggressive and made himself design director, and then tried to take over the business. Finally Dick told Mrs. Draper, "It's either *that* or me." Dick stayed, Willam went. If Willam was better liked than the acerbic Kent, the latter was more talented by far.

Glenn Boyles became Dorothy's chief designer. He made the big sketches and did a lot of her illustrations. Getting him to work for her was a real coup, for he was an artist's artist. His work was sensitive yet printable, and he understood her colors. Glenn was one of Parson's top design instructors and also taught at the Fashion Institute of Technology. He was the one who could translate Mrs. Draper's sometimes unfathomable concepts into art and then follow it into the mechanics of reproduction.

"Punch it up, Glenn!" she would say and thought nothing of tearing up his illustrations and making him start over like a school teacher at the desk of an idle pupil. Glenn put up with her. She paid well.

Leon Hegwood was her heir apparent. When she decided to retire, Leon could be trusted to carry on the business. A country boy from the South, he came to work for her as a young man in 1941. Insecure about his background, he had read Emily Post and was careful to avoid the smallest breach of etiquette. Mrs. Post said it was bad manners to eat on the street. Yet, when he had met Mrs. Draper at Grand Central Station early one morning during his first weeks on the job, she had come down the stairs and made one of her grand entrances, peeling and eating a banana, apparently not thinking a thing was wrong. Hegwood was puzzled. Mrs. Draper looked at him blankly and said, "I'm having my breakfast. I didn't have time to eat." He then understood that as a grande dame she was liberated from many of Mrs. Post's thou-shalt-nots.

But she observed other parts of the code. In twenty years of working with her, he saw her lose her temper only twice.

Isabel Berringer did new products; she brought in the Shenley and the Schlitz accounts. She took over Kerrs Department Store for Dorothy down to supervising the paint job on the delivery trucks. Isabel was a big, enthusiastic woman like her employer, a hearty type who liked her martinis. She was hired shortly after the Hampshire House job to ride herd on Mrs. Draper's expenses. When she arrived for her interview, Mrs. Draper said, "Thank heavens you're here. I understand you're going to take charge of me, give me a dollar when you think I should have it, and get my business in order."

However, Isabel quickly found that was not so easily done. She had her first major confrontation with Mrs. Draper over money when working on the Savoy Plaza Hotel. Like all those who came before her, Isabel lost. Mrs. Draper didn't like the way the dining room came out and told her, "It must be done over." Ted Muller was called in when Isabel couldn't get through to her that there was no money in the budget to do it again. But Mrs. Draper had no patience with the concept of budgets; the dining room was done over and the office absorbed the loss.

Isabel soon moved on to the creative end of the business. She was very imaginative and extremely neurotic. She had a great deal of difficulty with men. Although not beautiful, she had a persuasive drive and dynamic charm. She was great with clients, a skill Mrs. Draper was not so keen on possessing, particularly if the job was not a big, splashy one. DD did not really make friends with anyone, but Isabel became everyone's intimate.

Shortly after Ted Muller's experiences with Joachim Rolla, he and Isabel discussed going into the decorating business themselves and decided to open up their own office. Ted Muller left first. He and Isabel attempted to take over some of the Draper accounts, particularly the Mayflower Hotel. The executives there had not been at all happy with the Hollywood-type job Dorothy had done. Then Mrs. Draper found out what they were up to. The next morning she approached Isabel, who was sitting at her desk, and said in a voice that was cool but furious,

"Isabel, clean out your desk. You're fired." Then she stood by the elevator until Isabel was gone.

Loyalty was a virtue in an employee, and no one had ever proved to be more loyal to Mrs. Draper than Mabel Hakin, her social secretary. She had been in her employ since the 1930s. She kept Dorothy's date book and wrote the place cards and little notes that read, "I hope you enjoy the flowers." Mabel was known to write thank-you notes to thank-you notes. She worked in Dorothy's apartment at the Hampshire House.

Mabel could not handle money that was not new. She didn't like antiques because they had belonged to someone else. When she tried to explain this to Ted, he said acidly, "I have trouble buying new Louis XV these days."

Secretaries continued to come and go with great frequency. The pressure of the job was great. Glenn and Ted kidded Mrs. Draper about them, saying, "We can't remember their names. You've had three in the last two weeks. Do you think we could call them all Miss Smith?"

"But don't you think they'd mind?" she asked. It was often hard to know whether she caught a joke or not.

Then there were the mystery people. They would stay for a time, often at a high salary, perform unknown tasks, and then leave without a trace. Sometimes they turned out to be charlatans like an extremely voluble woman who said she was a countess on both sides. Her accent was uncertain and varied. She attached herself to Dorothy briefly, even traveling to Europe with her, and left with Dorothy's small Gainsborough. Some of these mystery employees were nice enough people, but no one seemed to know why they were working for her.

Penelope also worked in the office for awhile, after she had graduated from Garrison Forest. "Penny, dear, we don't have a desk for you, so you can just float around," her mother said. Penelope did her best to be helpful to Belle by putting fabric away and doing other chores, but she never had a place to call her own.

Another area of the business where people came and went with frequency was P.N.B., or the Possible New Business Department. Again, Mrs. Draper often hired people from her social set to fill these positions.

Brooke Marshall, an old friend and family member, was one. Brooke's sister-in-law was Evie Suarez, Penelope's godmother. Although her husband, Buddy, was Old New York money, Brooke made no bones about her background and even wrote about her life as an "army brat." Brooke had lived all over the world. She was an interesting person as well as being authentic. She had her own "touch" just as Dorothy Draper had hers. They were women who worked hard for a living selling their good taste. Brooke sold hers at *House and Garden.*

At one time she and Dorothy had been good friends. Mrs. Draper liked the way she gave dinner parties with round tables and special tablecloths. Dorothy was also a great admirer of Buddy, who she thought was one of the most handsome men of all time.

The Marshalls didn't have much money, but they did have a Mexican cook who made enchiladas that they served outdoors in the country, which DD said they did to perfection. Long on charm but short on money, Brooke and Buddy were one of the most popular couples around.

One Thanksgiving, while Brooke and her mother were washing dishes, they heard a terrible thump in the living room and found Buddy lying on the floor, dead of a heart attack. There had been no warning. Brooke was devastated by her loss. Her weight dropped to eighty-nine pounds. She wore her mourning clothes long past the usual year.

In 1939, when Brooke came to the Draper office, she was terribly vulnerable, a widow in her mid-forties without a job; she was also supporting her mother, who lived on a small army pension. Although Brooke had once made many blithe remarks about women being able to go out and get a job by making up their minds to do so, she did not feel so blithe about trying to get a job after losing one. Her wonderful little dinner parties had gotten her a job at *House and Garden,* where she did table settings, but they had let her go, in one of those political situations that occur in business, not because of the quality of her work or the success of her regular features.

Nevertheless, Dorothy was not eager to hire her old friend. Brooke made her feel colossal. Jean, who suspected why she was so reluctant, appealed to reason. People who were out of work had a hard time getting another job, she said. And it was better to be employed while looking for other work. Besides, Brooke might be able to bring some good contracts into the office. Dorothy reluctantly agreed.

Brooke brought her little dog Ziggy with her and sat in the desk next to her friend Joan Guggenheim Vandemaele, who was also in P.N.B. at the time, and doing very well.

Brooke was forever economizing, trying to look chic on very little money. One day she came back from lunch and told Jean Gordon, "I've just made the most wonderful economy move. I bought six polka dot dresses in different colors on sale at Bergdorf's."

"You're going to get so tired of them you'll have fits," said the sensible Jean. "Why don't you keep two, and we'll take the rest back."

"I don't think they will," she said. "They were on a special sale."

"I'll go with you," said Jean, who managed to talk the store into taking two of the dresses back.

Sometimes Brooke's mother would come by the office. She was a nonstop talker. "My husband always said I was just a rattle, and nobody can get a word in edgewise," she said, and people felt sorry for the widow who had to carry the extra burden of her mother.

But they all stopped feeling sorry for poor Brooke when she married Vincent Astor. He was about ten years her senior and about to marry another woman, but he was so charmed by Brooke that he changed his mind.

Basil Rathbone did a stint in P.N.B. He also shunned the rowdy Hollywood types at Ben Sonnenberg's, but with his height (tall), his sapphire blue eyes, and his great distinction, he was just the kind of gentleman Dorothy adored having around. He was a regular feature at her Christmas Eve caroling parties for awhile and would bring his wife, Ouida. A teetotaler, he drank glasses of tea that looked like Scotch to keep the drinkers happy.

They were a jolly crew at Dorothy Draper Incorporated. As head of the firm, Mrs. Draper was an excellent catalyst for these very talented people. Like a good city editor, she knew how to put all the pieces together and who to assign to what project. Dorothy came up with the big picture, and her staff executed it. In the meantime, she employed many secretaries to keep tabs on every pin and every measurement. She paid attention to every detail, no matter how small.

Dorothy made sure the people she surrounded herself with were interesting, lively, fun people. Some of them also flattered her a great deal and put up with her shortcomings for the sake of her generosity.

One of Dorothy's most obvious shortcomings was her intolerance for frustration. The office at 38 East 57th Street was on two floors, and waiting for the elevators never failed to irritate her. She was not afraid to reveal her impatience to anyone, even the famous portrait photographer Yousuf Karsh, who took her portrait for the 1948 Women of Achievement Award (which she won along with Katharine Cornell, Lily Dache, Elizabeth Arden, Bea Lillie, Marian Anderson, Eleanor Roosevelt, and Clare Booth Luce). He had this to say about her: "A handsome and very positive woman is Dorothy Draper. Used to having her way, I had to convince her that I would require more than just a few minutes of her time. . . . When I had finished the portrait I knew that I had met a brilliant and resourceful person—a dynamo of feminine energy."

While on a job she had a terrific fund of healthy energy, but after it was done, she tired of it immediately and didn't want to get involved in the boring details of maintenance. She didn't want to hear that her fabrics faded. Fortunately, there were a lot of people on her staff (too many, her business managers always told her) who could deal with what she had already done.

Another irritating shortcoming was Dorothy's undemocratic "If it looks right it is right" dictum, and her refusal to consider anybody else's opinion. Not that she wasn't sympathetic and understanding when she wanted to be—she was. But it was her enormous talent helped both clients and employees adapt to her strong personality.

For all her shortcomings, she was a generous employer. Before the financial Waterloos at Versailles and the Quitandinha, Dorothy liked to take her entire staff to dinner at places like the St. Regis and the Hampshire House. Even in lean times she would often take a secretary to lunch and talk business. One secretary had worked at Rambush, another decorating institution, where the very rich went for their custom-designed stained glass windows. "How do they do it at Rambush?" she would ask, all ears.

Her staff was invited to an annual Christmas luncheon at the Hampshire House. There was always a beautifully decorated table set for twenty or more, with Dorothy at one end and her mother at the other. Everyone was required to sing at least three carols, while sharing twelve red songbooks. If they didn't sing, she would shake a finger at them. After the songfest, a nonalcoholic punch would be served and then everyone would proceed into the dining room for a lovely catered lunch.

Perhaps due to the influence of DD's many teetotal ancestors, including the Reverend Doctor Joseph Tuckerman of Boston (who Justice Story said was "of prominent rank among benefactors of mankind" and who frequently lectured on the evils of alcohol), she rarely drank herself, except for infrequent bouts of pink champagne with her best friend Mae Davie. Although she didn't lecture, Dorothy made it obvious she didn't care to be around a lot of drinking. When traveling with Mrs. Draper, the staff hid the liquor in the top of the john. Dorothy was not naive. She was aware that quite a few of the people who worked for her, especially her sensitive artists, had drinking problems. She didn't mention it, but her frosty disapproval at the sight of a bottle of Old Grandad did little to enliven the atmosphere. People learned to do their boozing out of Dorothy's presence.

Dorothy also did not voice her opinions about the sometimes obvious sexual preferences of her "fellows." That Glenn was enamored of Ted Stewart was of no interest to her, nor were Isabel's tragic love affairs. Dorothy simply did not want to hear about them. Her concern was what it looked like—what people outside the office thought about her staff. It would not be any big surprise to people in the industry to discover that homosexuals worked for her, although a number of Clark Gable–type family men also worked for her. The Draper office was merely typical of the prevailing ratio in the decorating business. Nor did it concern Dorothy in the least that certain kinds of gay men were particularly attracted to her, for her flamboyance and her active pursuit of the fantasy life. Although she enjoyed their witty company, most of the time she didn't have the faintest idea what they were talking about. Dorothy kept her eyes on the road and ignored all the shenanigans. She knew the only important thing was appearance's sake, "What other people thought," and on the code of keeping up a good front she would not bend. Ted and his friends and lovers were definitely not meat-and-potatoes suburban types. Dorothy felt they could be as flamboyant as they liked as long as they were tasteful about it. But when there were big showings at Scalamandre or Schumacher, she would say to Ted, "Take Jean with you." Jean didn't mind. She was a good egg. She was also happily married to a man Mrs. Draper said was "better looking than Clark Gable" and had no concern about her image. Besides, Ted was great fun. She found his parties *after* the parties were often amusing, too—hilarious, in fact— but at a certain level it was also strictly business.

Elsie deWolfe also had her "fellows," but she brought them home with her, where they often entertained her on the weekends. On Sundays she played cards with her favorite fellows, always wearing white gloves because she thought her hands were ugly. Elsie's flamboyance went even further than Dorothy's, perhaps because she was so much smaller and could get away with going the limit. Tiny Elsie liked to play the imaginary invalid. Once in awhile they would play that game and attend a concert in the late afternoon. "Come on," she would announce to the card players, "it's time to go."

A chauffeur would bring around a wheelchair. Her chauffeur would then carry Elsie to a wheelchair, and wheel her to the car. Upon arriving at the theater, he would carry her out of the car, put her back in the wheelchair, wheel her into the lobby, and carry her to her seat. After the show, the whole process was reversed.

Home again, Elsie would get out of the wheelchair, walk back to the card table, and say, "Come on, let's finish the game." She had gone to the theater and returned without her feet ever touching the ground. She said it was her way of conserving energy.

On the serious side of the business, Dorothy Draper Incorporated was run by a system of revolving business managers, each of whom was going to make it efficient and profitable and none of whom ever did. They came and went like the seasons. One business manager was seen only when he came down the hall to sharpen his pencils. He would come out with a handful and then return to his office. The next day he did the same. By the third day the pencils were little stubs. By the fourth day he was gone.

Half of the business managers came in to try to take over the business, but with one exception, Mrs. Draper didn't seem to be aware of that. She had met him at a dinner party. He called himself Count Lovatelli, and he had a thick northern Italian accent. He lasted about five months. The count was charming, good-looking, and intelligent, but after a few weeks Jean told Mrs. Draper, "That count is as crooked as a dog's hind leg." He also coined the saying about Mrs. Draper: "The oats are good in her stable."

Like all business managers before him, the count became increasingly frustrated with Mrs. Draper's refusal to follow her budget, only he actually went so far as to address his grievances to her august board of directors. With considerable arrogance, Count Lovatelli presented his case against Mrs. Draper to her board and concluded that she was not reformable. Her rebuttal followed, which the count actually interrupted several times to dispute. Dorothy was developing a head of steam, but Count Lovatelli didn't know it. Few ever did, and even fewer ever saw her erupt. She went on the attack after he rudely cut her short with his third interruption: "Of course, I make that decision."

Mrs. Draper smiled and said quietly, "You did, Mr. Lovatelli, you did," which everyone around the table but the count heard as "Good-bye, Mr. Lovatelli, good-bye."

Slowly realizing that he was out of a job, Count Lovatelli departed with the indignant words, "Mrs. Draper, the fish it smell at the head."

Sometimes business managers were exposed to the somewhat wacky atmosphere of the office and were unprepared. One such incident involved Ted Stewart and some hats. Dorothy did a lot of public speaking. She often would be three days in one place, three days in the next, and so on, all the way out to the West Coast and back. On one such trip, she was supposed to have gotten her clothes together beforehand, including hats, but had not done so. Hats were a very important part of

207

Dorothy's life, for she wore one in the office every day. In fact, she was known for her hats, which were never inconspicuous.

On the afternoon of the night she was to leave, she came into the office with the hats and got on the phone to Jean. "Come here and bring your needle and scissors. I want you to trim my hats." When Jean got to her office Mrs. Draper was preoccupied.

"I have to have a head," protested Jean.

"Well, I can't give you any time," DD said. Jean began trying the hats on different people in the office, and the only person whose head was the right size was Ted.

He was very grumpy about complying. Jean worked as fast as she could, but there were five hats to trim. Fortunately for Mrs. Draper, Jean knew enough about hat trimming to do the job. She was working on the last one, adjusting a pair of beautiful gray pigeon wings from Mrs. Draper's mother, when the door to the main room opened and in walked the newest business manager. He was considerably shaken by what he saw, but not as much as Ted, who didn't think it was at all funny that he had been caught wearing Mrs. Draper's hat. However, for the business manager, it was a good introduction to Dorothy Draper Incorporated.

In addition to Mrs. Draper's revolving business managers, she had a board of directors to help steady the ship, which was quite unusual for the time. By the 1940's there were many women in the field doing the commercial jobs DD didn't get, but none of them had boards of directors. On her board sat powerful and influential people like Ben Sonnenberg and Peter Grimm of Douglas Elliman. Also on the board was her brother, Roger, known among the staff as "Bang-up," his response whenever he approved of anything. Although he had always taken second place to his sister the star, Roger didn't hold it against her or anybody else. He was a mild-mannered, devoted family man. Unfortunately, at board meetings there was often not anything to say "Bang-up" to. He also observed the many con artists busily plying money and favors out of his vulnerable sister, who was always in need of adoration. He worried about her.

Another valuable director on Mrs. Draper's board was her attorney, Frank Weil. It was because of Weil that Mrs. Draper never got sued. He was also one of her close friends. He admired her and thought she did fabulous work. There wasn't anything he wouldn't have done for her. He saw himself as her protector and successfully kept her from being involved in other people's mistakes.

For awhile even her son George was on her board. He had come East after quitting his job at the *San Francisco Chronicle* to work on the *Washington Post*. Between jobs he was in New York, and his mother put him on her board. He quickly sized up the situation: Very generous, and wanting to be liked, Dorothy had surrounded herself with some first-class flatterers with their own agendas. She seemed to be able to soak up endless amounts of gushing. At the time she was still trying to sell her correspondence course. A Miss Seaman, who appeared to be acting as the current business manager, had been influential in creating the course and keeping it an ongoing project over the years. Miss Seaman was a tall woman, one of the prerequisites for employment. She was also large, nearing fat, and had a powerful presence, the kind that seems to come into a room without opening the door.

Miss Seaman had a friend who was acting as an administrator on the all-but-defunct correspondence course. The friend was getting a double salary against future profits. George spoke up. He said he thought it was queer that someone should be getting double pay working for a company that was losing money. Miss Seaman exploded; tears flowed. George was quietly removed from the board. He had rocked his mother's boat. He realized his mother needed Miss Seaman and the others to give her positive strokes out of some great insecurity he had not been aware of until then. One of the smooth talkers among the designers on her staff had confided to George, "She *can't* figure out what's going on in your head." Dorothy Draper could be fooled by clever people. She was socially undeveloped in some areas, mainly because she rarely paid attention. She heard only what she wanted to hear, and that made her vulnerable to the sycophants.

Aside from Mrs. Draper's hand-picked family, there was another group of people who she was close to, who sustained her, and who were as loyal to her as vassals to a knight. They were her jobbers. It was a privilege to be associated with Dorothy, like those who sell to the British royal family and are allowed to display the crest of the rampant Lion, seal of the House of Windsor.

On the whole, her suppliers charged more. They provided custom-made goods and she paid accordingly. Mr. Handman was a great friend. He made all her curtains. She wouldn't even talk to anyone else. The Cinquinni family were cabinet makers as well as plasterworkers. Linquer and Wexler did her frames. Frederick Buck did her murals. She also relied on Rose Cumming, one of New York's most unique oddities. Originally a society florist who went into antiques, Rose had a shop across the street from Delmonico's on Park Avenue. All day she sat in the window of her shop in her Chinese robe and purple hair. Everybody in the decorating business used Rose Cumming because she had exquisite taste. Mary Pickford came all the way from California to buy from Rose. Her windows, entirely unarranged except for herself, held the most beautiful objects in the city. Her chintzes and chandeliers could not be found anywhere else. Nobody knew how she could walk into a room full of junk and go straight for the hidden treasure.

Dorothy's jobbers adored her and she them. They might privately tear out their hair as she constantly changed her mind, but their loyalty to her was unswerving. When she heard one of her fabric men, Jake Altman, had died, she wept and said, "We must send him flowers." Ted and Jean both told her that wasn't done at a Jewish funeral.

"Well, I'm going to take him some flowers anyway," she said and that ended the argument. Ted and Jean went with her to the funeral, bringing the enormous wreath she had ordered for her much loved Jake. She presented it with great emotion to Altman's son, who had been warned in advance by Jean about what Mrs. Draper was determined to do.

He and his sister met Mrs. Draper at the door. Tears streamed down her face over the loss of a real friend whose loyalty she had counted on and who had backed her up on many jobs. Altman's children took the wreath, thanked her, and sent it on to a hospital.

Mrs. Draper's ecumenicalism knew no bounds. In Rome, she had had an audience with the pope. Returning to New York, she gave Mr. Handman, her curtain man, some "prayer beads" which the pontiff had blessed. When Leon Hegwood informed her that Mr. Handman was Jewish, she gave him her blank look.

Once Mrs. Draper got it into her mind to do over Grossingers. Ted advised against it, but she was determined to go, so Jean went with her. The plan was to go in and have lunch with no bally-hoo, so DD could observe the surroundings and take some visual notes. They were turned away at the door. Dorothy's jaw went slack.

"You can't turn me away," she said. "I am Mrs. Tuckerman Draper, and I have come to discuss doing a decorating job for this hotel."

"I am sorry, madam."

"Then I wish to make an appointment for a future visit."

"I am sorry, madam."

"Couldn't we just buy a sandwich and eat it in the car?" asked Jean. No, they could not.

How Dorothy Draper survived in business at all with her extravagance and generosity is a miracle. So many people fleeced her. She always picked up a tab and never failed to overtip. To her, the worst sin in the world was being stingy. For some reason it was anathema to her. Her lack of business sense made her brother shudder, but over the years Dorothy persisted in maintaining her Edwardian point of view, which was to think about money as little as possible and never discuss it. With each new business manager, she hoped for one who would tell her good news, but it never came. Basically, Dorothy didn't understand the concept of money.

Dorothy didn't think she lived lavishly. She owned no furs or property and entertained on a large scale only once a year, at her Christmas caroling party. Dorothy and her brother shared a trust fund that was set up so that their children would share it after their deaths, but the money didn't last that long. Today, it would take a monthly income of somewhere between forty thousand and fifty thousand dollars to live the way Dorothy did.

Every month, when Mabel read her the monthly list of bills, she would vow to reform. "I'll have to cut down," she said. It was a ritual. Living without fresh flowers, for instance, was unthinkable.

Mrs. Draper's payroll expenses were also way out of line. She hired before it was justifiable economically and kept people on the payroll long after she had a use for them. Part of her concern was altruistic—she truly cared about her staff—and part was fear of their being hired by one of her rivals.

In bad weather she had her chauffeur drive her employees to the subway station. Every afternoon the receptionist came around and asked what people would like for refreshments, and DD paid the bill. When the Mayflower Hotel opened in Washington, D.C., she brought down the entire office. She underwrote the cost of flying the staff, including the secretaries, to the Arrowhead Springs opening.

And then there were her sudden whims, like the time she missed the Italian Shoe and Leather Show in Brooklyn. "It was marvelous, but now you'll never see it," Joan Vandemaele told her.

"Oh yes I will," Dorothy replied, and took a plane to Chicago, where it was going next.

Another expensive taste was her preference for the one-of-a-kind item. Someone else might make a thousand of the same item for half the price, but it simply wouldn't do. Or if a job had been inadequately supervised or details had been executed without her approval, she would cry, "It's terrible! I'm ashamed of it." If someone protested, she would raise her voice slightly. "Rip it up! Start again!" Perfection was the thing, not profit. Dorothy was not in business to make money, but to do something beautiful! And when there wasn't enough money to pay for what she wanted, first she badgered the client, and if that didn't work, she badgered her brother. One way or the other, she usually got what she wanted. In fact, she generally approved of the way she handled money. She spread it around. She made a lot of money and spent a lot of money and paid good wages. That way money circulated as it was meant to. Who knows? She may have been right.

Once, after completing a particularly costly project, in order to free up some extra cash, she decided to sell her pearls. Her father had willed her a double strand of matinee-length matched pearls, real, not cultured, worth sixty thousand dollars in 1940s dollars. Not even Tiffany would buy them. Cultured pearls had knocked the bottom out of the market. Over the years, these pearls became her nemesis. She used to wear them with imitation strands, and left them out on top of her bureau saying, "I hope a burglar comes and takes them. Then I won't have to insure them anymore." Shortly before entering a nursing home, she gave them to her doorman, who returned them to the family.

On the positive side, Dorothy often received perks, like living at 30 percent off at the Hampshire House. She got cars from her automotive jobs and enjoyed going out in her black Ford that resembled a taxi. The rear passenger doors were painted yellow, and there was a yellow band all around the car. People were forever flagging her down. She painted the greyhound on the hood black with white spots to look like Dewey, her dalmatian. She thought that was very chic.

She had also been promised a little run-about car in bright red from a company that had hired her to do a room for them for the Detroit motor show. But they didn't deliver, even though she had her secretaries send note after note. Finally she went to Jean and asked her to try.

"I just want the civility of a reply," DD said. Jean wrote a cryptic letter and Dorothy signed it. The office got a reply by telephone. The car was on its way.

"What did you do?" asked Dorothy.

"I sent it to the president by name, registered mail, receipt requested, and marked personal." Jean smiled.

Unfortunately, Mrs. Draper was a menace on the road. Her ex-husband's two dictums—never fight with machinery, and keep your eyes on the road—had never penetrated her consciousness literally. Finally Ted convinced her she could not drive in New York, and she sold both cars.

Dorothy was also a menace in shops. She entered, nose in the air, sweeping others aside, and demanded immediate attention. But underneath the queenly attitude was a shy and insecure woman who never felt she knew all the things she should have known. Lacking that, she wore her imperial presence like armor and put on the dowager's voice to protect herself.

One of the areas where she was especially vulnerable was in her dealings with the second Mrs. Draper. It was difficult with two Mrs.

Drapers in the decorating business, especially on a personal level. For years Dorothy had any mail that came into her office intended for Elisabeth Draper thrown away even though they rarely competed for the same jobs. Elisabeth's clients were mainly conservative people and retail, but every now and then there would be a confrontation. Once Dorothy had signed to do a hotel in New York and then lost it to Elisabeth.

"We're sorry," came the explanation. "We meant the other Mrs. Draper." Then there was the bank on the corner of Park Avenue and 59th Street, not two blocks from Dorothy's office, which Elisabeth Draper had done in black and red. That galled Dorothy because she thought she had patented the combination.

DD nearly lost her cool over the Eisenhower job. Ike and Mamie had taken an apartment near Columbia University. The job had come to the Draper office and gone through the preliminaries. According to Jean, one day the Eisenhowers phoned Elisabeth Draper by mistake and she snapped up the job. Dorothy contemplated a lawsuit, but Mr. Weil said, "It's not worth it. How do you know you'd even like the job? Besides, it won't bring much publicity."

Dorothy had her revenge without doing a thing. Mrs. Eisenhower was a horror, Jean heard. She had the master bath changed seven times, and each time all the tile had to be ripped out and replaced.

Dorothy's staff and her board were her comforts, a buffer between herself and the world; they helped close the gulf that lay between her and her real family. In return, she was a true motherly type to her friends. The milk of human kindness that had not always flowed for her children flowed in abundance for her friends and substitute family.

Her real family was scattered by the four winds. When George came East, he would pay his mother a visit and they would have a jolly chat for a couple of hours. He would ask her about business, and she would reply that everything was going well or not going well. She could not comprehend her son's newspaper career because the salary was so low, so she could not ask him how his business was for long. Then, having had a meal together and having run out of things to talk about, he would be off for a couple of years.

Dorothy was even more estranged from her older daughter. Diana was a Southwesterner now, full of zeal about the transplant. Life in the Land of Enchantment was beautiful, she said, a rich, cross-cultural polyglot. In Taos, Santa Fe, and Albuquerque the Spanish, Indian, and Anglo-Saxon elements mingled freely. Servants were cheap, and the heirs of the old pre-income tax fortunes could live the good life somewhat like their forebears had, if not in quite as splendid style. Mabel Dodge, the auto heiress, was one of the socialites around which the Nelson Jays gravitated. There was a constant stream of artistic people at her salon in her ranch near Taos: D. H. Lawrence and Baroness Frieda von Reichtoven, John Marin, the watercolorist, and lots of English blue bloods. Mabel shocked the conservative Indians by having an affair with the governor of New Mexico, Tony Lujan, and he was excommunicated from the pueblo even though they eventually married.

The New Mexico lifestyle was definitely Bohemian; peyote was the drug of choice after alcohol. Partying was central to the lives of Nelson and Diana, although they were strained by it as they tried to find the meaning of life around the cantina of the La Fonda Hotel. Nelson had become a licensed pilot and had enough flight time to qualify him to fly passengers on commercial trips. Diana followed suit, although she was never terribly enthusiastic about flying.

When World War II broke out, Nelson was encouraged by his flying buddies to join the RAF, and Diana, who was pregnant for the third time, moved back to New York. While Nelson enjoyed the romantic life of the RAF with its "Live today tomorrow we die" ethic, Diana coped with living in the Hampshire House with her mother. Diana had dreaded Dorothy's visits to New Mexico because her mother was so critical and talked to her about taking out more insurance. It wasn't anything Diana could pinpoint, but one thing was obvious: Dorothy's visits took a toll on Diana and it took time to recover her self-esteem after Mama had departed. But Granny D was a completely different person from Dorothy the critical mother. She was proud of her children's offspring and nearly smothered them with hands-on affection. She loved to hug and kiss her grandchildren, particularly her favorite grandson, George, and would introduce him at parties as the next governor of New Mexico.

Granny D took her grandchildren to F.A.O. Schwartz and bought them nifty toys. She gave them money, packets of fresh dollar bills. "Here's your filthy lucre," she would say. Granny D took care of everything. At restaurants when the menu came, she ordered for them. Because George was the favorite grandson, he enjoyed the way his grandmother comported herself in public, but his brother Dean was embarrassed by her grand entrances and the way she talked and gesticulated—it was so boisterous! People at other tables would stare.

The grandchildren were awed by the Hampshire House, with its fantastic view of the park, the doormen in the wonderful uniforms designed by their grandmother, and the elevators that moved so fast their ears would pop.

The Christmas party of 1944 was particularly festive; twenty children were gathered around a gorgeously decorated table while the adults congregated around the eggnog in the next room. At each place was a present. After the creamed chicken and rice came the Christmas carols led by Aunt Penny, followed by excited roughhousing with cousin Roger Wolcott. Granny D's trumpet lamps were used as basketball hoops, and wild tumbling took place under the Christmas tree with the Leroy boys.

Mrs. Draper was upset when the Jay family moved after the war. Packing up kids, dogs, and birds, making a caravan of their two cars, they went back to New Mexico, more or less never to return.

Over the years, only Penelope remained close. Her mother had always tried to give her her heart's desire. At fifteen Penelope had wanted to be an opera singer. Dorothy arranged for her to meet Madame Lucrezia Bori, a soprano with the Metropolitan Opera, who lived in the Hampshire House. Penelope, in the full flower of adolescence, gangled in and unfolded herself on Madame Bori's couch. Her mother had taken great pains to decorate the room according to the diva's wishes, framing ten of her costume sketches, designing a book case that covered an entire wall, and painting her bleached coffee tables black and giving them black

Carrara marble tops. But Madame Bori began to talk passionately about opera and singing, so passionately that she forgot to ask Penelope to sing, and she left the interview without being heard.

Although Dorothy was not the least bit musical, she tried to get closer to her youngest child by sharing her interest. One day she said, "I want to take you to an opera. What would you like to see?"

"*Siegfried!*" Penelope said without hesitation, because she had been reading the Norse myths. The stage would be full of Valkyries singing at the tops of their lungs. Dorothy bought two seats in the dress circle and dropped off to sleep in the first act while Penny watched the opera, enraptured. Dorothy slept peacefully throughout the performance, with a restful stretch during the intermission.

When they went to see *South Pacific,* however, Dorothy remained fully awake. This time she got seats in the fourth row of the orchestra. After Ezio Pinza made his first entrance, during a lull, Mama said in her voice, which carried so well, "Isn't he a handsome man?" Her daughter quietly slid under her seat.

Mrs. Draper did not approve of the way her six-foot daughter loped through the halls of the Hampshire House. There were four steps that led from the hallway into the dining room and Penelope used to take off from the top step and attempt to fly into the dining room. That was simply not done, admonished Mama. Nor was swooning in the elevator after bumping into Brian O'Hern.

Glamorous Diana had had a coming out party. As Penelope put it, she didn't come out. She leapt out. Although Diana was very social, Penelope had a terrible self-image. That her mother expected her to be a social butterfly was beyond her.

"Penny, stand up straight for heaven's sake," Dorothy would order. Slouching always made her cross.

"Have fun with men!" she urged. Dorothy tried to be accommodating, and even indulgent about some things. Penelope loved dogs. Mrs. Draper adored Dewey, her dalmation, for his chic, but she was not wild about dogs as a general rule. Yet she allowed Penny to have a succession of dogs in the apartments they lived in. First there was James James Morrison Morrison Weatherby George Dupree, a cross-bred bull terrier puppy. One day as Dorothy was lying in bed under her wonderful red-lined comforter, James James hopped up on the covers and lifted his leg.

"Out," DD ordered. He went. Then came Bonnie. She eventually went, too, to cousin Bayard.

Penelope had one-and-a-half sets of parents. She also spent time with her father and Elisabeth. Her stepmother had no trouble giving affection, but her father was definitely not the hands-on type. One day shortly after graduating from high school, Penelope telephoned him at work, which infuriated him. When he cooled off, he wrote her a marvelous letter explaining the meaning of one's work. He was not an intimate man, although he was loving in his way. Dorothy loved to hold a person's hand and hug and kiss (once she tried to take Penelope, then approaching thirty, on her lap), but she remained a closed book—one copy made, privately printed, and the pages uncut.

The Tuckermans as a clan were not close. Up in Boston, the interests of Paul Tuckerman's nephew Bayard, a true huntin', shootin', fishin' type of stock broker-cum-country squire, could not have been more different from those of the New York branch of the family. Uncle Bayard was consumed with breeding, and he couldn't get over the fact that the current generation broke all the rules and brought the line to rack and ruin.

There was one Tuckerman family member that Dorothy was close to, her mother. Susan Tuckerman was very beautiful, even as an older woman, with her strong nose and facial bones. In her day, she had been daring in her own way. As a philanthropist she was not content to meet with her friends at Sherry's to lay plans for the next charity ball. Rather, she conducted her philanthropy in prison kitchens and marched up Fifth Avenue when she was eighty-four at the head of her Red Cross contingent. She was a standard feature at Dorothy's Christmas parties, where it was obvious Susan had a sharper wit and keener interest in the goings-on of the outside world than did her daughter.

After the death of Paul Tuckerman in 1940, Susan learned to drive. Until she was eighty-nine she drove around Tuxedo Park, intrepid to the end, wearing her Queen Mary hat, bolt upright behind the wheel,

honking her horn at every corner. She was not a menace like Dorothy on
the road: Although heavy on the horn, Susan was a good driver and
never had an accident.

In her widowhood Susan became one of those lonely old ladies who
feel free to express their eccentricity to the fullest, liberated at last to do
as they please and not concern themselves with what anyone else
thought. She prided herself on keeping up with the times, even the
changing sexual mores, and was more liberal than Dorothy on that
point. Hearing one of her grandnephews had become engaged, she told
him to live with his fiancée for awhile to make sure he liked her before
considering marriage. She could even cook, and every now and then
made a wonderful rice pudding.

When Penelope was studying at the Dalcroze School of Music in New
York, she used to stop by on her way home for tea with her grandmother,
which Mrs. Tuckerman served at four o'clock in the nineteenth-century
manner, complete with cake stand, enormous silver tea service. The
hostess wore a marvelous tea gown.

"And what did you do today?" she would ask. If Penelope got down on
the floor to show her a new exercise, she would join her.

Once Penny said to her, "Oh, Margee, you wouldn't understand."
That made her grandmother cry.

Thirty-four floors above 59th Street, Mrs. Draper also observed high
tea, minus the elaborate tea gown, on her terrace overlooking the park
whenever weather permitted. When Penelope moved into her own
apartment, DD's household was reduced to herself, her social secretary,
Mabel, her personal maid, and a live-in cook. The cooks came and
went, but her maids were loyal. Jessie was with her for years, a stabilizing
factor in the house. She was followed by Isabel Blanchard, or Bella, a
tiny and resolute Scotswoman. When Mrs. Draper traveled, Bella was
part of her entourage. Her head was the same size as Mrs. Draper's, so she
sat for all of Dorothy's hat trimmings, and when her employer tired of the
hats she gave them to Bella. Bella and Ben Sonnenberg's steward had
been lovers for years, and when the steward's wife died, they married.
DD thought that was awfully romantic.

*   *   *

Getting Mrs. Tuckerman Draper ready to go out every day was much like launching a ship. Bella scurried around to get her clothes out and Mabel instructed the cook and took notes on what DD had to do that day. If Mrs. Draper was entertaining that evening, Bella stayed. Over the years Mabel perfected her role as social secretary, knowing without being told that she was to do place cards if the guest list was more than sixteen, unless Grace Vanderbilt was coming. The eternal parvenue, Mrs. Vanderbilt expected place cards no matter how many were dining.

Dorothy never learned to cook, although she was known to make cornbread from a box when she invited friends for the weekend in the summer places she rented in Newport or East Hampton. "I have always lived near a great kitchen," she explained. The first week on the job at the Hampshire House, Mrs. Draper handed Mabel a menu and said, "Order the most expensive thing you want because I get all the food here at 30 percent off."

One day the cook was gone, and Dorothy decided not to order downstairs but to make herself some bacon and eggs. She figured it must be a simple enough matter, although she had never actually observed them being prepared. When Mabel smelled grease burning in the kitchen, she ran in and found Mrs. Draper putting the strips of bacon right over the burner.

"You need a pan," Mabel cried, at which point DD gave up and called room service.

Once, watching Penelope prepare vegetables DD said, "You really like cooking, don't you?"

"I do."

"I didn't teach you, did I?"

"No," Penelope said. "Jessie and Aunt Alice taught me. Root vegetables go in cold water and above-the-ground vegetables in hot."

Once Mrs. Draper became involved in her business, she became less and less enamored of society life, although she did maintain a preference for members of the social register no matter what she said about not being snobbish. Still, the life of the idle rich had become terribly boring to her. All they did was gossip about each other. She dropped most of her society friends as the years went by with the exception of Mae Davie, her best friend since her Washington days. In the afternoon, the two of them would get together, drink pink champagne (the only time Dorothy really imbibed) and giggle like two girls in school. Mrs. Davie was an old-fashioned hostess who loved to throw formal sit-down dinners for thirty-six. They also went to parties where there was going to be dancing, the one physical activity Mrs. Draper performed well, thanks to her training. Mrs. Davie considered herself a fashion trend-setter. She was one of the first to wear Balenciaga in New York. One evening dress had a skirt that stuck out so much she couldn't get into her limousine and had to change.

When she went out, Mrs. Draper did not depend on the kindness of her hosts to provide her with male companionship. She believed that a woman in her position needed to be escorted by *two* men, for the fusty old days of "You be faithful to me" were gone. It was more a question of having a roster of male friends whose social schedules coordinated with her own busy schedule than it was a question of romance. She had her standards, of course—tall, good-looking, and well bred.

There was a handsome, blue-eyed Swiss with a dual passport named Wagner, who drove racing cars, and a fabulous-looking ski instructor with curly black hair. Stroheim Roham used to come up for cocktails. In the 1930s she had a serious romance with a Connecticut architect who couldn't divorce his wife. The relationship went on until the early 1940s, coinciding with her rise to fame. She once said she had done her best work when she was in love. The love affair with the married man ended in tears. Her last serious romance was with a man who was younger than she was. In a rare moment of confidentiality, she asked Penny, "Do you think I ought to marry him?" Penelope, who didn't like him for her own reasons, answered, "He has fat ankles," and for years afterward wondered whether she had blighted her mother's love life.

It couldn't have been more obvious that DD adored men. Having received bountiful affection from her father from the day she was born, she was willing to take risks and not worry too much about rejection. And she was a flirt, fluttering her lashes at handsome men long after her romancing days were over. Her complete acceptance of men as delightful creatures who would never particularly hurt her feelings was why her husband's rejection of her had been devastating.

She liked jokes of a sexual nature as long as they didn't cross a certain line. She enjoyed talking about sex, but never on a personal level. Her vision of herself was one of high romance. Had she had her way, she might have wished to live the life of a Grand Horizontal of her favorite century. Even in her worst moments, if she could read a juicy romantic novel she immediately felt better.

Her female friends were also of a romantic nature. One of her favorites was Hope Hampton, who still got a few cents on every foot of celluloid film that was sold, even though Mr. Hampton was dead. Hope believed she had earned the royalties because Mr. Hampton had definitely not been a joy forever. Dorothy regarded the widow Hampton as one of life's most amusing people because Hope thoroughly enjoyed herself and had none of the usual angst that could be so wearisome in people.

Dorothy had first met her through the business. Hope had come to the office and wanted the company to do an orangery for a house she had designed herself up in Scarsdale. Ted Stewart and Jean Gordon went to see the house. Mrs. Draper rarely got involved in residential jobs since the Dodges had kept her cooling her heels in Grosse Point for three days and then didn't hire her.

Hope had a new boyfriend, and said she had gotten rid of the old one by giving him a Jaguar. "I always do well by them," she said. Aside from the orangery, there was another small job Hope wanted done.

"I don't want to upset the servants," she said, "so I want a sliding door put on the back of my clothes closet so my boyfriend doesn't have to run out into the hall."

Mrs. Draper thought that was uproarious, and she approved of the tiny woman wholeheartedly. Hope had star quality and had always worked hard for her money. When Hope married Hampton she was a lowly showgirl, not even a featured artist, but she was gorgeous, like a rhinestone kewpie doll. Her husband had a terrible temper, though, and used to give her black eyes, but when he died he left her all his money, which Hope joyfully spent. Hope was as entertaining as could be, and DD liked to be entertained.

* * *

Throughout her life, Dorothy continued to think of herself as a great beauty. One day when well past her prime, she went into Bergdorf's with her maid, Bella, and announced to a saleswoman, "I am a very pretty woman and I want a pretty hat."

Dorothy was increasingly vain about her looks. Her hats often had veils that rubbed against her nose, creating a troublesome rash. While at the dermatologist, she inquired as to the possibility of getting a new nose; she had never been satisfied with the old one. One nostril was rounded and the other elongated. She said it made her look like a fox. The doctor strongly recommended that she keep the one she had.

"You are out of your mind," he said. Still she persisted, collecting opinions from friends and associates.

"You have a beautiful nose," she was told by her office staff. "It would be a shame to have a nose job on such a lovely nose." Her friends agreed. Why she was so determined to have it reduced was a mystery. Maybe she thought it would make her smaller, or young again. Then, after making everyone in the office promise they would never reveal why she was going to the hospital, she phoned all her friends while she was conva-lescing after surgery and told them about her nose job.

The new nose did not make her look any smaller. Dorothy was of heroic proportions—all over. She was not only tall, she was large of bone. She always made the big, bold gesture because anything else would have made her look silly.

"It was as if she had decided that as long as she was tall anyway, she might as well be a colossus," said one of her friends. "So she made herself into the Statue of Liberty." In her youth, being big wasn't held against a woman. It was not yet the era of small, thin, sticklike figures. Because Dorothy had beautiful shoulders, a wonderful complexion, and glorious eyes, and as long as it was the fashion to wear skirts to the floor, she did not look heavy as well as big.

Dorothy was not obese by any means, but even her large frame could not accommodate the amount of food she would have liked to consume, particularly when food became her main sensory indulgence. As a result, she was constantly dieting. Even when the days of counts in racing cars were gone forever, she still made trips to Elizabeth Arden's spa in Maine Chance, Arizona, where Dorothy reported women lost weight by leaping barefoot in the grass while wearing cheesecloth.

The extra lunches and secret snacks took the place of amour. The wife of one of her business associates frequented the same hairdresser as Mrs. Draper. Early one afternoon while having her hair done, the hairdresser mentioned to the woman that Mrs. Draper had been earlier and had ordered a sandwich.

"That's odd," she said. "She's having lunch with my husband now." When the woman asked her husband that evening what Dorothy had ordered, he said, "Just a salad."

Jean Gordon was once sent to the hair salon to get Dorothy to sign something and discovered Mrs. Draper eating a massive piece of triple-layer chocolate cake. Dorothy had told everyone in the office how much she was losing on her new strict diet. She asked Jean repentantly, "Are you going to tell on me?"

"No, I'm not going to tell," said Jean, "but it's going to show on the scale."

"Well, that's my business, but are you going to tell?"

On the whole, her dieting regimens were no more successful than her budget-pruning sessions.

As time went by, DD maintained her self-image as a woman of great beauty by looking askance or not at all into mirrors or at the numbers on the bathroom scale. She had greater worries on her mind, like keeping a roof over her head. Having lived for nearly ten years at the Hampshire House at 30 percent off, the management had finally screwed its courage to the sticking point and told her she had to leave. She was on excellent terms with Mr. Coyle, for whom she had done the Carlyle Hotel and the Essex House. Nevertheless, she had been acting like a live-in landlord for too long. From the beginning of her stay, she had failed to live up to the terms of her maintenance contract. As far as anyone could determine by the way she acted, she was just another high-paying guest. If approached about new lampshades, she would say breezily, "Yes, I'll take care of that," and sail on, never to follow up. Management asked her to

check a room on the second floor they used for small parties but she
didn't. In fact, the Hampshire House job hadn't interested her in years.
She loved having people admire her work, but once it was completed it
bored her. She had thought of a hundred other ways to do the place
since the redecoration.

Her lack of concern annoyed Ted especially because he was often the
one sent out in a big hurry to do what should have been done months
earlier.

"Why can't you pay attention to these requests?" he would ask, but
she ignored him, and them.

When management finally booted her out, Dorothy had no choice
but to go to her mother's apartment at 555 Park Avenue, where Susan
turned her library into a bedroom for her daughter. It wasn't the first
time DD had lived in one room. They got along splendidly, but there
may be something to be said about the old adage of two women living in
one house. When Susan put up ten thousand dollars to buy a very nice
cooperative apartment in the Carlyle, DD was grateful, and perhaps her
mother was too. The Carlyle had been the scene of one of her daughter's
earliest triumphs, and the lobby was still just the way she had done it in
1929.

A joyful Dorothy moved in, decorating the place with Auntie Mee's
precious things: the Angelica Kauffmann chairs, the family portraits by
Stuart and Thomas Sully, and the eighteenth-century inlaid cabinet,
the doors of which she had hinged to the horror of her mother, because
they swung out too far into the room. The cane seats of the chairs were
worn, and Dorothy had had them lovingly replaced by one of her
jobbers. Dorothy Draper was one of the first designers to restore
antiques; she didn't think of them as sacred. She thought it was silly not
to hinge a cabinet door when it took up half a room when opened.

Inside the precious cabinet was the "Famille Rose" Lowestoft china
which had crossed the Atlantic on the *Flying Cloud* packed in green tea.
On the shelf below was the crested etched stemware from the Tuxedo
Park days, when her mother's tables were set with rows of glorious
swanlike stemware in various colors and sizes.

The living room also displayed the hurricane globes from the Newport house of her great-grandfather Gibbs. The most impressive object in the room, however, was the massive mahogany secretary that had once belonged to Oliver Wolcott. A person could not sit at it without having a thought that wasn't elevated.

Next to the desk stood an item that illustrated the Draper touch: a $5 grandfather clock bought at auction.

Dorothy was happy in the Carlyle. It was convenient. There was a seamstress who altered her things, and the beauty salon went out of its way to fit her in when she forgot to make an appointment. She had a strong feeling that the bad times were over, and it wasn't just Peale's inspiration. It was the culmination of a lot of very hard work, and the process had been harder than she had ever thought it would be. This was her reward for keeping her business going through a decade of hard times, from the Crash, through the Depression, and then through five long years of war. Soon the business would be flourishing amid the explosion of postwar building and spending, as "we the people" cashed in our war bonds and went on a historic spending spree. Stores couldn't keep Dorothy's goods in stock. The time was hers to seize. The fusty old Greenbrier would be her pièce de résistance; the reopening of that hotel would be her finest hour—she could feel it and almost taste it.

What a Swell Party It Was

Going into World War II, southern society had never been more secure than it was at the Greenbrier. The customs of the antebellum era had been revived and were so popular that a General Lee week was held annually. But Pearl Harbor changed all that. Hours after the bombing the government claimed the Greenbrier for its own use because of its strategic location.

By December 21, 1941, the first trainload of Nazi diplomats arrived at the White Sulphur Springs station to stay at the Greenbrier, which the government would temporarily use as an internment camp. Because of its isolation (not even Chandler's Br'er Rabbit could have gotten through the miles of brier patch that surrounded the Greenbrier) and because diplomats were treated *quid pro quo* even by Nazis, housing them in luxury would help assure that U.S. diplomats in Germany, Italy, and Japan would be housed accordingly while exchanges were being worked out.

Aside from some bad feelings in the local community, there was no particular problem with housing the diplomats. Roy Sibert was put in charge of their care. He got along with them except when they had too much to drink. Then it was touch and go.

It was a lonely life for the 1,100 Nazis in the world's most exclusive prisoner-of-war camp. Telegrams were received at the end of each day. The *quid pro quo* situation provided that while American diplomats were kept under house arrest in Italy, the Italian diplomats at the Greenbrier were denied the privilege of going to town. The FBI confiscated of lot of their belongings, which was also part of the arrangement. The diplomats could not take dollars out of the country, so they bought out everything in the expensive Greenbrier shops, down to the last twenty-dollar hand-crocheted baby bootees. The only newspaper they were allowed to buy was the *Baltimore Sun* because it didn't carry a financial section from which the Nazis could deduce what was going on in the outside world.

The Nazis stayed seven months before the exchange was complete and were treated like normal guests in every way, except for the presence of FBI agents and the border patrol that secured the perimeters of the resort. There wasn't any way for the diplomats to escape; the police were there to protect them from the local community.

Immediately after the last diplomat was exchanged, the internment camp became an army hospital. Roy Sibert was made executive officer for the hospital. The army brass came down and told him how they wanted to run things. Sibert sometimes argued with them but other times he saved his breath.

Officers ate mess-hall style under the dining room chandeliers and they turned the Virginia Room into an officer's lounge where they played darts against the muraled walls. A bigger problem, however, was how to keep the army from taking a chunk out of the ballroom for an operating room. He lost that round, too.

During the Greenbrier's stint as an army hospital, the exiled duke of Windsor and his duchess were frequent visitors of a semiofficial sort. White Sulphur Springs had been one of the royal couple's favorite haunts even before their marriage. Wallis Simpson, for whom King Edward VIII had forsaken his throne, was of the Baltimore aristocracy, impeccable to the bottoms of her shoes. As a belle, she had come frequently to her family's favorite cottage on Baltimore Row and had spent both her prior honeymoons at the Greenbrier. Wallis was a Warfield and a Montague, patrician families from the seventeenth-century migration.

In 1919, after performing bravely in World War I, the gay and debonair golf and sport aficionado, Edward Albert Christian George Andrew Patrick David Windsor, then the Prince of Wales and heir to the British throne, visited the Greenbrier and posed while drinking water. He was dressed in his natty plaid golfing clothes, for he was a great fan of the Scottish game of golf. When he arrived in his private railroad car, he walked from the station to the hotel—merely several hundred yards, but an unheard-of gesture for an official.

From the beginning, his little democratic touches endeared him to Americans. Striding like an American populist past the banks of red roses, which the hotel had been informed were his favorite flower, the prince passed them without notice and headed for the links. He also enjoyed the Old White Club and the many belles. The reputation of the southern belle, he said, was everything he had heard and more.

As was the custom in the bistros of London, band leader Meyer Davis asked the prince to play the drums, and he cheerfully complied, mumbling to the orchestra, "You *know* I can't play these damn things." They knew, but it was one of high society's little "spontaneous" rituals. Blue bloods love their amateur hour.

What the Prince of Wales really came for was golf. Over the years golf had become the main attraction of the Greenbrier, particularly after the arrival of a golf pro named Sam Snead. While still a new employee, Snead was fired for hitting a member of C&O's board of directors with a golf ball that Snead hit not from the fairway, but from the tee 335 yards away. Once the injured party had become convinced Snead was telling the truth by playing a game with him, Slamming Sammy was rehired, and soon White Sulphur Springs became an international golf mecca. To play a game with Snead was a spiritual experience. In the hushed atmosphere of the green, the golf widows barely dared to breathe for fear of breaking the players' concentration.

The former king and his tiny wife, plus their many small cairn terriers they addressed as "the old men," were frequent visitors to White Sulphur Springs. The couple had not been treated well by the Royal Family of England, but the exiles were warmly embraced by American society, especially the aristocrats of the Old South, for the duke of Windsor had blessed their line by choosing Wallis. Anyone from Baltimore could prove that the duchess's blood was more blue than that of some members of the current Royal Family.

Although the duke had distinguished himself in World War I, he did not do so in World War II. After consorting with the Third Reich, he was not given a wartime assignment of importance. Then he botched an appointment in Canada and was finally made governor of the Bahamas, which both he and the duchess saw as a form of exile. The duke and duchess escaped the boredom of the Bahamas to pay semiofficial visits to the army hospital, but they were primarily interested in being entertained and spent much time in the cottage of General Beck.

The duke was fascinated by American entrepreneurs, people who went out into the world and made a fortune by their wits. His favorite was Robert Young from Texas; Young's being a Texan doubled the romance in the eyes of the king without a country.

Robert Young was a classic entrepreneur. He came out of the Texas Panhandle at the age of twenty-five with the proverbial one suit of clothes to make his fortune on Wall Street. Ten years later he owned the largest block of preferred stock in the Allegheny Railroad, of which the coal-rich Chesapeake and Ohio branch was the big money-maker. By an uncanny sense of buying and selling at the right moment, Young now owned homes in Newport, Palm Beach, and the Waldorf Towers.

Young called himself a true capitalist—someone who took risks, with profit as the reward. As a businessman and a populist, he had a special mission: to save capitalism from the capitalists. He believed that a small group of men who were members of "The Four Hundred" had assumed control of the United States by becoming trusts and interlocking to control all capital through the Wall Street banks, thereby dominating the corporate, political, and social arenas of the country. Capitalism, he said, had been corrupted by the trusts, which removed all risks, and had been monopolized over lunch in the exclusive clubs of the Wall Street bankers.

Young captured the attention of the ordinary citizen by his denunciations of the oligarchs of Wall Street who controlled most of the wealth in the country. He said these "private governments" of the established order were strangling the little man and had to be crushed before they destroyed the free market altogether. Young would slay the dragon by leading forty-four thousand common shareholders in the New York Central Railroad against the giant trusts.

All his life Young had had it in for bankers, ever since his small-town banker father sent him to a foster home at the age of twelve upon the death of his mother. Because he was convinced that the powers against him controlled both the political and the legal structure of America, Young didn't go to battle with them in those arenas. He went public. His secret weapon was advertising. Young was more successful than even Ben Sonnenberg because he didn't pay for his ads. He made the news.

Robert Young dreamed of supermodern trains that would cross the country like Joachim Rolla had dreamed of casinos: trains with movies and libraries and no tipping, which had annoyed train travelers since the beginning of the railways. He dreamed of credit cards, an efficient reservation system, and, most of all, transcontinental service without switching at the Mississippi.

Young feared the postwar travel boom would favor the airlines while the railroads became mired in entropy caused by monopolized service. To prevent that scenario, he waged a vigorous media campaign for improved railroad passenger travel. He sent an ad featuring a picture of a well-dressed pig with a suitcase about to board a train; the caption read, "A hog can ride cross country without changing trains but you can't." The ad was sent to everyone of importance in the press, every elected official in Washington, D.C., every cabinet member, and forty thousand members of *Who's Who*. The press ate it up, and the result was miles of column inches of publicity—all of it free—an avalanche of public support, and his face on the cover of *Time*.

Young's vision of a people's railroad needed a theater of operations, and the logical choice was the Greenbrier. He had had some trouble convincing C&O to buy it back, even though the railroad had owned it since 1910. Over the years the resort had maintained its quaintly southern atmosphere, even after it went international.

Shortly after buying back the Greenbrier in 1945, Young mounted the takeover of the New York Central Railroad, with the duke of Windsor as one of his backers. Young, through the Allegheny Corporation and C&O, had become the largest shareholder. An intense publicity battle followed, and Young was winning. The Vanderbilts and the Morgans were portrayed as the villians and Young as the hero, defender of the small investor and the champion of improved passenger travel by rail for the common man. Some C&O executives who had opposed him on buying back the Greenbrier changed their minds when they saw everything fall into place.

Under the management of C&O, the Greenbrier became the playground of the industrial elite, and the northern twang became predominant in its corridors. Young saw no reason why it could not regain its popularity now that the war was over. He didn't even care whether Old White made a profit. He wanted it to be a lovely backdrop against which he could play Pygmalion as the rich, the powerful, and the blue bloods mingled together. In order to do that, he needed someone who could transform the Greenbrier into something that surpassed even its past glory, and that someone, said his wife, Anita, had to be Dorothy Draper.

Although Robert Young and Dorothy Draper didn't see eye to eye (he was 5'6"), they were on the same mental track. Both were successful merchandisers and knew the value of free publicity. They had reaped a fortune in free advertising between them. Both used a technique new to the scene called mass saturation: Young used direct mail, Mrs. Draper, mass-market magazines.

Mrs. Draper's specialty, he knew, was making the society columns. News about the rich and famous was what everyone wanted to read. Win over the society press, especially the syndicated columnists in the Hearst press, and the public followed right behind.

Young wasn't interested in Mrs. Draper's aesthetic as much as her showmanship. A woman who could get the Marx Brothers to perform had showmanship. Young's plan for the opening of the new Greenbrier was to invite everyone who counted to a lavish three-day on-the-house party and get C&O to foot the bill as a business expense. It would be a revival of postwar social life, and he'd see to it that the party made the cover of *Life*. And at the center of it, like the bride and groom on top of the wedding cake, would be the duke and duchess of Windsor. It would be a kind of coronation.

Mrs. Draper was well acquainted with the duchess. Dorothy had earned Wallis's gratitude when Betty Thornley had sent care packages of fabrics to the duke and duchess during the war. Dorothy also knew about Anita Young through Betty, who had advised Anita frequently on matters of taste. Her goal in life was simple: to get into high society. She wanted Mrs. Draper to transform the Greenbrier, not for business reasons but for personal ones: in her moments of self-doubt, she was still just a little girl from Texas. It was a comfort to be able to buy the kind of taste that made no mistakes (even when it did).

In January 1946, Mrs. Draper and Robert Young held a joint press conference in New York to announce plans for the new Greenbrier. Rumors were already flying about secret plans to go ultramodern.

"Nonsense," replied Mrs. Draper.

"The Greenbrier will be done in only one style," announced Young, "Great Beauty."

Meanwhile, five hundred extra workmen were hired at White Sulphur Springs and the major construction began. A new entrance had been cut in the porte-cochere, and the main hall was broken up into livable portions. Such a fuss was made about what they were doing to the hotel that Mrs. Draper sent Jean down to smooth everyone's feathers. Jean stayed in General Lee's cottage where it was warm, because the rest of the hotel was full of open holes. When the job of supervising got to be too much for Jean to handle alone, Dorothy sent down Ted, Dick, (whom she had hired for the job), and Glenn. They all moved into the Baltimore cottage. Next to them lived the Greenbrier's housekeeper. The fellows had hired a cook, so the housekeeper came over frequently and had dinner with them. It wasn't long before she was making passes at all three men. They used to ask Jean for advice, not wanting to hurt the housekeeper's feelings. She was particularly crazy about Hurley, who was very good-looking. Finally, when the housekeeper discovered she was not going to get very far with any of the men, she decided to be their chum. They were interesting company, and Ted was always making people laugh.

But the complexities of the job grew with each passing day. Mrs. Draper came down and stayed in one of the cottages on Baltimore Row. She brought a landscape architect from Long Island who knew how to construct a Jeffersonian serpentine wall. They found the old brick needed for the wall at a South Carolina plantation house. Construction was tedious. Each brick had to be numbered and laid out like a giant puzzle.

Mr. Lawless persisted in disagreeing with Dorothy about the obstructed view in the front of the hotel. She finally ordered the grounds crew to cut down the offending oak, but Lawless came on the run just as the men were turning on the power saw. A compromise was made. The giant oak stayed and several of the smaller trees were transplanted. (Years later, Dorothy was vindicated. The obstructing oak was removed by the hotel in 1987.)

Mrs. Young also came down. Although Mrs. Draper was genteel at all times, even when driving everyone crazy, Mrs. Young was not. She was nasty. She wanted a romantic curve in a staircase for the duchess to walk down. When the consulting architect, George Smith, said he didn't recommend it for structural reasons, she said menacingly, "I'll have my staircase or hire another architect!"

Dorothy wanted to install a canopy over the freshwater swimming pool, which she said was about as cheerful as a mausoleum. The executives protested again. High divers would catch their heels in the shirring. But that skirmish was minor compared to what happened to the elaborate wedding cake plaster ceiling of the Cameo Ballroom. Right after Cinquinni put it up, half of it came down with a terrible crash. Cinquinni redid it, and then built Dorothy several furniture reproductions she had given up hope of finding.

Sooner or later the Greenbrier executives succumbed to Mrs. Draper's charm. As they began to see what was happening to their hotel, they developed a new respect for her. She also tempted them into the drama. "We must look at this project as a producer of a theatrical production puts on a play," she told them. No one had to ask who was the star.

After she redid the railroad station in green and white, she told

Robert Bowman, president of C&O, that she didn't want any of his locomotives stoking up within two miles of her nice, clean depot. He just laughed. The governor of West Virginia did not have to intervene in her plans to paper over the murals in the Virginia Room, because Dorothy finally reneged on the repapering.

Although she was able to mesmerize the executives, she did not please the unions. The problems started innocuously enough with chauffeurs' caps. Dorothy had designed new caps to replace the soft-crowned ones they wore, which she thought were sloppy. She thought the new caps were very smart, with their white tops, red bands, and white patent leather visors, but the chauffeurs wouldn't wear them. They were too stiff, they said. Dorothy insisted. They refused. The stalemate continued.

Next to revolt were the caddies. They refused to wear the red shirts and green caps she had designed for them. Some agreed to wear one or in some cases both, but only for an increase in pay. Others refused under any circumstances.

Doormen, she had always believed, should be cast for their part like actors in a play. They should look like the cheerful old family coachman. She thought the head doorman, Jim McKensie, looked stunning in his red and green uniform, which was patterned after the liveries she had seen worn by footmen in Italy. However, the unions protested again because the other doormen and porters didn't like the ornate round buttons she had designed.

She had no trouble with Big Florence over what Dorothy called her "mammy" costume, which she wore when serving coffee to guests while their luggage was being tagged and brought upstairs. It was a full-skirted costume, with hoops, lace petticoats, and special jewelry. Big Florence said she didn't mind because all she had to do was serve coffee. The parlormaids, however, refused to wear their Annabella costumes, which were short-skirted versions of what Big Florence wore. They said they were too constricting to wear when cleaning rooms. Around the time the ceiling fell in, the unions issued a joint statement: Wearing Mrs. Draper's costumes was to be optional and required extra pay.

As the problems mounted, the opening date of fall 1947 was pushed back. Dorothy had told Young from the beginning that his plans for a fall opening were unrealistic. Spring of 1948 was more likely.

With all the setbacks, somehow she had managed to make the Greenbrier look cozy, even the twenty-foot-high passageway from the terrace dining room to the president's parlor (one-fifth of a mile long), which she had broken into smaller spaces with fireplaces and movable screens. The executives even liked her "Yankee" touches—English mantles, English chintzes, the Jane Stuart portrait of Washington over the massive wood-burning fireplace. With her red-and-green color scheme, all that was lacking was snow on the windowsills.

They also appreciated how she respected the few antiques she found usable, such as a table from the army hospital era which had been used for cooking by the officers. She had the top fixed, pronounced it fit, and put it in the President's Parlor. She made one of her few relatively expensive purchases for the floor of that room: a five thousand-dollar, 145-year-old Aubusson rug. She also chose a marble mantle for the fireplace with a theme of Bacchus and vines, which came from an English manor house. It called for a painting on either side, but Ted had difficulty finding a pair. Then her eyes fell upon a large Georgian landscape.

"Oh, that's nice," she said to Ted. "A lovely river, and trees with hills in the background. Cut it in half."

"Certainly," he replied, for nothing Mrs. Draper told him to do surprised him anymore. Little did it matter to her that the lovely scene was actually the battle of Ticonderoga, where both Draper and Tuckerman ancestors had fought against the little flashes of red she liked so much in the background. What mattered was it worked as a pair of pictures flanking the mantle.

Having won over the White Sulphur Springs people and even some of the C&O executives who had previously been her sworn enemies, Dorothy returned to New York and her next mission: designing a private car for C&O, a pet project of some of the members of the board. They said they wanted something luxurious. She gave it to them: French beaded curtains lined with sateen and trimmed in braid, a high-pile green carpet, hand-woven Siamese silk cushions, solid brass and white porcelain knobs. But she was designing an impossible dream for what was fast becoming an anachronism, a future for life whose time had passed. She might as well have tried to breathe life back into Tuxedo Park. The days of train travel by luxury private car were over, and the days of comprehensive passenger travel by rail were waning.

Robert Young had tilted at windmills when he had tried to save the passenger rail service for the small investor and the common man. He had no way of knowing that he was living in the dawn of the space age and the corporate empire. Still, he was strong enough by 1948 to be talked about as a presidential candidate, and the C&O became the largest single investor in New York Central Railroad. For a man who had come up the hard way, those accomplishments put Robert Young in a kingly position.

As Dorothy Draper rushed to get the Greenbrier ready for the big opening, Robert Young was going full tilt at several windmills—the Interstate Commerce Commission for one. In a hostile confrontation with them, Young laid out his plans for his Federation of Railway Progress, whose goal was to modernize the rail system and improve passenger service. Young promised to abolish monopolistic practices and eliminate tipping. He was hoping for one million members who would join for a low fee of two dollars. Already on his advisory committee were Admiral Halsey and Clare Booth Luce.

Young promised to do what the government and the railroad industry would not and seemingly could not do: "Give service to labor, stockholders, shippers, and travelers. And we aren't going to do what they do—lobby for noncompetitive practices!"

Then Young took on the Wall Street establishment. His name and fiesty nature were as well known by then as the name and nature of Will Rogers.

The Greenbrier opening was set for April 1948. Young and his wife Anita began to draw up the invitation list in their Palm Beach house. By the time they were finished they had more than five hundred names. The invitations went out as the press began to grind out copy about the impending party to end all parties. Then the responses started pouring in.

Absolutely *everybody* was coming.

Mrs. Draper went down to White Sulphur Springs on the Thursday before the opening to inspect the premises. Everything had to be perfect. There were only three things wrong:

Smelling the soap in the duchess's bathroom, she said, "That's not the soap I ordered. The scent is wrong."

"I'll replace it as soon as we open," said one of the Greenbrier people.

"You're not going to open unless the scent is correct," she said mildly.

"What can I do about it, Mrs. Draper, two days before we open?"

"If you don't do it, I will," she said, and she did.

Then there was the ghastly mistake about the garden hoses. They were brown! They were green by the following morning. The next day, as she walked through the massive rooms and gardens, she could not find one other thing wrong except the green slime around the drain in the Spring House. Dorothy Draper had outdone herself. The job was perfect. She could hardly wait for the party to begin.

Approaching dawn of April 19, 1948, a convoy of ten sleeping cars on a special train sped through the West Virginia mountains toward White Sulphur Springs, carrying a considerable number of the Youngs' three hundred fifty guests, a roster of the rich, the famous, and the powerful of the postwar era, plus a smattering of blue bloods.

The train had left Penn Station, New York City, at nine o'clock the night before, the cars filled with laughing, joking, drinking people whom Young cared about for one reason or another. None were as important as the members of the working press—the slick and zany, hard-drinking columnists, the newspapermen, the news service photographers, the editorial and camera crews from *Town and Country*, *Life*, *Time*, *Harper's Bazaar*, *Esquire*, *Vogue*, and other less prestigious magazines. Young wanted to impress the columnists most of all, especially the syndicated Hearst columnists, for they were some of the most powerful people in the world. For many a provincial, the wit of Walter Winchell and the series of writers who wrote under the name of Cholly Knickerbocker was as close as they would ever come to urbanity.

"A bowling alley by Dorothy Draper is something I gotta see," is what Cholly said.

For months the columnists had been wagging about what Mrs. Draper was doing to the Old White. Young had taken out ads in all the national magazines, which showed a picture of the Spring House under wraps with the caption, "We've embarked upon an extraordinary project of transformation designed to surpass even the Greenbrier of Old." One day soon the "New" White would open in the sparkle of a glorious sunrise. Still, rumors persisted, supplied most likely by hostile sources within C&O, that Dorothy was trashing the place, which served to deepen the intrigue. Hundreds of column inches had appeared in the press well in advance of the opening concerning the wonderful/awful things Dorothy was or was not doing to the venerable shrine of the Old South. Trying to get an interview with her was impossible.

"I haven't time to discuss anything," she told the inquiring press. "I'm doing the Greenbrier."

Meanwhile, the working press whetted their appetites in anticipation of another wingding. DD always got her clients to give great openings— with considerable help from Ben Sonnenberg, or so he said. But this was one party the columnists were especially looking forward to because Robert Young was picking up the tab for *everything*. They could have themselves a good time and not spend a nickel on à la carte.

Shortly after sunrise, the travelers began to make themselves presentable in the cramped quarters of the roomettes as the special train ground its gears uphill, approaching the White Sulphur Springs depot near the pinnacle of the mountain range. The train was met by an old-fashioned tallyho Tuxedo-style, drawn by a pair of magnificent Greenbrier Valley horses. It was like stepping off the train into the past. Even the jaded gasped: "Is this a movie?"

Across the road and through the gates, immense and gleaming white at the end of a circular drive, shaded by ancient oaks and holly trees, was Tara.

The press pulled out their notebooks: "The first impression of the hotel is that you are approaching a perfect Southern mansion, right out of the Old South. The decorative Draper touch is obvious from the time

239

you sight the charming little white station. Uniformed bellboys and the cars that await the train are in elegant Draper green."

Two enormous trucks filled with luggage followed the passengers to the guest register, where a "mammy dressed like Aunt Jemima" greeted them with cups of New Orleans coffee.

All through the morning and the afternoon special trains, private planes, and long sleek cars arrived at the gates of the Greenbrier and deposited the well-known guests. In no time there was chaos at the front desk. First came the problem with the Hearsts. The publishing czar (and head boss to most of the syndicated columnists present) had recently divorced Mrs. Hearst, who arrived at the Greenbrier first. She was shown to the suite set aside in the Hearst name, to which Mr. Hearst and his new bride were later ushered.

Then came the mix-up with the society reporters. Igor Cassini, the Hearst press's current Cholly Knickerbocker, walked into his room with his new wife and found it occupied by his recently divorced former wife Austine (now Bootsie McDonnell and also a columnist). They compromised civilly on adjoining suites and got good copy out of it: "Ex-husbands, ex-wives, ex-wives of ex-husbands, and ex-husbands of ex-wives among the three hundred guests have been rubbing elbows like olives in the same bottle," reported the first Mrs. Cassini.

Settled into their brightly decorated Dorothy Draper rooms, the press was appropriately given the large children's playroom to set up in, and they then stampeded boisterously into the dining room for lunch. As they looked around, they realized they had turned out in numbers comparable to coverage of a presidential convention. There were nearly as many photographers as guests.

Next came a press conference with "the dynamic and intensely dramatic" Dorothy Draper, who pointed out to them that she had not gone modern as they had accused but had used "a modified Victorian style" suitable to Old White's historic past.

"There is a terrific lot of hooey built up about decorating," she said. For the transformation of the Greenbrier she had simply "Let my imagination run wild, then gradually toned down my ideas to conform to eighteenth-century tradition." (Had she told the whole truth, she might have included a certain spectral assistance along the way, but that slightly unpleasant encounter with General Lee and his horse had been forgotten long ago.)

One of the comments that amused her most came from those who said, "At least the chandelier in the ballroom is the same." Mrs. Draper chortled. She had designed the 1,800-pound Czechoslovakian drop crystal chandelier using an old Russian print of the winter palace of Catherine the Great as a guide.

The reporters said they had heard that some of the old-timers had gasped in horror when she painted over fine mahogany chairs and bureaus. Wasn't it true that she had upset some of the dyed-in-the-wood antique lovers by "Draperizing" precious antiques with a coat of white paint?

Mrs. Draper laughed airily. "I don't mind objections, and I don't listen to other opinions. When a piece of furniture needs a coat of paint to fit into my scheme, it gets it."

And speaking of dyed-in-the-wool, was it also true that she told people to dye their precious Oriental rugs?

Mrs. Draper said thoughtfully, "I always thought there were three things you could do with Oriental rugs. First, you can bleach them so the colors are softened or blurred. Second, you can have them dyed to achieve a dark, one-tone effect. Third, you can give them to your mother-in-law."

Antiques were not sacred cows, she insisted. "I think persons who collect antiques simply because they are old are insecure, striving for something other than beauty. But this passionate interest will never make beautiful rooms."

"But isn't it true that you write at home on the desk of your great-great-grandfather somebody?"

"Oliver Wolcott, signer of the Declaration of Independence. That's entirely different. If you have real sentiment for your grandmother's chair because when you were little you sat on your grandmother's lap, then, for heaven's sake, keep it. If it has no meaning for you, throw it out. Just don't be dull. Jumble periods cheerfully. We don't have to think about what is traditionally correct. Instead, we can be as daring as an abstract artist."

The most commented upon Draper touch was the scarlet washcloth. "How to get some color and stick to the white idea demanded by the powers-that-be was a problem," she said. The answer was found in the outsize brilliant red washcloths which soon appeared everywhere as the eyes of the staff rolled heavenward—neckties, halters, belts, turbans, and dangle accessories. Before the weekend was over the guests had helped themselves to an average of nearly two each.

By evening, the gathering of the elite was as thick as clotted cream. The Palm Beach, Newport, and Tuxedo crowd had come *en masse* in a state of deep tan: the Aldriches, the Amorys, the Astors, the Bakers, the Grenville Kanes, the Bernets, the Biddles, the Burdens, the Binghams, the Cushings, the Cuttings, the Pells, the Fishes, the Guests, the Phippses, the Tuckermans, the Vanderbilts, the Van Burens, the Van Pelts, and the Whitneys.

Southern society was there, too: Duponts galore, the Floyds of Texas, and the Hardys of Richmond. Publishing was well represented: Hearst, Forbes, Luce, Pulitzer, Oakes, and Paley. From Hollywood came William Morrow and Bing Crosby and from England, Arthur Rank. All the nouveau were also present, hostesses like Elsa Maxwell and Pearle Mesta. There was a smattering of royalty—counts and countesses, and a princess or two. It was a Kennedy family reunion: Rose and Joseph, Jack and Eunice, Kathleen, the Marchioness of Hartington, and Patricia. "The Lady Hartington looked like a twelve-year-old in pale pink tennis dress, turquoise blue ribbon binding her blonde hair." (Kathleen was killed three weeks later in an airplane crash in the south of France.) Grace Kelly's parents were there representing Philadelphia. There were senators and governors, old money and new, café society and Boston society, true blue bloods and those who didn't care. They were all there, and it was as if nothing had ever happened.

Pearle Mesta found the mix to be too chichi. "I really don't belong here with all these rich people," she said. Columnist Elsie Morrow also had a negative response: "With a few notable exceptions, the Palm Beach rich, the café society, Eastern-International set, it is the class to whom gracious living means being gay with your ex-husband and your ex-husband's new wife. It is neither a superior group of people nor a nice group of people." The women were a disappointment to her. "The only real beauties are young. You would think that women with everything at their disposal to preserve their beauty would age well, but they don't. Mrs. Winston Guest (he's in polo) is a dazzling blonde. But so many of the others, whose faces shine in *Vogue* and *Town and Country,* look like depraved ghouls or bloated fish." Said one wide-eyed woman reporter from Cleveland: "It's a good thing they have money, because they sure don't have anything else."

Slowly the press began to realize they were part of an event, a solid silver scoop, an unusual occasion that actually lived up to their own hyperbole.

"It outshines the dreams of Haroun-al-Raschid," cried Elsa Maxwell.

"We doubt that even the sultan of Turkey, the emperor of China, or the czar of Russia, when those fabulous courts were at their peak, ever attempted anything on a more colossal scale," said Cholly Knicker-bocker, outdoing even himself.

"Out of this planet!"

"An aurora of society too brilliant to dismiss with one telling!"

"Surpasses the Hadley-Martin Ball of 1897!"

"Anybody who shows up at the Colony this weekend is a social outcast."

Even Cleveland Armory of Tuxedo Park, not given to hysterical prose, called it, "The outstanding resort society function in modern social history."

But where were the duke and duchess of Windsor? That question was on everybody's lips.

The following morning, the golf widows lounged in their links wear, looking as if they were not posing for the photographers who were literally crawling over them. Suddenly the links were buzzing. The royal couple America had adopted as its own had arrived. Their car was waiting on the siding.

Many gathered about to glimpse the most romantic couple in the world. First out of the car was the duke's man, then the duchess's personal maid, then a mountain of luggage, and then the royal couple—two immaculately clad, tiny, smiling people and their little dogs.

The duke did not walk to the hotel as he had on the previous visit. His present circumstances were too complicated for that. However, he was the model of relaxation, and his attire was the perfect example of what a gentleman of leisure should wear to a sporting weekend in the mountains. The press counted the pieces of luggage (forty-two) while the duke and duchess proceeded to the Presidential Suite (larger than Blair House). Its seven rooms would be shared by their hosts, Mr. and Mrs. Robert Young.

Meanwhile, in her room directly above the porte-cochere, where she could watch the front door from her window, Mrs. Draper saw the royal entourage arrive. The duke and duchess made her nervous. They were both such tiny little people.

She called for Jean on the telephone.

"Get *yourself* dressed and go downstairs and mingle. Find out what people are saying."

"Now? I'm not through in the President's Wing."

"Never mind. I want you to go now."

Beneath the sweeping canopy of the porte-cochere, the press crawled all over each other to get a view of the couple now disappearing from sight. The crowd followed them into the hotel. Then they fanned out to absorb the full effect of what Dorothy Draper had wrought.

Jean reported back fifteen minutes later.

"What did you hear?" DD asked.

"Three women, very well dressed and staying at the Homestead, said they were so thrilled that you saved the one thing that was beautiful here, the garden."

"But there wasn't any garden," Mrs. Draper said. "Just a heap of rubble and old timber. Did you tell them?"

"Why should I tell them? They were thrilled that it's still there, and they both remembered it completely." They both laughed heartily. That was the thing about magic. People couldn't tell reality from illusion. Dorothy loved that. It just tickled her pink.

Dorothy Draper had decorated the suite for the duke and duchess of Windsor expressly for their tastes, as she had once done for King Carol's morganatic wife, but their tastes ran to the Carolingian. The duchess's bathroom was wallpapered in sprigs of violets in soft purples, mauves, and greens that the duchess preferred—nothing too bright and with a high French cast. The duchess's maid put out the many photographs of the former king and his family, which he always traveled with, and the duke's man lay out his photo opportunity clothes.

On the 1919 visit nearly thirty years before, the monarch had posed in his knickerbockers, cap, and boutonniere down by the Spring House, tumbler in hand. His man prepared for a repeat pose. Meanwhile, the duchess's maid stripped the hotel bedclothes and replaced them with special ironed linens in preparation for the duchess's afternoon nap; she then instructed the kitchen regarding the duke's special marmalade. Then she assisted in the dressing of the duchess while the duke selected from the three sporting outfits his man had laid on his bed.

The first photo session was indeed down by the Spring House.

"Twenty-nine years ago this smelled like (unprintable)," said the duke, endearing himself to the press. He struck the desired pose, sniffing the sulphur water but not tasting it. "And it still does."

The man had perfect timing, too.

The next photo opportunity was at the first tee of the Old White golf course, where Bing Crosby, Sam Snead, and Robert Young were waiting. There they posed for photographers as the press shouted questions:

"What do you think of this place, Bing?"

"My maid uses a mink dustmop," he said. "And she checks for dust with a lorgnette."

"Hey, Duke, is it true the duchess's dresses start at $400?"

"She never pays more than $350," replied the duke, indignantly.

"Hey Mr. Young, who's picking up the tab, you or C&O? How much do you think it's going to be? We heard the champagne alone will run you three grand."

"You know, last night I did my laundry before I gave it to the laundry," drawled the beloved "Der Bingle."

Bing teed off with a handicap of six and, with a gallery of close to two hundred following, the four men played a round of golf. At one point, the duke, who knew the scenario in his sleep, asked, "What's the name of that creek down below?"

"That's Howard's Creek," said Sam Snead. Snead then told him that George Washington had once explored Howard's Creek while it was still a frontier, his services paid for by a baron loyal to George III. The duke enjoyed that.

Sammy liked to tease the duke by imitating his golf stroke. When the duke made a bad play, he wouldn't tear his hair or curse loudly like some famous people, but make a small clucking sound like "tut-tut-tut."

The hotel staff had prepared for the event like it had been an invasion. So far things had gone smoothly, although the guests were taking anything that wasn't locked up. The staff had been drilled by Mr. Lawless on orders from Mr. and Mrs. Young. They must be careful to call both the duke and his wife "Your Royal Highness." Also, they should wait for the duke to speak. The word was, however, that he made the protocol easy for the staff. The executives of the hotel and C&O had been given the same briefing, but bluff Bob Bowman was in the men's room at the time. He got back just in time for introductions, stuck his hand out to the duke and said, "Hi, I'm Bob Bowman," endearing himself immediately to the duke.

That kind of behavior endeared Americans on the whole to the duke. He wanted to be on their team nearly as much as he wanted to improve his golf game. Like the rest of the common shareholders of New York Central Railroad, he was rooting for Robert Young. The party was a bold adventure, peculiarly American, and the duke was there to give it the royal seal, which meant so much to Americans. As for the duchess, she was thrilled by the party. It was a triumphant return to her home turf, where everybody had to call her "Your Royal Highness." It was like a fairy tale.

The postwar period was not a high point in the career of the duke of Windsor. But the most shocking snub of all came when he wasn't invited to the wedding of Elizabeth, to whom the line of succession would pass upon the death of his dour brother. It was now obvious to one and all that the Queen Mother was *never* going to accept the duchess into the Royal Family.

Shortly after the war, Robert Young had taken the duke in hand and given him a sense of direction. He told him about his plans for C&O and his grand scheme for improved passenger rail travel. The duke thought it was a brilliant scheme. Young had learned the tactics of guerrilla warfare: Never attack your adversaries head on, or on their turf, and always have the majority at your back. It took the skill of a samurai warrior and the strength of King Kong, but it could be done. In fact, Young had done it all his life and had never picked up the tab! The two men were very much alike in the way they finessed a situation.

Robert Young and the duke had gone to Cleveland, home base of John D. Rockefeller, to study American business methods. The duke bought a fair amount of stock in New York Central Railroad, becoming a royal common shareholder, a fact which the American press spread as thick as margarine. The duke served as a helpful ally during Young's battles with "The Four Hundred," among whom were the duke's distant relatives. There was that delicious if slightly bitter irony to the whole affair.

At the Greenbrier, strolling on the links with Bing Crosby, Robert Young, and Sammy Snead, all three immensely popular Americans, the duke of Windsor created a new image for himself, or it created him. Everything was public relations. No one knew that better than English royalty. The Greenbrier event, which was already being called the "swellest party that ever was," helped him become strongly identified with the common shareholder, led by a populist who was fighting the ruling establishment. A purpose was one of the few things that could have been given to the duke that he didn't already have, and Young gave him one.

The Diamond Ball was held on the third and last night of the party. It was the icing on the cake on top of which the duke and duchess twirled for the syndicated columnists. Judy Garland, Robert Merrill, and even Bing Crosby sang that night.

"When Bing sings to the duke of Windsor's drumming—now that's a party. Nothing even the slightest bit brawley," wrote the columnist from the *Brooklyn Eagle*. Yes, everybody behaved themselves very well under Dorothy's new chandelier in the Cameo Ballroom, which many insisted had been there since the days of General Lee. They danced on a parquet floor suspended on chains while crystal light sprinkled diamonds streaking like meteors along Dorothy Draper's rhododendron walls; the deep red-and-pink satin of the draperies blurred in the background. Those watching the waltzing said the duke and duchess were more graceful than Ginger Rogers and Fred Astaire.

The duchess wore a gown of oyster white satin embroidered with crystals and brilliants, her skirt slim around her birdlike body and draped in a romantic bustle behind.

Guests gathered for the drawing of a diamond-studded cigarette case, a raffle that was held for the benefit of the Salvation Army. Bing Crosby thought the ten gallon hat that was to have been used to draw the winning ticket wasn't chic enough, so he picked up one of the huge, precious antique China vases in the lobby, dumped out its contents (one hundred fifty dollars worth of perfumed rose petals) and carried it back to the ballroom floor for the drawing as the Greenbrier people held their collective breath.

When Bing Crosby sang at the ball, he broke his long-standing rule about singing at social affairs. He just didn't like to do it. Robert Young had talked him into singing "for charity, for the Salvation Army."

That evening, Young Clark Clifford, special counsel to President Truman, came over to one of the new C&O public relations people. He looked very serious.

"If His Royal Highness plays the drums with the band, you must not allow it," Clifford said.

"I beg your pardon, sir?" said the young PR man.

"There are press photographers here wall-to-wall," he said. "Photos are sure to reach London."

The PR man laughed at the idea of telling the duke that he must not do something, and the special counsel to the president sought out higher authority.

It didn't matter. While the earnest young Clifford was looking for Robert Young, the duke was already making his way to the bandstand, where a smiling Meyer Davis was waiting with engraved drumsticks to commemorate the last time they had played together at the Greenbrier thirty years ago. As the press photographers came forward in a wave, the broadly smiling duke seated himself at the drums, and Meyer Davis struck up "How Are Things in Glochamorra." The duke's face fell. He apparently expected something easier. Trying to keep up, he spilled both drumsticks on the floor and retired in confusion to great applause; most of the guests were unaware of what had happened. Returning to the duchess, he was heard to say, "My hands went numb."

Meanwhile, the columnists were doing their jobs hopping from table to table and consuming more than their fair share of the three thousand dollars worth of champagne. Elsa Maxwell, wearing starched gray lace and rhinestones, reported that the duke was in wonderful form and that the duchess was enchanted with the Greenbrier. Moving on, she told Margaret Duke, Melissa Bingham, and Peggy Talbot, "It's hard to write about you gals, for I've known you all so well for twenty years, and I adore you but it's hard to find anything new to say."

To this Mrs. Duke murmured, "You had better look out, Elsa. You are slipping on that 'Worst Dressed' list."

Another columnist investigated Robert Young's hidden motives for throwing the party in the first place: "There are several schools of thought. Of course, you can't ask a man if he's a social climber. There's another school which says the whole thing is strictly business—invite all the flotsam and jetsam from the freewheelers of the social set, throw a lush party for them and send them back to tell their friends 'what a divine place it is, darling.' "

They were probably all correct. But from the vantage point of hindsight, the one who had the most accurate view of all was an anonymous blue blood, thoroughly stewed, who, according to Cleveland Amory in his book *Who Killed Society?,* had gone up to Meyer Davis at the height of the bash and said, "I feel like this is the end of the old era."

"Oh yeah?" said Davis. "How's that?"

"I don't know," the man replied. "I just have the feeling nothing will ever be like this again."

Meyer Davis's alleged comeback was "Well, whenever civilization is dancing at the brink of disaster, it's always to the music of Meyer Davis."

It was one of those prophetic moments. The 1950s were going to be as different from the 1940s as the 1940s had been from the 1930s. A new age was being silently ushered in that would have little room for the tycoon, an age of small-mindedness that would not allow the big gesture and the grand illusion. The 1950s ushered in the age of the "Man in the Grey Flannel Suit" and corporate decision making; no one would look higher than the bottom line—time when everything would be reduced to the common denominator. The party was definitely over.

The Party's Over

If the Greenbrier opening hadn't brought back society as it had been known, it wasn't Robert Young's fault. The war had changed everything. Resort life as it had been known was over. Tuxedo Park was a ghost town. So was the Greenbrier, at least for the era the party had meant to revive. When the guests departed and Mrs. Draper's magic faded along with the brilliant red washcloths, the hotel's roster was filled to capacity until 1949, with a new kind of guest—the corporate customer—not the social elite that Young had hoped to attract.

The Crawfords and the Tafts did not come back. The Crawfords went to Newport, but many others of the Old Guard abandoned resort life completely in favor of the Hyannis-style private enclave. The remnants of the southern elite had moved back to Charleston and Richmond. The postwar new money came to society's former hunting grounds and found cadres of businessmen going to meetings, all dressed alike. There was not a society dweller to be found.

Saratoga was also taken over by the common denominator. Society no longer moved in for the summer. The dust was terrific, as was the wild beer drinking of the crowds. And there were no more private railroad cars, except for people like the duke and duchess, who could still afford to live grandly. Old Wealth just didn't have it to spend anymore. Many of them had never recovered from the last plunge of the stock market, and with so many unions on strike they found little to be enthusiastic about for the future.

The party had been a disappointment to Mrs. Draper, too. *Life* had come to her party, and put the duke and the duchess of Windsor on the cover instead of her! She was fit to be tied. *She* was the one who had done the Greenbrier. She pleaded with Ben Sonnenberg to move mountains if he had to, but Sonnenberg failed her. It irked her for years that when her time came to grasp the gold ring, it was the duke and the duchess of Windsor and their foolish little dogs who got on the cover of *Life* instead of the person who had created all the magic.

The world was changing and Dorothy had to change along with it. World War II had the end of many things, and one of them was provincialism. What they said about farm boys who had seen "Paree" was true. In fact, postwar designers had to hail from Europe or the public wouldn't buy. American women wanted French labels in their clothes, and American designers were left out in the cold. Some actually adopted a French-sounding name, or went to France and sold their clothes from there.

English imports also sold well, but certain English companies in Ireland did not do well in the American market and couldn't figure out why. Therefore, they called Dorothy Draper. She flew over at their expense, went through their mills, and was madly enthusiastic. Their linens, she predicted, could become huge money-makers. The reason why they hadn't was obvious, she advised: The colors were all wrong. Drab beige, pale brown, and faded pink and yellow simply wouldn't do in the U.S. market.

Nevertheless, the company went ahead and printed their goods in the "gravy" colors she despised, and she was devastated when she found out they hadn't taken her advice. When she complained, they said, "Sorry, that's not what our clientele wants."

"You asked me what this clientele would like and I told you," she replied, but the English businessmen would not waver. Fortunately, the fee had been generous, and she had seen some three hundred-year-old lace curtains in one of the great houses and had reproduced the pattern from memory back in New York.

Soon after the failed Irish promotion, she got another call to go international. In pursuit of the American dollar, Louis Boulin, head of tourism for Spain, came to the United States to ask Dorothy if she would do a line of fabrics that portrayed the Spanish spirit. If she would consent, the Spanish government would pay for her trip and all expenses, plus a car and a chauffeur who would take her all around Spain on a two-week trip.

Making the trip with her would be her designer, Glenn Boyles, and Rene Carillo of Schumacher, the fabric company that would be manufacturing the line.

Boulin was a great friend of Spain's dictator, Francisco Franco, and he had given Boulin carte blanche just after World War II to do something about Spanish tourism. Picasso's *Guernica* hadn't done much to increase the tourist trade, and the war-ravaged country badly needed money.

Boulin had instituted the *paradors*, "stopping places" throughout Spain: former convents, monasteries, and castles with from five to twenty rooms. The meals were good, and the cost was inexpensive. They were very popular (and can still be rented today). The Spanish government wanted to get publicity for the *paradors* concept, which was where Mrs. Draper came in.

Of course, Dorothy scarcely knew more about what was going on in Spain in 1949 than she did in 1936, when she cautioned her son not to fight on the side that wore overalls. Fortunately, the flight to Spain in a constellation with piston engines took about fourteen hours with a fueling stop in Portugal, which gave her plenty of time to be briefed. It was Mrs. Draper's first long continuous flight. All the others had been short hops that took forever. As Carillo briefed her about the situation in Spain, her ignorance amazed him. He began with the conquistadors and ended with the Spanish Civil War, explained who Franco was, and how he, Hitler, and Mussolini had tested their weapons for World War II on the Spanish citizenry. Carillo's family had been thrown out of Spain for being part of the revolt, so he was keenly familiar with the situation.

"Oh?" she would say, her mind obviously on something else.

The economy in Spain in the early 1950s was pretty grim. Everywhere else in the world the Fascists had been defeated (except in certain countries in South America), but Franco continued to rule with an iron fist, even without assistance from his friends in Italy and Germany. He knew the Spanish people would put up with a lot. Although terribly poor, they had the reputation for being among the friendliest people on earth to visiting foreigners. Hence the push to improve Spanish tourism.

Arriving in Madrid, Dorothy and her delegation were given the full red-carpet treatment. Mrs. Draper seemed oblivious to it, as if she expected it. It didn't take Carillo long to realize that for Mrs. Draper everything had to be of a large scale—literally. In fact, he wondered whether he would be accompanying her if he had not been more than six feet tall. Glenn, he noticed, was also tall; their guide, however, was not. The guide spoke terrible English and wasn't more than 5′3″. Carillo, who could speak both languages fluently, brought the guide over to Mrs. Draper, who was busy engaging the officials in conversation, for introductions. She took one look and said to Carillo in a low voice, "I won't have him."

"Why not?" asked Carillo.

"He's too small."

"Dorothy, they don't hire guides by their height. They hire them for how well they know the country."

She would not budge: A guide who was that short was unacceptable.

"We can't be rude here, not about a thing like that," said Carillo; he would not back down. Dorothy finally relented. The man turned out to be a terrible guide, and, as they were to discover, was drunk most of the time, too, but there was no way Carillo was going to insult the Franco regime.

The red-carpet treatment continued; they stayed at the Ritz. Along the route Mrs. Draper saw her first Spanish roses.

"Look!" she exclaimed. "They have roses in Spain!" The guide laughed heartily when Carillo explained to him in Spanish that Dorothy thought she had created the rose.

Carillo discovered traveling with Mrs. Draper produced a lot of laughs. She was a comedienne without knowing it, someone who didn't have a clue in the world as to why she was funny. For instance, Dorothy assumed that the Spanish should change their eating and sleeping routines to fit hers. She kept regular American hours, including high tea, and had dinner in her room at seven o'clock because the dining rooms didn't even open until half-past nine or ten o'clock. Mrs. Draper disappeared into her room just as the evening was beginning for Carillo and the guide. The cocktail hour started at nine, just as Mrs. Draper was removing her daytime face. Then, after her leisurely dinner in her room, as she was well into her second decorating dream, Carillo and the guide were just ready to go out and have a good time on the Spanish government. They sought out working-class bars where farmers came in from the country. Farmers were the poorest of the Spanish people, but they didn't seem to resent that foreigners had money and they did not. Carillo never ordered a round unless someone insisted on buying the next one.

Mrs. Draper knew the Duchess of Lerma, and she and her delegation went to the duchess's house to see her collection of uncataloged El Grecos, including one with a hand mark made when the paint was still wet. They toured the streets of Toledo and visited a monastery where they saw a beautiful cloister where a profusion of Spanish roses grew. An abbot picked one and gave it to Mrs. Draper, saying, "Here is a rose for a lady as beautiful as a rose." She was enchanted.

Wherever they went Dorothy insisted on having Rhode Island–style picnics. Carillo thought it was fun traveling with her. She could be amazed by the most mundane detail, such as the fact that the sweet potato and the yam did not originate in America. She was ecstatic over a pot of geraniums on a sun-washed windowsill. Her color sense was great, but Carillo discovered she knew very little about the details of the manufacturing of her creations, so he learned to communicate with Boyles.

Dorothy's ideas were few but inspired. The geranium on the windowsill was one. Carillo would tell Boyles which ones he thought would sell and Boyles would draw up a rough sketch which Dorothy would examine and approve or reject. Either it was right or it wasn't. Dorothy trusted Carillo's choices, however, because she had learned that manufacturers often weren't as interested in producing a quality product as in making a profit. Carillo had overseen the production of the Brazilian line inspired by the Quitandinha fabrics, and they were breaking sales records. The "Fazenda Lily" became Schumacher's all-time best seller. Dorothy had insisted that Brazilian names be used for the line, even though the fabric was all roses. Schumacher printed in five combinations of colors, but the one that sold best (one hundred thousand yards in one year) was on a white ground with the typical punched-up Dorothy Draper reds and greens, huge roses and lush tropical flowers, plus even a lily or two. Schumacher also sold hundreds of miles of her Hampshire House rose chintz that home decorators had broken sales records buying to spruce up Depression-era living rooms. The partnership had been good for both parties. Dorothy liked to think she put Schumacher on the map.

Glenn was good at capturing both the Draper and the Spanish spirit. The *Olé* design was a black etching on a white ground that looked like an early Goya etching of a bullfight in the old style, used with chairs. It became popular, as did a cotton print of ironwork with geraniums on a balcony on a white ground. Dorothy trusted Carillo and let him have a free hand, but he thought she was pretty rough on Glenn. Dorothy took advice more graciously from professionals outside her business.

It wasn't long before the three travelers succumbed to the dread *la tourista*. Carillo had had amebic dysentery in World War II and suffered badly. One morning, from the balcony of an ancient Arabian *parador* in Granada, Dorothy inquired about his condition.

"Are you all right, Rene?" she shouted. The tourists in the courtyard looked up from their guidebooks. "What medicines are you taking today?" Carillo was forced to enumerate—aspirin and Kaopectate.

The trip went very well, which did not seem to surprise Mrs. Draper. Her trips always went very well. Several weeks after returning to New York, she called Carillo and said, "Gee, Rene, let's go to Spain for the weekend. Now that I know you can do it in twelve hours each way, we can go any weekend we want. And we can stay at the Ritz."

"Sure," he said. "Who's going to pay for it this time?" The idea that you could fly off to Spain any weekend would never have occurred to Carillo. The only problem Dorothy seemed to have was finding a company—or a country—to foot the bill.

But what had surprised him most was that someone with a name as big as hers wouldn't know how furniture and fabrics were made. She knew only vaguely whether something was sixteenth or seventeenth century, but she got away without knowing for sure; it was the *impression* she got from the depth of a swoop of a line. Nor did she care whether a color was going to fade or not. The famous red oversize monogrammed Greenbrier washcloths turned the water bright vermilion when they were laundered, but that did not concern Dorothy. They had been great advertising, and now hung in the private bathrooms of major columnists as well as in those of the most rich and famous people in the world.

After Glenn finished his sketches for the Spanish "Espagne" line, they were turned over to Schumacher, where professionals arranged the design so that screens could be made. Mrs. Draper wanted her name on the selvage printed much bigger than it was. She said it would help to sell the product. Although Carillo never argued aesthetics with her, the size of the selvage was another matter. Because of strikes, cotton cloth was still hard to come by. In the years after the war drapery goods were still being printed on bed sheeting. There was no way the company was going to widen the selvage to make room for a larger loop in her famous double *D* signature. Had she lived to see the current fashion, with the names of designers written large across the bias of their designs, DD would have been thrilled.

Nevertheless, Mrs. Draper got preferential treatment because she was a very big customer, and Schumacher had gotten a lot of mileage out of her splashy fame. If business associates understood that she was going to be difficult and that she was going to expect everyone in the world to know who she was, and if they were ready at all times to have her glide into a room like Queen Mary, pushing people aside, and if they were tall enough, then they could get along with her and share her fame.

Despite all that she expected from others, when Dorothy loved you, she really loved you. She could even be a great friend. She invited

Carillo and his wife to Newport, and they went to dine in the finest places. The Carillos often invited her to their house in New Canaan, Connecticut. DD loved the way Mrs. Carillo used wicker, and said she had excellent taste. Around the kitchen table Dorothy was a completely different person from the imperial woman of business, and she couldn't have been more attentive. After observing the Carillo children playing in the backyard, on the next trip up Dorothy brought a basket with an attached rope pulley that would act like an elevator for the family dachshund, enabling the children to lift their dog up into their tree-house. It made a cute photo opportunity and wound up in a magazine, but that was not at all Dorothy's motivation. She truly wanted to please. The publicity was a consequence of the quality of her pleasing.

In the 1950s the decorating business changed in a significant way. Architects now insisted that they do the interior as well as the exterior design. They had an easy time convincing the corporate client to take on one bill and less overhead, curtailing much of the commercial decorating business by the end of the decade. The American Institute of Decorators (AID) was up in arms about what the trend meant for its profession. For a long time Mrs. Draper didn't belong to AID. Although she was the uncrowned queen of her industry, other designers didn't want her in the organization. She was unschooled, they said. Although many others in the association also lacked education and professional training, the fact that Dorothy got all the big contracts and most of the publicity made her anathema, so a different standard of admission had been set for her. What that most galled the association was that she didn't care whether or not she belonged.

One of the members of AID was "family." His name was James Amster. He was a good friend of Muriel Draper, and he was rather fond of Dorothy, too. Amster saw the potential embarrassment that exclusion of Dorothy might cause AID, and he managed to coax the membership into letting her join.

In 1952, AID threw a big party on the roof of the Waldorf Astoria honoring the most famous architect of the day, Frank Lloyd Wright. It was a peace gesture because Wright had led the fight against the decorating profession, going so far as to design his own line of fabrics for Schumacher.

Because of Wright's fabric line, Rene Carillo had worked closely with the architect for a year. He found Wright even more difficult than Mrs. Draper. If Wright didn't get his way, he reportedly would have *terrible* temper tantrums and storm out of Carillo's office. As Carillo put it, "He was a great man, but boy, he did some dumb things." For Dorothy, if the quality of the mass-produced item was often less than what Dorothy would have liked, she was often miffed but never threw a tantrum.

The AID dinner took place shortly after the Wright fabric promotion (which turned out to be almost but not quite as successful as Mrs. Draper's line). Wright had asked Mr. and Mrs. Carillo to sit with him and his wife at Wright's table. Although DD was a bit disappointed that Carillo wasn't sitting with her, she realized that it was Wright's dinner, and he could hardly turn the guest of honor down.

Then Wright did a dumb thing. Addressing the AID members after the dinner, he began his speech by insulting the decorating profession. "I don't call them *interior decorators*," he said. "I call them *inferior desecrators*. And the greatest inferior desecrator of all is Dorothy Draper. She doesn't know anything. All she knows is God made some flowers."

As people around the room began to boo, Mrs. Draper rose to the occasion. "Yoo hoo, Mr. Wright." She waved. "Here I am." Then she thanked him graciously for noticing her and said she was a great admirer of his architecture and was glad he was acquainted with her work.

When she sat down, people applauded. Her remarks had been extremely well made. Carillo was uncertain; Dorothy could be on occasion very dumb. Her delivery had been so ingenuous, but it was almost impossible to believe she had been unaware Wright had been viciously insulting her. But it was just as possible that she hadn't been listening and had heard only her name. Or she might have intentionally saved the day.

Regardless, for once DD got some recognition from members of her own profession. For the moment there was someone in the room the decorators hated more than they hated Dorothy Draper. Their applause soon turned into loud boos and the throwing of chairs. Such an uproar was created that Wright could not go on with his speech.

The 1950s had ushered in another significant change. The tycoon was being replaced by the corporate board. In the 1930s and 1940s Dorothy had dealt with individuals who owned their own companies and controlled them by the strength of their personalities. Now she had to deal with a corporate hierarchy whose major preoccupation was not glamour and romance and risky derring-do but protecting themselves and maximizing profits. Dorothy's commercial jobs were becoming more and more prosaic—tacky little rooms in motor lodges and corporate hotels. Gone were the days of the silk or satin lining. Despite Dorothy's powers of persuasion, she could never talk a group of corporate executives into spending any more money than they had to, and who had to vote about every little decision.

She missed the wild and brilliant Robert Young, with whom she was going to decorate railroad cars, and even the irksome Joachim Rolla who had cost her so much money, for they had all had exciting concepts. The corporate mind-set was doing her in. Business simply wasn't any fun anymore. Worse than that, it was boring. The risks were just as high— higher because of inflation—but the thrill was gone.

For many years Young was the last tycoon of his kind, until the 1980s brought a fresh crop of them, this time in real estate. He took his life in Palm Beach in 1953. He went out like Hemingway. Many people speculated on why he killed himself, and there were several explanations. People who knew him around the Greenbrier say he had nothing but trouble after the big party.

Roy Sibert remembered his last board of directors meeting: "It was held at White Sulphur Springs. Robert Young was supposed to be there from Palm Beach. He sent a telegram to Mr. Bowman, the president, telling him he was sick, which made Bowman angry. They were all suffering from nervous tension."

Tension plus grief for his only child, a daughter, who had been killed in a plane crash, was Roy Sibert's theory for Robert Young's suicide.

Another was the tragic ending to Young's dream for passenger rail travel and "Train X," the supercomfortable passenger car, designed by Dorothy Draper shortly after the Greenbrier party, with all the amenities, like a little shelf for your purse behind the bathroom door. Young was going to make passenger travel by rail the wave of the future—economical, safe, and readily available everywhere. But his dream never got off the ground because of the growth of air travel. Other things happened too, strange things that looked like sabotage.

"The railroad [industry] built all those bridges too low and his cars wouldn't go under them and sold all the equipment to South America at ten or fifteen cents on the dollar," said Sibert.

Another theory as to why Robert Young took his life may have been apocryphal: On his desk at the time of his death was a letter from a common stockholder, a widow, who had lost her life savings by believing in him.

Gone with him was the glamour of the romantic flower-strewn postwar period. The 1950s were small times, run by small-minded men who thought in a group and decided in a group. The individual was a rare bird and getting rarer. Dorothy hardly ever had the opportunity to lock horns with one powerful man anymore.

One exception was Harry Rosenthal. He was known as the Henry Ford of the dress business, for he mass-produced dresses which never cost more than twenty-five dollars and sold them in twelve thousand stores. Dorothy loved his modest chic and had done one of her most spectacular white plaster environments for his showroom, quite possibly her most surreal. She turned it into a labyrinth of mirrored hallways and baroque staircases with elaborately carved white balustrades lit by dozens of baby spotlights in the ceiling. Buyers complained they needed a map to get through the showroom. She spent a staggering two hundred fifty thousand dollars on the rooms. A tycoon like Rosenthal always did things in a big way, and she rewarded him richly in kind.

Another exception was Mr. Davies, the head of the Mormon church in Salt Lake City, Utah. The Mormons were building a skyscraper hotel. Meeting with Mr. Davies had reminded Dorothy of her audience with the pope, but Mr. Davies had not cowed Dorothy. Although he said he was only interested in her decorating the top floor, a revolving restaurant called the Sky Room, she told him, "I have decided I want to do your entire hotel." Then she had her staff draw a portfolio of sketches on each public room and a series of plans for the bedrooms and sent them out to Salt Lake City.

Mr. Davis postponed making a decision for several years. Then one day one of Dorothy's friends came back from Utah and described how the hotel had been done over. The economical Mr. Davies had had someone else execute her sketches.

Most of the commercial work that came Dorothy's way seemed piddling compared with her big jobs. She had been used to dealing face to face with individuals on whose desk the buck stopped rather than messing around with "Mr. In-Between." Dorothy had enjoyed going into combat with tycoons, staring them down until they gave her carte blanche. She did not enjoy cooling her heels while a group of men all dressed alike huddled and worried and scratched their heads around her sketches, nervously taking notes and then leaving to consult with unseen higher-ups.

Then along came Convair. The company offered her five hundred thousand dollars to redesign an airplane interior, which she had always dreamed of doing. When she signed the contract she took her entire office and was still outnumbered two to one by Convair executives. The fee made her wild-eyed; she immediately went into her Napoleonic phase. Dorothy said she would do for the rapidly growing airline business what she had not been able to do with Young for the railroads. She would do it the way she always had, controlling everything, designing everything in sight from uniforms to china to trays right down to the discomfort bags.

The company gave her two hundred thousand dollars to start, and she went through it in a month. She hired all kinds of people, and most of them didn't know how to interpret what she wanted. The rapid expansion was dangerous, but there was no stopping her.

The more insecure she felt, the more money she spent, and the more people she took to the Convair meetings. Once she went with Dick Kent, Leon Hegwood, Belle Clark, and her new man, Gary Pizarelli.

The meeting was held in a Convair boardroom, and about fifteen executives tried to understand what on earth Mrs. Draper was talking about when she waved her arms and went on about "treillages around the top." During a break, one of the executives approached Leon Hegwood and said, "Maybe you can tell me. What in the hell is a treillage?"

In the end, after all that money had been spent and all those meetings attended and all those votes taken, the company didn't actually execute one of her ideas. But TWA's new jets, conincidentally or not, had the Dorothy Draper look—black, white, and red.

Every year the corporate cast expanded, and the numbers of executives taking votes on decisions did as well. Making a profit was all they cared about. For instance, in 1952 she did seven gorgeous designs for Golding Brothers, a textile company, on a two-year contract at twenty-five thousand dollars a year. They canceled after the first year, citing not enough volume. The cost of the patterns was prohibitive and the royalties less than hoped for. "This project," they advised, "was a very disastrous one."

Dorothy hadn't lost her magic touch, however. The Mark Hopkins Hotel, across from the Fairmont on San Francisco's Nob Hill, was a financial success. The liquor volume in the Lochinvar Room increased eight times when she redid the room in 1954. But the hotel business had also changed. It no longer depended on society but on conventions. A giant corporation might spend a half-million dollars in three days. What private individual could top that?

Hotels all looked the same now. It was as if everyone had started ordering from the same catalog. Across the United States there was a proliferation orange and brown—Dorothy's least favorite color combination. The sight of it was enough to make her lose her appetite. There was a hotel tycoon around in the 1950s, Conrad Hilton, but he wouldn't hire Dorothy Draper. He thought she would eclipse him, and she would have—her image was that strong.

If her grand gestures, which were so appealing to tycoons like Robert Young, didn't appeal to Conrad Hilton, they made the corporate man very uneasy, to say nothing of her eccentricities. While doing over a lowly motor inn in New Jersey, she insisted that the cows in a nearby field be changed from brown to black-and-white to match her color scheme. No one in the cadre of dress-alike executive officers that followed her around the site was amused, although Ted and Glenn had to leave the premises to keep from laughing out loud. Her plans for doing over the old Penn Station was another instance. The station had an enormous terminal restaurant and architecture Dorothy approved of. Her idea was to have a canopy stretched over the area where the trains pulled in to the station. She was told it was impractical. But a canopy would be the perfect solution to the cavernous gloom, she argued. They wouldn't even listen.

The private client had also changed. She no longer had the stomach for dealing with some of these new *parvenus*, no matter how much money was involved. She went to Newport, once so glorious, and became aware of the decline of her little "family" more than at any other time. She went to look at a house owned by Frazier Jelke, whose son Mickie was behaving badly with call girls. Neither Jelke nor the care-taker was there, but the door was open. She took one look at his poky little rooms and narrow high windows with heavy, musty curtains and walked right out, declaring there wasn't a thing she could do for such a house. Not even gutting it would help.

Dorothy's treatment by the press also changed after the 1940s. The jet set took the fancy of the syndicated columnists, and Dorothy Draper became a person from a lost era in their eyes. Her vision did not fit into their streamlined world. Within her profession, opinions of her work were as hateful as ever. A canopied dining tent she did for a merchandis-ing show was reviewed harshly:

"Hits you in the eye."

"Posh pup tent."

"Careful placement of the air conditioning unit will prevent suffoca-tion when draperies are closed."

"Extravagantly amusing . . ."

One of Dorothy's few memorable jobs of that era was designing The Metropolitan Museum of Art's cafeteria, a cavernous room with a Roman pool on the ground floor. She had won a competition for the job, much to the grumbling of those who said she got the prize by knowing someone on the board. Dorothy designed the cafeteria to be a monument to herself. In fact, it became known as the "Dorotheum." The walls were painted an eggplant color she called aubergine, and the vastness of the space (127' × 96') suddenly became mysterious and intimate. A canopy of translucent white rayon was draped tentlike over the ceiling; it concealed a skylight to give it an effect of "lighting like that from a cloudy sky warmed by sunlight." She painted the twenty-five-foot classic columns of the villalike room black and white. She also designed 8'6" wrought iron birdcage chandeliers and painted them white. Pools of light and hedgerows formed cozy eating areas.

But the centerpiece of the room was a tableau designed by the Swedish sculptor Carl Milles. He was commissioned to do a work for the pool, and it was an early example of site-specific sculpture at a time before that concept was in vogue. Inspired by Mrs. Draper, the sculptor turned out a mythical scene of the goddess Aganippe and a group of spindly smaller-than-life figures gliding away from her over the waters of the pool. According to Greek mythology, the goddess Aganippe had been turned into a fountain and became a source of creative inspiration for anyone who drank from it. Milles's figures glide across the surface of pool, fresh from their visit to the goddess. She is portrayed larger than life, full-bodied, splendidly proportioned, her arms outstretched. Deliberately or not, perhaps inspired by Dorothy, the sculptor had received her vision and displayed it as he saw it, center stage, in the Dorotheum.

Then in mid-job, the museum cut her budget in half. Long gone were the days when she could underwrite the cost of implementing her ideas when all else failed. She had to change much of the original scheme, and she was not happy with the result. The statues had been installed in a way that distressed her. They looked as if they were either jumping in or leaping out of the pool, she complained, instead of gliding its surface. The beautifully carved animal friezes she loved had to be put above the entrance, where they were unnoticed. She said she learned something on that job. "I've discovered people don't see things that are up over their line of vision. I'll never do it again."

At a certain point, she lost interest in the Metropolitan job and turned it over to Ted and Glenn. In spite of her disappointments, the cafeteria was well received and loomed in importance because it was done at a time when grand scale had already been diminished to a great extent.

The Metropolitan job was Ted Stewart's last, for upon its completion tragedy struck the office. Ted and Jim Roebottom had been lovers ever since Ted had brought him home from Germany after World War II. Although Ted's wife Betty had tolerated his other lovers, she kicked up a terrible fuss over Jim. This was not just a spring romance, she said, it was marriage!

The relationship had spelled trouble for Betty from the beginning. Ted had never been happy riding the Staten Island ferry to Betty's new house after he brought Roebottom home. He complained that it was too cold in the winters. But Betty believed he probably would have felt the same way had he been taking the train to any house. The fact was, Ted wanted out.

When Ted took his things out of Betty's house to move into a Chelsea brownstone with Jim, she told him to take everything they had bought together or she would throw it out, and she would have, too. They had been married for twenty years and had both loved auctions, so a lot of their possessions went with him. Ted's new apartment in Chelsea had eighteen-foot ceilings and bay windows and fireplaces in each drawing room. The two men had done it all in off-white and antique ivories, colors that were good backdrops for Ted and Betty's large collection of *objets d'art.*

Roebottom was by that time in his late twenties, and Ted was in his late forties. They were a perfect match for a guaranteed conflagration. Although neither alone was a heavy drinker, together they drank like there was no tomorrow, and they fought a lot when they were drunk. They tried to make each other jealous and were very successful at it, throwing big parties for the purpose of making or receiving passes until one or the other blew a fuse. They seemed to need the conflict. Some of the parties got wild, and a drawer in the drawing room was filling up with photographs in which, as Jean put it, "People weren't exactly dressed."

Still, no matter how crazy Ted and Jim drove each other, they didn't split up but kept coming back for more.

Betty was also drinking too much at this time. She had run through her money. A relative had plied her with martinis and had taken her stock. Betty said she wasn't going to worry about money for her future because she was destined to die young which, unfortunately, she did.

Mrs. Draper didn't care much for Jim. She didn't find him attractive. He slouched, and if he put on a new suit, in no time at all it looked as if he'd slept in it for a week. He was clean, but didn't look as if he'd scrubbed. The "hippie look" was not typical of the kind of people who worked for the Draper office; after all, clients expected to partake of the good taste of those more refined than themselves. But Jim stayed on the staff primarily because Ted insisted on it.

One day Mrs. Draper was consulting with Ted and Jim when suddenly Jim began to hang on to her and jerk himself about in an alarming manner.

"What's the matter with him?" she asked.

"He's just got the flu," said Ted.

"Get Jean," she commanded. Mr. Stoll, the current business manager, ran to find Mrs. Draper's trouble-shooter.

"Mrs. Draper wants you," he told Jean. "Get upstairs in a hurry."

Ted had managed to get Jim back into his chair and was still insisting he was alright. "He's just sick to his stomach," he said. Jean got angry because she knew what was going on. Jim kept falling off the chair and Ted kept putting him back into it.

Mrs. Draper immediately absented herself, leaving the problem to Jean. She didn't like to be around sick people. She was a very healthy person and didn't understand why other people had to get sick. Her standard advice for anyone with a health problem was "Think clear, positive thoughts and get to a psychiatrist."

Finally she fired Jim, something she hated to do, but he kept coming to work drunk. After he lost his job, he drank even more until Ted became very disturbed. Jim started acting crazy, and Ted would be on the phone with him endlessly at work while Jim had the d.t.'s down in Chelsea. Finally, Ted, knowing Jim would never forgive him, had him committed to Bellevue Hospital for his own good.

Ted was racked with guilt over what he had done. Frequently he threatened to commit suicide to put himself out of his misery.

One morning shortly after the opening of the new Metropolitan Museum of Art cafeteria, Ted didn't come in to work, even though he had an early appointment with some clients. After they had cooled their heels for an hour, Belle Clark had called Ted's landlady, who lived upstairs, asking her to check in on Ted. Her husband called back because his wife was downstairs crying. Ted Stewart was dead.

Jean was home that day. Mrs. Draper had Belle call her immediately upon hearing the news. After telling her that Ted had died, Dorothy said, "Now, Jean, I want you to go over there and make sure there's nothing lying around that shouldn't be. We don't want any publicity, no reporters. We have to protect poor Ted."

Jean knew what she meant. She had a large black handbag that she always carried when she went to lunch with her boss. In it there was ample room to hold the samples of forks, small plates, and napkins that Mrs. Draper collected for her files. The first time she made Jean take an item Jean wished she could have died on the spot. She felt nothing now. The sudden death of her good friend had put her in a state of shock that would make possible the job of coolly removing certain evidence under the nose of the police.

Just as Jean feared, the police had arrived first. She was greeted at Ted's apartment door by a kindly fat sergeant, who got her a glass of water and a wet cloth to put over her eyes after she had seen Ted, who was still lying on the bathroom floor in his dressing gown. While the sergeant was in the next room filling out his report, Jean moved toward the drawer in the drawing room with her big black traveling bag open. Undetected by the police, she scooped the incriminating photographs into her bag.

The official report was that Ted had died of a heart attack, but his friends in the office who knew how depressed he had been wondered whether he hadn't taken too many pills. It would have been Ted's way out. When Jean went to the office that day, it was in turmoil. Belle was hysterical. Glenn was crying. Ted had been everyone's favorite, and they all felt terrible. But Mrs. Draper did not allow turmoil, although she was as grief stricken as the rest. Ted had come into her life needing a good motherly figure to guide him, and she had been that person. She had loved Ted as much as if he had been family.

In 1952 the *New York Times* polled fifteen thousand women in the metropolitan area and asked them what was the best known name in decorating. Dorothy Draper won hands down, although they never featured her in their ultrachic Sunday magazine. Then they asked what was the best source for decorating, and Schumacher won hands down. A second choice was not even mentioned.

One of the highlights of Dorothy's career at that time (along with finally getting on the covers of *Life* and *Time*) was being interviewed by Edward R. Murrow on "Person to Person." Mrs. Draper was excited about her interview because it meant that everybody would get to see how she lived at home. She had done radio shows for years, but the prospect of having so many guests pay a visit to her living room thrilled her and made her terribly nervous at the same time.

Her nervousness grew when she saw what being on television meant. Cables were strewn all over the apartment. Equipment filled the kitchen and the hall. She was frightened when the sound men wanted to wire her for a microphone above the knee, and giggled most uncustomarily. Meanwhile, Mabel, who was also nearly beside herself with excitement, ordered sandwiches, coffee, and pastry from Longchamp's for the crew.

In spite of Dorothy's nervousness, she came off magnificently. Murrow asked her about her historic appointments in the apartment, and she replied with just the right touch of self-denigration, even pointing out how she had shaved off the sideburns of the bust of her illustrious ancestor, Robert Minturn, because she thought he looked better without them. If the show had been in color, the television audience would have seen what this shade called aubergine, which they had been reading

269

about in the papers, looked like. Her walls in the Carlyle were painted that deep, rich color, with white trim. They would have seen the peacock blue of the satin sofa and the two bright red velvet chairs in front of the fireplace, and how the colors all blended together to look natural. At least they could see the high contrasts on their television screens: the juxtaposition of the aubergine wall and the snow-white draperies, which were extra full and a little too long, the way Dorothy liked them. They could see the high-density contrast of the white fur rug against the oak floors, which were stained umber. And they saw how nothing managed to look new or cried out "Look at me!" but melted into something so pleasing that Mrs. Draper, knowing there was perfection all around, relaxed in the middle of it all like a gracious queen. For once she didn't act the part of the Marx Brothers matron but was herself, and Murrow knew just how to bring her true personality out, center stage. Her happy face beamed into the living rooms of America.

By the time Dorothy had reached the age of retirement (although she had no intention of retiring), there was little in the way of accolades she had not received. She had been Woman of the Year in 1948 and had had her portrait done by Yousuf Karsh. Her face had smiled down on the masses from the Kodak mural high above Grand Central Station along with the other reigning syndicated columnists of her day.

Dorothy also enjoyed the rewards of grandmotherhood. Although Diana dreaded the infrequent visits of her mother, the grandchildren looked forward to them. She was a hugger, a full-figured motherly type who projected lots of power, and when they were engulfed in her bosom, they felt for awhile that everything was going to be alright.

It was when her grandchildren actually lived with Granny D that they came to realize what being taken care of really meant. George tasted his first caviar with her. The contrast with his stark New Mexico life was a sharp one. At the Hampshire House all was luxury, which Granny D enjoyed to the limit without even a touch of guilt. She loved to throw an extravagant party and relished the rough-and-tumble play of children under foot. Sooner or later she would grab George by the collar as he was wrestling with the Leroy and Tuckerman boys and bring him into the adult party.

"I would like you to meet the next governor of New Mexico," she would say, and with a grandiloquent flourish bring him out from behind her skirts. It was her way of letting her favorite grandson know that she had high expectations for him. He, too, would be a star in the firmament.

When George graduated from Millbrook School in June 1955, only Granny D was there. She arrived in the DD Special, the Chrysler she had been given as a perk for decorating a sensational exhibit for the auto show, complete with driver, having been convinced she was a menace to the road. She told her grandson how thrilled she was that the hit of the auto show had been a Dodge pickup she had painted with bright pink-and-white circus dots and filled with roses. People had gasped and applauded, she said.

George's cousin Tucky (Roger Wolcott Tuckerman) was not thrilled so much as awed over the presence of his famous aunt. When the boys were eighteen, Tucky was having the male equivalent of a debutante party at the River Club, which had been organized and decorated long ago by Dorothy Draper.

"M'gawd, George, Auntie Dodo is coming tonight!" Roger said. When Dorothy arrived it was like a film star making an entrance to a preview.

George admired her zip and flair and her ability to pull together an outrageous outfit that would have made people laugh if she hadn't had the charismatic animation to carry it off. As she took over the party, George wondered how she got that way. Was she actually shy at the core and fought against it so successfully that she shot out the other end like a rocket? What was to be made of the loneliness in her eyes in those rare private moments when she revealed herself to him? Once she cried on his shoulder, just like his mother did, and tears fell like rain over how the men in her life had abandoned her—husband, father, lover. It was obvious that the tears were those of a woman who had loved frequently and with passion.

When George was still in prep school, she gave him a book on marital relations. She marked a passage which stuck in his mind: "To make love without adequate foreplay is like serving a banquet on bare boards." Even though approaching seventy, Dorothy kept her boudoir a highly romantic place. She reclined on her four-poster canopied bed like a grand courtesan, her dressing table crowded with photographs of her intimate male friends. George especially remembered one: It was a country scene—wicker basket, bottle of wine, and a good-looking man with a well-loved look gazing toward the camera, DD at his side. His favorite was a drawing with watercolor highlights of a train chugging along, the flat cars behind towing her four poster bed, dressing table, and a little privy with a quarter-moon on its door, its smokestack belching enormous cabbage roses.

George admired the way she handled being interviewed. Once at the Carlyle a female reporter from an Arizona newspaper came by, and he was fascinated by the remarkable way with which Dorothy avoided answering the reporter's personal questions. As she dug for that tidbit (it was what she had come for) Granny D remained the professional, veering her back skillfully each time, and revealed nothing of an intimate nature. At the conclusion of the interview the reporter slipped a camera out of her handbag and aimed. Dorothy sprang to her feet and said, "Absolutely not!" If the reporter wanted a picture she could call her office. She then ushered her out the door forthwith.

George got married in Charlestown, Rhode Island, to Sandy Mowry. His grandmother arrived from New York just in time for the ceremony in her custom-made Chrysler driven by her chauffeur, wearing a fantastic red cape rimmed with black rooster feathers. She came through the reception as if she were the woman of the hour. When she reached the bride, whom she was meeting for the first time, she gave her a big hug and whispered in her ear. The bride turned Granny D's favorite shade of red.

"What did she say to you?" George asked Sandy later.

"George, she's definitely your grandmother. She told me the best part about marriage was going to be having sex with you!"

George's younger sister Susan was awed by her grandmother, but her nature was so different from Granny D's that she was never perfectly comfortable in Dorothy's presence. Susan even had trouble sleeping in her Hampshire House room. She thought the stripes on the wallpaper were too bold, too colorful. But she adored her grandmother nevertheless and tried to comprehend her.

Years later, Dorothy's fabulous red cape rimmed with black rooster feathers would come into Susan's possession. By that time she was a married woman with children. The red cape was a most wonderful, practical, and appropriate legacy. DD would have appreciated its use with an explosion of laughter. Dorothy's spectacular cape was worn to so many children's costume parties and Halloween night festivals that Susan had to mend it many times.

Dorothy grew to appreciate her own son, George, the way he lived his life, and his closeness to his sons. She was proud of the way her son the newspaper reporter had managed to nudge a few crooked politicians and unscrupulous businessmen into the bucket where they belonged. George had done many unusual things in his life. He had been a cowboy, ran away to the circus, learned to play the harmonica, worked in a steel mill, and painted and sculpted. He was a romantic like she was, and he had done much to break out of the societal mold just as she had done. Dorothy couldn't understand his choices, but she liked his style, and when he came to visit he seemed to be happy with the way his life had turned out.

Penelope was also happy. She met Harvey Buchanan, a professor of art history at Case Western Reserve University in Cleveland. When they were married, Dorothy hosted the lunch and the second Mrs. Draper had the party. Elisabeth went to the lunch and DD to the party, staying a full half hour and displaying her most beguiling *joie de vivre*. Time had a way of healing wounds to the point where the past could be forgotten and the present enriched for it.

Unfortunately, Diana was not happy. It was no surprise to anyone that Diana's marriage to Nelson Jay didn't last. There were too many problems that never got resolved, among them getting married at a young age. When Dorothy heard that Diana was getting married again, this time to a Bigelow, she was delighted, assuming he was of the carpet family. That, unfortunately, was not true.

When Diana came East to get married in the Carlyle, she and her husband-to-be stayed with Dorothy, which irked her. Unlike DD's mother who had suggested premarital cohabitation as insurance against failing at marriage, DD did not approve at all. "Why can't that man stay somewhere else?" she complained. "Does he have to check in before they're married?"

It was a lovely wedding, like the first one, and Diana's beautiful face, which Sir Cecil Beaton had captured in its rounded innocence, was now sculpted, revealing the classic bone structure of the women in her line, which would cause her to look *more* lovely as she got older, or lovely in a different way. Those who knew her, however, saw the ravagement beyond the obvious beauty.

After ten years of incapacitation with Parkinson's disease, Dr. Draper died in 1959. That year Dorothy was doing the Westhampton Beach and Tennis Club, which she called a "boatel." She had been doing the work on weekends with her crew. One night she sighed and said to no one in particular, "Isn't it nice to go out to Westhampton for the weekend instead of home to a dying man?"

Shortly after Dr. Draper died, Elisabeth came to one of Dorothy's Christmas parties. It was possible for the two women to be social by that time. Ruth had died in 1956. Both Dorothy's father and mother were gone; they now lay with Nanny in the family plot, overlooking Newport harbor. The family that remained began to see themselves more and more as survivors, and the circle began to draw itself in a little. Besides, DD respected Elisabeth; she, too, had always had to work hard for a living.

After the 1960 elections, another member of the Tuckerman family became well known to the public—Dorothy's niece Nancy Tuckerman. She became social secretary to the new First Lady, Jacqueline Kennedy. Dorothy saw Nancy frequently during that time because the Carlyle became the New York White House during the Kennedy Administration. There the Kennedys occupied an enormous suite on the thirty-fourth and thirty-fifth floors where JFK received a steady stream of the best and the brightest. The apartments were furnished in authentic Louis XV, according to Mrs. Kennedy's wishes. The hotel had a convenient back entrance. John Kennedy used to sneak out to see late movies by taking a back elevator to the second floor and walking one flight to the street, returning around three o'clock in the morning to the chagrin of his Secret Service agents.

The Carlyle became the address of world leaders in town as well. Prime Minister Nehru of India had a party there in 1960 to which Khrushchev and Castro showed up. It was a very short party because Mr. Nehru did not serve liquor.

The lobby of the Carlyle was still the way Dorothy Draper had done it in the 1930s with Vincent Coyle, and it had become an institution over the years. Its oversize black-and-white marble tiles laid on the diagonal were still covered with the Savonniere rug, and the gorgeous French tapestries she had found at Rose Cumming's shop still hung from ceiling to floor. Dorothy was delighted that among the jewels in her crown was this backdrop for Camelot.

The Last Grande Dame:
A Retrospective

In 1960, Roger Tuckerman insisted that his sister sell her company. It was eating into her own money at the rate of twenty-five hundred dollars a month, and she owed more than she could pay out. The time had passed when she could underwrite her jobs in order to satisfy her own high taste. Dorothy, already disillusioned with the new crop of clients, sold her company to Leon Hegwood and Carleton Varney and retired. Every now and then, people from the office would see her on the streets, for she loved to take walks around the neighborhood to keep in touch with the changing scene. Someone who did not know who Dorothy was might think it odd to find an elegantly dressed elderly woman, gesturing in her animated way, full of questions, in the middle of a construction site among the hod carriers and plasterers and the construction men taking sand and plaster in and out.

Dorothy Draper died in 1969 at the age of eighty. She was buried in the Tuckerman family plot at St. Mary's Episcopal Church in Portsmouth, Rhode Island, close to the graves of her mother and father and that of Frances Somson, her children's beloved nanny. The church had been built by her great-great-grandfather George Gibbs, whose farm, Oaklands, which was five miles outside of Newport, had once been the summer quarters of the Old Guard. Her final resting place overlooks the harbor once filled with the clipper ships of her ancestors. At the conclusion of the graveside ceremony, her son George pulled out his harmonica and played the "Battle Hymn of the Republic." It was her favorite song.

If Dorothy were to return to her old haunts today, she might be surprised to find the scene both the same and radically different from the one she had done much to change in the 1930s.

Although the building boom of the past twenty years has drastically changed Manhattan since Dorothy's death, the enclave between 57th and 79th Streets, and Fifth Avenue to Third Avenue has remained virtually intact. New towers rim the enclave on every side like the fence that once surrounded Tuxedo Park.

Of course, Dorothy would have seen the positive side. She would have loved Philip Johnson's AT&T building. She would have applauded the change in New Yorkers' eating habits; there's a fresh fruit and vegetable stand on every block, even on Park Avenue at the illustrious Mr. Choi's. Had the Tuckerman ladies been around when the presence of his luxury delicacy store broke the residential code on Park Avenue and 70th Street, causing an uproar, they would have championed Mr. Choi, because the ready availability of fresh, premium-quality produce was a basic feature of the quality life. The ability to buy arugula at two in the morning on both sides of the street would throw Dorothy into rapture. Only in Manhattan could such a thing happen—which, of course, was why everybody wanted to live there, especially the new crop of international go-getters who have arrived in droves.

Dorothy would cry out in rapture over the proliferation of croissant shops and old-fashioned ice cream counters; every walk to the corner would be a severe test of her resolve. She would agree that city street eating had come a long way since Ben Franklin walked the streets of downtown Philadelphia eating penny buns.

If I were able to enter her time warp I would say, "Come with me to the Far West Village, Dorothy. I've got to show you something."

We would get out of the car at Hudson Street, Greenwich Village's antique row, and I would laugh with delight when she saw the draperies hanging in the window of a retro shop called Second Hand Rose.

"My two-toned banana frond from the Quitandinha! Done by that dear Glenn Boyles. How I miss him!" Many of Dorothy Draper's drapery prints from the 1940s still exist and are snapped up by knowledgeable antique fabric dealers in yard sales across the country. In good supply is the Fazenda Lily, which still adorns the massive upper lobby of the Greenbrier, where she would be glad to see the management has finally taken her advice and removed the offending oak. The popularity of the 1940s style she helped create is rapidly growing as it begins to emerge as an Age of Innocence which people yearn for and want to re-create in their lives.

Returning to the Upper East Side for a tour of the enclave, Dorothy would see that the Essex House still flies the Rampant Lion over Central Park South. She would be distressed to find that the Hampshire House next door has muted the colors of "her" lobby. Her gleaming white doors and molding have been painted ecru. She would undoubtedly demand to see somebody about it at once. Still, she would be relieved and touched to see that the rest of the lobby remains exactly as she did it: the curvaceous doors with center knobs too big for one small hand to turn; the oversize black-and-white marble tile, whose gleam has developed the pearllike patina of aging marble, still in the right angles of her prediagonal phase; and the bust of the unknown Roman dignitary, who still peers down upon the head doorman.

Lester Grundy's oversize Grinling Gibbons plasterwork, executed by the Cinquinnis, is still intact, as is the Art Deco curved glass, whose cold touch is a surprise, when one expects warm lucite. Her massive ebony tables, heavy as stone, still line the lobby walls.

By standing in the Hampshire House lobby and absorbing the quality of all those surfaces, it is possible to learn the difference between glint and gleam. The glint of the new will be more recognizable after experiencing the understated gleam of quality. For the most part, that quality is gone now. Mr. Cinquinni, who once made her marvelous plaster friezes, retired long ago, as have all the other artisans listed in her precious black leather notebook of "sources." Most of the suppliers of quality are long dead. What they made cannot be bought new today, with very few exceptions. There is precious little of the "real thing" on the market now. It must be retrieved from the past.

Countinuing her swoop of the southern border of the enclave, Dorothy would gasp at the sight of Trump Tower. She would probably have something to say about a man who autographed his buildings. Dorothy was also a mover and shaker with a monumental ego, but not even she would have gone that far!

Dorothy would have delighted at the chance to work with a tycoon again, appreciating Mr. Trump's height and good looks. If given the opportunity to sell him the Draper touch, she would take him enthusiastically by the arm on a stroll through his public space.

"It looks like a mausoleum, dear, like those dreadful spooky old Cairo museums. And all this orangy-tannish marble simply has to go." If Donald Trump agreed to her demands for carte blanche he could then announce to the press that the most famous decorator of her time was redoing his lobby in Great Beauty, as she had once told a mesmerized Robert Young.

"It all looks too new, dear. Too shiny. We need to flood the place with sunshine and bright, clear color and a few good things."

DD wouldn't find Rose Cumming on Fifth Avenue. The town has no room for eccentrics anymore, unless they are well subsidized. The divine clutter of Rose's shop would be out of place in the ultrachic atmosphere. Oddity shops like hers, a jumble of treasures hidden among piles of junk, have been driven out by high commercial rents, replaced by banks and sweet-shop franchises. The mystery is long gone.

Dorothy would not be thrilled with the luxury towers rising around the fringes of the Upper East Side (even the all-powerful developers cannot break into the enclave). For years these buildings have been getting taller and taller; when the wraps are removed, monuments of ugliness to the recent barbarian age are revealed. Dorothy would be shocked to find the buildings are made of such unattractive materials, to say nothing of the style—something called Memphis, which is already passé; lines fragmented and jumbled at odd angles for no reason. The buildings have funny Lego tops and turrets, with tiny jumpseat terraces to enjoy the view in lieu of those who have lost theirs. The painted metal of their surfaces is sure to discolor and stain. No patina will slowly develop with the passage of time. The surfaces are sadly devoid of all adornment, molding, or trim, a cost-cutting feature of bottom-line architecture. The buildings look for all the world like children's toys, painted nursery shades of green, red, blue, yellow, and that trendiest of colors, turquoise. They are permanent examples of the invasion of the 1980s: ugly and cheaply built but sold expensive, they are stacked as high as the law would allow or could be bent or bought.

Moving up Third Avenue, Dorothy would see that thoroughfare has become another Tombstone Alley like Sixth Avenue. The sight of 186 East 64th Street would be the biggest shock of all. Nothing could prepare her for it. The Upside-Down House is no more. The Royale, "Dedicated to the remembrance of things past," which rises from the site of the house where she raised her children, is made of a pinkish granitelike material that resembles cinderblock. It is set in painted metal. Across the street rises another monster high-rise in two-tone beige; on the downtown side is plopped the Phoenix, in Quitandinha-style poured-and-pressed concrete. The corner next to where her house stood is a maze of meaningless columns, a symmetrical Stonehenge, brutal in its newness. The commercial life of the corner, once lined with tiny specialty shops, has been reduced to savings banks and parking. The view down 64th Street framed by the tall buildings looks like a mural of "Olde Manhattan," barely real next to the hugeness of the corner, and in its permanent shadow.

If Dorothy Draper were commissioned to do over the lobby of one of these new luxury apartment houses, she would find them very much like the ones she tackled in the 1930s: cold, funereal, too plush, the colors grayed-out and dull. She would treat the project the way she had treated the Quitandinha, with blinders on regarding the outside of the building because nothing could be done. Then she would call for floors to be ripped out to create a space big enough to work in, and fill that space with sunshine, color, lots of gleaming white and black, and a few quality things. But where she would find these things would be her biggest problem.

Escaping from the shock of the eastern border and moving west to Park Avenue, she would discover that Bobby Short still entertains at the Carlyle. Rose Cumming's fabulous tapestries still hang in the lobby, although the decor has been "Frenchified." Some of the ornate plaster molding has been gilt. She would shudder at the sight of the paper flowers on her glass-topped table with the massive gold eagle base.

Looking downtown from 76th Street and Park Avenue, she could note that nothing new or garish has gone up since the Pan Am Building nearly ruined the vista in the 1950s. Since then the neighborhood has said no to conspicuous construction—and won. The Ritz Towers on 57th Street is restoring its lobby to the way Dorothy did it in the 1940s. Many other lobbies along Park Avenue in the seventies are still exactly as she did them because there is no reason to change perfection. Signs of the Draper touch are big, dark green wing chairs, ornate plaster wall brackets, big gold eagles, big black side tables, and oversize black-and-white marble floors.

Uptown at The Metropolitan Museum of Art, Dorothy would be shocked to see that the Dorotheum is no more. The pool has been drained and is now a sunken restaurant where food is served at a high price. The Carl Milles sculptures commissioned for the pool, and around which Dorothy planned her design, are no longer leaping just above its surface. The pool developed a leak and no one could be found to fund the repair. It was drained, and the sculptures were loaned to a museum in St. Louis with a similar Roman pool. The walls of the museum cafeteria have been repainted beige, ruining the effect of the aubergine mystery, but her massive bird cage chandeliers are still in use.

There are other vestiges of Dorothy Draper about, which in this age is pretty unusual. After a few years or a decade or two what is left behind of anyone? But Dorothy Draper left much behind that others valued enough not to change. The Greenbrier is a Dorothy Draper museum, conserved just the way she did it, and on tours of the famous building, the hotel historian will tell guests many amusing anecdotes about Mrs. Draper.

The lobby of the Fairmont hasn't changed either; it was used as the design for the television series "Hotel." All that is still missing from its famous lobby are the red lanterns and some honky-tonk music.

Arrowhead Springs is now a religious retreat. Little there has changed either. They are still using their Dorothy Draper double bolsters in the bedrooms. After World War II the Quitandinha became the biggest white elephant south of the equator. Guides took people through the state-owned property and snapped their fingers in the huge empty exhibition halls, setting up echoes that reverberated all the way to its crystal dome. "The roulette tables are silent now," wrote one columnist, "and the magnificent casino [is] an overdressed corpse." Brazil went through its own barbarian age, from which it has recently emerged. The Quitandinha reopened, first as a budget-price resort and today as a health spa.

Best of all, vestiges of Dorothy Draper can be seen at home, on late-night reruns of "The Honeymooners." On Ed Norton's unrenovated, early 1950s Bensonhurst, Brooklyn, kitchen wall bloom Dorothy Draper's large-scale, free-form, broad-leafed rhododendrons of the 1940s—the quintessential Draper touch. As she would say herself, "Simply perfection!"